Conversations with Mary McCarthy

Literary Conversations Series

Peggy Whitman Prenshaw
General Editor

Photograph by Carlos Freire, Paris, 1977. Courtesy of Vassar College Library.

Conversations with Mary McCarthy

Edited by
Carol Gelderman

University Press of Mississippi
Jackson and London

Library of Congress Cataloging-in-Publication Data

Conversations with Mary McCarthy / edited by Carol Gelderman.
     p.   cm. — (Literary conversations series)
   Collection of reprints of interviews originally published
1963-1989.
   Includes bibliographical references and index.
   ISBN 0-87805-485-5 (alk. paper). — ISBN 0-87805-486-3
(pbk. : alk. paper)
   1. McCarthy, Mary, 1912- —Interviews.   2. Authors,
American—20th century—Interviews.   I. McCarthy, Mary, 1912-   .
II. Gelderman, Carol W.   III. Series.
PS3525.A1435Z6   1991
818'.5209—dc20   90-49282
                                                           CIP

British Library Cataloging-in-Publication data available

Books by Mary McCarthy

The Company She Keeps. New York: Simon & Schuster, 1942.

The Oasis. New York: Random House, 1949.

Cast a Cold Eye. New York: Harcourt, Brace and Company, 1950.

The Groves of Academe. New York: Harcourt, Brace and Company, 1952.

Venice Observed. Paris: G. & R. Bernier, 1956.

Sights and Spectacles: Theatre Chronicles, 1937-1956. New York: Meridian Books, 1957.

Memories of a Catholic Girlhood. New York: Harcourt, Brace and Company, 1957.

The Stones of Florence. New York: Harcourt, Brace and Company, 1959.

On the Contrary. New York: Farrar, Straus and Cudahy, 1961.

Mary McCarthy's Theatre Chronicles, 1937-1962. New York: Farrar, Straus and Company, 1963.

The Group. New York: Harcourt, Brace & World, Inc., 1963.

Vietnam. New York: Harcourt, Brace & World, 1967.

Hanoi. New York: Harcourt, Brace & World, 1968.

The Writing on the Wall. New York: Harcourt, Brace & World, 1970.

Birds of America. New York: Harcourt Brace Jovanovich, 1971.

Medina. New York: Harcourt Brace Jovanovich, 1972.

The Seventeenth Degree. New York: Harcourt Brace Jovanovich, 1974.

The Mask of State: Watergate Portraits. New York: Harcourt Brace Jovanovich, 1974.

Cannibals and Missionaries. New York: Harcourt Brace Jovanovich, 1979.

Ideas and the Novel. New York: Harcourt Brace Jovanovich, 1980.

The Hounds of Summer and Other Stories. New York: Avon Books, 1981.

Occasional Prose. New York: Harcourt Brace Jovanovich, 1985.

How I Grew. New York: Harcourt Brace Jovanovich, 1987.

Contents

Introduction

The Group, Mary McCarthy's fifth and best-known novel, was published on 28 August 1963. It immediately appeared on the best-seller lists, first in the United States and then in several European nations, including Great Britain and Germany. Although Harcourt, Brace's promotion and publicity people had pushed the book long before publication, they had to work without much cooperation from McCarthy. In June, two months before publication, she wrote to William Jovanovich, her close friend and publisher, explaining why she objected to interviews of writers.

> *Life* has rung me up here about doing a "Close-Up" story. They sent me some samples this morning, which made me very uneasy. They were Dr. Spock, Rachel Carson, and Dame Edith Sitwell. The first two were not so bad, but Dame Edith was grotesque, and not the less so because of the gushing admiration the *Life* writer expressed for her. It seemed to me the reason for the difference was not simply Edith's nonsense but was inherent in the literary profession. Spock and Rachel Carson belong in *Life* because he is a public health figure and she's a biologist who's fighting for a cause. There's no discrepancy between what they do professionally and a *Life* interview. But it's not so for a poet or a novelist. A picture-story cannot help vulgarizing a writer because the part of himself that writes is invisible by its nature. The best they can do is to make a connection with the writer's exhibitionism, his worst side.[1]

Unfortunate that she should have used just that word, for many critics have labeled her unusual outspokenness exhibitionism. From the time she first appeared on the literary scene in the pages of the *New Republic* in the mid 1930s until her death in 1989, her brutally honest exposure of literary ineptitude and of people's foibles drew the ire of countless commentators. The recurring sameness of their criticism prompted a Ph.D. candidate, preparing to write a disserta-

[1]Mary McCarthy to William Jovanovich, 6/20/63. Courtesy of William Jovanovich.

tion on the critical reception of McCarthy's work, to ask if in a hundred years textbooks on American literature will still be using nouns and adjectives like knives, stilettos, switch-blades, cold, heartless, clever, cerebral, cutting, acid, exhibitionistic in discussions of Mary McCarthy.

It seems surprising that a person so "ready to take up arms" as her brother, actor Kevin McCarthy has described her, was also so reluctant to give interviews. And she was reluctant, but when she did agree to an interview, she answered questions honestly, outspokenly, sometimes outrageously. Asked by a fellow Vassar alumna if she would send a daughter to Vassar, she replied that she thought Radcliffe was the better school today. To a feminist interviewer she said she "sometimes felt oppressed by one man but never by men in general." Asked how she liked living in Paris, she berated Parisians for being disagreeable. "Everybody gets on each other's nerves. They're in a permanent state of irascibility."[2]

Mary McCarthy seemed to have a need to say exactly what was on her mind and to get everything down accurately, a manifestation of the meticulousness and honesty of her nature and of a natural tendency that forbade her to hold anything back. Yet she granted few interviews in her lifetime. She rarely appeared on television, for example, but when she did, she was liable to say something unexpected. In the television interview with Edwin Newman that appears here, she admitted that the controversial Pullman-berth seduction scene in her story "The Man in the Brooks Brothers Shirt" was autobiographical, down to the detail of the missing button on the protagonist's underpants. On the "Today" show and again in a *Nation* interview that appears in these pages, she blurted out that she had had several abortions. On the Dick Cavett Show, in a fateful aside, she called Lillian Hellman a liar, prompting Hellman to sue.

Honesty was her absolute rule, even if it hurt others and herself, and it got her in trouble again and again, accounting for her reputation as the "enfant terrible" of the literary scene and later as its "lit arbiter," "broadsword," and "headmistress," as Norman Mailer described her compulsion to uphold standards.[3]

[2]Eugenia Sheppard, "Pity the Men," *New York Post*, July 12, 1971, p. 39.
[3]Norman Mailer, "The Mary McCarthy Case," *New York Review of Books*, October 17, 1963, p. 1.

When people first met Mary McCarthy, they often commented on the contrast between this reputation and her real self. William Tuohy, who had met her in Saigon when he was bureau chief there for the *Los Angeles Times,* had expected her to be difficult, even grim. "I had heard about McCarthy's being able to cut someone verbally, and she wasn't like that at all. She was pleasant, witty, charming, gossipy in the best sense of the word—chatty about people and about things. Obviously she was a brilliant person with wit that could be acid and biting, but she was not that kind of person who relied on that."[4] Indeed, her great friend and political philosopher Hannah Arendt said that the discrepancy between the public image and actual person was greater in McCarthy's case than in any other she had known of. This public image resulted from her inability to suppress the whole truth as she saw it when asked a question.

When McCarthy turned sixty on 21 June 1972, the producers of French television's "Variances" taped a special thirty-minute interview. A newspaper commentator, recalling an earlier television interview during which she had called Paris "a city of notaries and concierges" where "love and youth are as short-lived as the mating season of birds," marveled at her present amiability. He called her "a new Mary McCarthy," a "mellowed, smiling woman who talked for half an hour without drawing a drop of blood."[5] No blood was drawn because the interviewer had asked few questions. Right up to the end of her life she gave her opinion—only if asked—straight off and unedited. Sometimes when she saw what she had said in print, she was horrified and blamed the interviewer for not showing more discretion than she had.

"I do not seem to live and learn,"[6] she told Edmund Wilson after what she thought was an unpleasant article about her by Brock Brower, with whom she had cooperated, appeared in *Esquire.* She echoed herself a few years later in a letter to Doris Grumbach after reading the galleys of Grumbach's critical biography of McCarthy called, at McCarthy's suggestion, *The Company She Kept.* "Unfortunately," McCarthy wrote, "I am not discreet, and I do not seem to

4Carol Gelderman's interview with William Tuohy, London, 1982.
5Irving Marder, "The Face Was Familiar," *International Herald Tribune,* August 30, 1972.
6Mary McCarthy to Edmund Wilson, 10/n.d./66, Edmund Wilson Papers, Beinecke Library, Yale University.

learn. I enjoy talking."[7] The book included several cutting remarks about people and events that McCarthy had made in a taped interview.

In October 1965 when Doris Grumbach had finished two-thirds of her book about McCarthy, she wrote the author in Paris to ask for an interview. The women met in early January 1966 at McCarthy's Paris apartment. Grumbach interviewed her subject a few hours one afternoon, using a tape recorder, and later mailed the transcript of the interview to McCarthy for corrections. McCarthy was alarmed. In the interview she did what she had so often done before: having started talking, she got carried away, revealing more than she had intended.

McCarthy drew up a list of imprudent disclosures recorded on the tape that she did not want to appear in the book—chiefly cracks about Edmund Wilson—and then left it up to Grumbach not to quote "some things I may say later in this letter as well."[8] Having said that, she drew up a year-by-year chronology of her life, including again, a few more startling revelations. When she got the galleys of the book, she was angry to discover that Grumbach had reported unkind remarks about people that she had made on tape, intimate details of her life and her husbands' lives, and details of her love affair with James West (her fourth husband), although she admitted to William Jovanovich that she had given Grumbach "a sad mixture of confidences and dry chronology."[9]

Grumbach's publisher, nervous about some of McCarthy's quotes, sent the galleys to Edmund Wilson, who exploded. McCarthy assured him that she had never meant her remarks to appear in print and then consulted William Jovanovich, who turned the matter over to a lawyer. Jovanovich warned her that a lot of damage had been done, owing to "your unfortunate candor in the course of the intervew" and "your subsequent correspondence, including the long biographical letter."[10] Her "unfortunate candor" had apparently confused Grumbach as to what was and what was not all right to publish.

The matter was settled, but the episode illustrates how her directness and openness were often mistaken for desire to attract notice. Once she had agreed to be interviewed, she conversed for

[7]Mary McCarthy to Doris Grumbach, 9/26/66, courtesy of Mary McCarthy.
[8]Mary McCarthy to Doris Grumbach, 2/22/66, courtesy of Mary McCarthy.
[9]Mary McCarthy to William Jovanovich, n.d., courtesy of William Jovanovich.
[10]William Jovanovich to Mary McCarthy, 10/31/66, courtesy of William Jovanovich.

four hours with a perfect stranger while a tape recorder preserved every word, and then, despite concern over the disposition of the tapes, supplied a single-spaced eleven-page letter in which she listed exact dates of crucial events in her life, including the specifics of early sexual experience. McCarthy admitted, "I talk too much," when she saw the transcript.[11]

Mary McCarthy's candor—recording the kind of perverse thoughts most people entertain at one time or other, but never give voice to or admit to having had, even to themselves—is one of the characteristics that makes her and her writing memorable. An intransigent and fearless honesty was a basic trait of her character. She was, to quote writer Thomas Mallon, "the most uncompromising—and uncompromised—writer of her time."[12] She was also gregarious, devoted to her friends, competitive, an indefatigable student of languages and of art, a dedicated cook and gardener, in short a perfectionist. Quite naturally these traits show up in her interviews.

The Literary Conversations series reprints uncut interviews, and for this reason, there is some repetition. Not surprisingly, Mary McCarthy was asked the same questions by several interviewers. Nevertheless the twenty-six interviews included here give a picture of how multi-faceted a writer Mary McCarthy was—novelist, short story writer, essayist, journalist, memoirist, critic. The interviews are arranged chronologically according to the dates they appeared in print. They are also reproduced as they originally appeared; obvious errors have been silently corrected.

I want to thank all the interviewers and publishers who have granted permission to reprint the material in this book; Maria Zeledon of the University of New Orleans who helped prepare the book for publication; Beatrice Calvert, also of the university, who proofread and prepared the index; and Seetha Srinivasan and Peggy Prenshaw who asked me to do this project.

[11]Mary McCarthy to Doris Grumbach, 9/26/66, courtesy of Mary McCarthy.
[12]Thomas Mallon, "Mary McCarthy, A Mind in Perpetual Motion," *USA Today*, October 27, 1989, p. 40.

Chronology

1912	Mary McCarthy is born on 21 June in Seattle, Washington, to Roy and Therese McCarthy.
1918	Roy McCarthy dies 6 November and Therese McCarthy 7 November in Minneapolis. MM and her three younger brothers move to Minneapolis to live with a great aunt and uncle. MM attends St. Stephen's parochial school.
1923	MM moves to Seattle to live with her Preston grandparents. She attends Forest Ridge, a Sacred Heart Convent.
1925	Attends Garfield High School
1926	Goes to boarding school, Annie Wright Seminary in Tacoma, Washington
1929–33	Attends and graduates from Vassar College
1933	Marries actor Harold Johnsrud in June; begins publishing in *The New Republic* and *The Nation*.
1936	Divorces Johnsrud and moves to Greenwich Village
1937	Lives with Philip Rahv; Rahv, Dwight Macdonald, Fred Dupee, William Phillips, and Mary McCarthy revive *Partisan Review*. McCarthy is made drama critic.

1938   Marries critic Edmund Wilson in February; Reuel Kimball Wilson is born on Christmas Day.

1939   Wilson teaches summer school at the University of Chicago. Wilsons move to Truro on Cape Cod.

1940   The Wilsons buy a nineteenth-century farmhouse in Wellfleet on Cape Cod. MM starts writing fiction.

1942   *The Company She Keeps,* her first novel, is published.

1945   In January Mary McCarthy leaves Edmund Wilson. She accepts a teaching job at Bard College.

1946   Makes her first trip to Europe with Bowden Broadwater; she marries Broadwater in December.

1948   Takes a teaching job at Sarah Lawrence. MM and other New York intellectuals start the Europe-America Groups to give help to European intellectuals.

1949   MM's fable *The Oasis* wins the Horizon Prize; it satirizes the bitter factionalism surrounding the Europe-America Groups. In June the Broadwaters move to Portsmouth, Rhode Island.

1950   MM does a ten-part series on night life in Greenwich Village for the *New York Post.*

1952   Publishes *Cast a Cold Eye,* a collection of short stories and memoirs and *The Groves of Academe,* a novel that satirizes academic life

1953   MM convinces Arthur Schlesinger, Jr., Hannah Arendt, Dwight Macdonald, and Richard Rovere to help her start a magazine. She works all year to raise the necessary money, but the *Critic,* as the magazine was to have been called, does not materialize.

1954   The Broadwaters go to Europe, where MM finishes *A Charmed Life,* a novel that satirizes Wellfleet.

1955   MM goes to Venice to write *Venice Observed.*

1956–59   MM in Europe frequently, doing work on *The Stones of Florence; Memories of a Catholic Girlhood* is published in 1957; McCarthy resumes work on *The Group* in Libya.

1960   McCarthy accepts invitation from the State Department to give a series of talks in Eastern Europe and the British Isles. She meets James West, public affairs officer for the American Embassy in Warsaw. Both secure divorces and marry in 1962.

1962   The Wests move to Paris; James West becomes the first director of information of the recently formed Organization for Economic Cooperation and Development (OECD).

1963   *The Group* is a run-away best seller.

1967   *The Company She Kept,* Doris Grumbach's study of MM, is published. McCarthy goes to Saigon to write about the Vietnam War for *The New York Review of Books.* The Wests buy a house in Castine, Maine, where MM will spend part of each year for the rest of her life.

1968   MM goes to Hanoi to write about the war for *The New York Review of Books.*

1972   Publishes *Birds of America,* part of which satirizes life in Stonington, Connecticut, where the Wests with his three children, spent two summers

1973   McCarthy makes ten transatlantic crossings, several to report on the Ervin Committee's hearings on the Watergate break-in for *The Observer.*

1975   Hannah Arendt, MM's close friend, dies. For the next two years she edits her friend's *The Life of the Mind.*

1979   *Cannibals and Missionaries,* McCarthy's last novel, is published. In October she appears on the Dick Cavett Show and calls Lillian Hellman a liar.

1980   Hellman sues McCarthy, Cavett, and station WNET, which broadcast the show, for libel. McCarthy gives the Northcliffe Lectures at the University of London; these become *Ideas and the Novel.*

1985   *Occasional Prose,* a collection of reviews and essays that appeared in *The New York Times Book Review* and in *The New York Review of Books,* is published.

1986   McCarthy accepts the Charles Stevenson Chair of Literature at Bard College, where she will teach each fall.

1987   *How I Grew,* a memoir, is published.

1988   *Mary McCarthy, A Life,* a biography by Carol Gelderman, is published. McCarthy receives an honorary degree from Tulane University and is inducted in the National Academy of Arts and Sciences.

1989   Mary McCarthy dies on 25 October. She is buried in Castine, Maine.

Conversations with Mary McCarthy

The Art of Fiction XXVII:
Mary McCarthy—An Interview
Elisabeth Niebuhr/1962

From *Paris Review,* 27 (Winter-Spring 1962, 59-94). Interview reprinted in *Writer's at Work: The Paris Interviews,* Second Series, ed. George Plimpton. Viking-Penguin, 1963. Copyright © 1963 by Viking-Penguin. Reprinted by permission.

The interview took place in the living room of the apartment in Paris where Miss McCarthy was staying during the winter of 1961. It was a sunny, pleasant room, not too large, with long windows facing south toward the new buildings going up along the Avenue Montaigne. A dining-*cum*-writing table stood in an alcove at one end; on it were a lamp, some books and papers, and a rather well-worn portable typewriter. At the other end of the room were several armchairs and a low sofa where Miss McCarthy sat while the interview was recorded. On this early spring afternoon (it was March 16), the windows were open wide, letting in a warm breeze and the noise of construction work nearby. An enormous pink azalea bloomed on the balcony, and roses graced a small desk in one corner.

Miss McCarthy settled down on the sofa and served coffee. She was wearing a simple beige dress with little jewelry—a large and rather ornate ring was her one elaborate ornament. She is of medium height, dark, with straight hair combed back from a center part into a knot at the nape of her neck; this simple coiffure sets off a profile of beautiful, almost classic regularity. Her smile is a generous one, flashing suddenly across her face, crinkling up her wide-set eyes. She speaks not quickly, but with great animation and energy, gesturing seldom, and then only with a slight casual motion of her wrists and hands. Her sentences are vigorously punctuated with emphatic verbal stresses and short though equally emphatic pauses. In general, she impresses one as a woman who combines a certain gracefulness and charm with positively robust and somewhat tense assurance; it is typical of her that she

3

matches the tremendously elegant carriage of her arms and neck and handsomely poised head with a deliberate, almost jerky motion in taking a step.

While Miss McCarthy's conversation was remarkably fluent and articulate, she would nevertheless often interrupt herself, with a kind of nervous carefulness, in order to reword or qualify a phrase, sometimes even impatiently destroying it and starting again in the effort to express herself as exactly as possible. Several times during the interview she seized upon a question in such a way that one felt she had decided upon certain things she wanted to say about herself and would willy-nilly create the opportunity to do so. At other moments, some of them hilarious—her gifts for pitiless witticism are justifiably celebrated—she would indulge in unpremeditated extravagances of description or speculation that she would then laughingly censor as soon as the words were out of her mouth. She was extremely generous in the matter of silly or badly worded questions, turning them into manageable ones by the nature of her response. In all, her conversation was marked by a scrupulous effort to be absolutely fair and honest, and by a kind of natural and exuberant enjoyment of her own intellectual powers.

Interviewer: Do you like writing in Europe?

McCarthy: I don't really find much difference. I think if you stayed here very long, you'd begin to notice a little difficulty about language.

Interviewer: Did you write about Europe when you first came here after the war?

McCarthy: Only in that short story, "The Cicerone." That was in the summer of 1946. We were just about the only tourists because you weren't allowed to travel unless you had an official reason for it. I got a magazine to give me some sort of *carnet*.

Interviewer: Did the old problem, the American in Europe, interest you as a novelist?

McCarthy: I suppose at that time, at least in that story somewhat, it did. But no, not further. For one thing, I don't know whether I cease to feel so much like an American or what; New York is, after all, so Europeanized, and so many of one's friends are European, that the distinction between you as an American and the European blurs. Also Europe has become so much more Americanized. No, I no longer see that Jamesian distinction. I mean, I see it in James, and I could see it even in 1946, but I don't see it any more. I don't feel any more this antithesis of Young America, Old Europe. I think that's really gone. For better or worse, I'm not sure. Maybe for worse.

Interviewer: What about the novel you're writing while you're here—have you been working on it a long time?

McCarthy: Oh, years! Let me think, I began it around the time of the first Stevenson campaign. Than I abandoned it and wrote the books on Italy, and *A Charmed Life,* and *Memories of a Catholic Girlhood.* When did I begin this thing again? A year ago last spring, I guess. Part of it came out in *Partisan Review.* The once called "Dotty Makes an Honest Woman of Herself."

Interviewer: Is it unfair to ask you what it will be about?

McCarthy: No, it's very easy. It's called *The Group,* and it's about eight Vassar girls. It starts with the inauguration of Roosevelt, and— well, at first it was going to carry them up to the present time, but then I decided to stop at the inauguration of Eisenhower. It was conceived as a kind of mock-chronicle novel. It's a novel about the idea of progress, really. The idea of progress seen in the female sphere, the feminine sphere. You know, home economics, architecture, domestic technology, contraception, childbearing; the study of technology in the home, in the play-pen, in the bed. It's supposed to be the history of the loss of faith in progress, in the idea of progress, during that twenty-year period.

Interviewer: Are these eight Vassar girls patterned more or less after ones you knew when you were there in college?

McCarthy: Some of them are drawn pretty much from life, and some of them are rather composite. I've tried to keep myself out of this book. Oh, and all their mothers are in it. That's the part I almost like the best.

Interviewer: Just the mothers, not the fathers?

McCarthy: Not the fathers. The fathers vaguely figure, offstage and so on, but the mothers are really monumentally present!

Interviewer: Does it matter to you at all where you write?

McCarthy: Oh, a nice peaceful place with some good light.

Interviewer: Do you work regularly, every morning, say?

McCarthy: Normally; right now I haven't been. Normally I work from about nine to two, and sometimes much longer—if it's going well, sometimes from nine to seven.

Interviewer: Typewriter?

McCarthy: Typewriter, yes. This always has to get into a *Paris Review* interview! I very rarely go out to lunch. That's a rule. I've been accepting lunch dates recently—*why* didn't I remember that? My excuse—the excuse I've been forgetting—is simply that I don't go out to lunch! And in general, I don't. That was the best rule I ever made.

Interviewer: Once you've published part of a novel separately, in a magazine or short-story collection, do you do much work on it afterwards, before it is published in the novel itself?

McCarthy: It depends. With this novel, I have.

Interviewer: Speaking not of a novel, but of your autobiography, I remember that you published parts of *Memories of a Catholic Girlhood* as one section in *Cast a Cold Eye*. You changed the story about your nickname a great deal, reducing it to just a small incident in *Catholic Girlhood*.

McCarthy: I couldn't *bear* that one! It had appeared years ago in *Mademoiselle,* and when I put it in *Cast a Cold Eye,* I didn't realize how much I disliked it. When I came to put *Catholic Girlhood* together, I simply couldn't stand it, and when I was reading the book in proof, I decided to tear it out, to reduce it to a tiny tiny incident. As it stood, it was just impossible, much too rhetorical.

Interviewer: When you publish chapters of a book separately on their own, do you think of them as chapters, or as independent short stories?

McCarthy: As chapters, but if somebody, a magazine editor, thought they were what *Partisan Review* calls a "self-contained chapter," all right, but I've never tried to make them into separate units. If one happens to be, all right—if they want to publish it as such. The *New Yorker* has given me surprises: they've printed things that I would never have thought could stand by themselves. But *they* thought so.

Interviewer: Did you, when you saw them in print?

McCarthy: Surprisingly, yes.

Interviewer: What about in your first novel, *The Company She Keeps?*

McCarthy: Those chapters were written originally as short stories. About halfway through, I began to think of them as a kind of unified story. The same character kept reappearing, and so on. I decided finally to call it a novel, in that it does in a sense tell *a* story, one story. But the first chapters were written without any idea of there being a novel. It was when I was doing the one about the Yale man that I decided to put the heroine of the earlier stories in that story too. The story of the Yale man is not a bit autobiographical, but the heroine appears anyway, in order to make a unity for the book.

Interviewer: Were you also interested simply in the problem of writing one story from various different points of view, in experimenting with the different voices?

McCarthy: There were no voices in that. I don't think I was really very much interested in the technical side of it. It was the first piece of fiction I had ever written, I mean I'd never made any experiments before. I was too inexperienced to worry about technical problems.

Interviewer: You hadn't written any fiction before then?

McCarthy: No. Well, in college I had written the tiniest amount of fiction: very bad short stories, very unrealized short stories, for courses, and that was all. I once started a detective story to make money—but I couldn't get the murder to take place! At the end of three chapters I was still describing the characters and the milieu, so I thought, this is not going to work. No corpse! And that was all. Then I simply did *The Company She Keeps,* and was only interested in the technical side from the point of view of establishing the truth, of trying to re-create what happened. For instance, the art-gallery story was written in the first person because that's the way you write that kind of story—a study of a curious individual.

Interviewer: You imply that most of the stories were distinctly autobiographical.

McCarthy: They all are more or less, except the one about the Yale man.

Interviewer: Is this distinction between autobiography and fiction clear in your mind before you begin writing a story, or does it become so as you write? Or is there no such distinction?

McCarthy: Well, I think it depends on what you're doing. Let's be frank. Take "The Man in the Brooks Brothers Shirt"; in that case it was an attempt to describe something that really happened—though naturally you have to do a bit of name-changing and city-changing. And the first story, the one about the divorce: that was a stylization—there were no proper names in it or anything—but still, it was an attempt to be as exact as possible about something that had happened. The Yale man was based on a real person. John Chamberlain, actually, whom I didn't know very well. But there it was an attempt to make this real man a broad type. You know, to use John Chamberlain's boyish looks and a few of the features of his career, and then draw all sorts of other Yale men into it. Then the heroine was put in, in an imaginary love affair, which *had* to be because she had to be in the story. I always thought that was all very hard on John Chamberlain, who was married. But of course he knew it wasn't true, and he knew that I didn't know him very well, and that therefore in the story he was just a kind of good-looking clothes-hanger. Anything else that I've written later—I may make a mistake—has been on the whole a fiction. Though it may have autobiographical elements in it that I'm conscious of, it has been conceived as a fiction, even a thing like *The Oasis*, that was supposed to have all these real people in it. The whole story is a complete fiction. Nothing of the kind ever happened; after all, it happens in the future. But in general, with characters, I do try at least to be as exact as possible about the essence of a person, to find the key that works the person both in real life and in the fiction.

Interviewer: Do you object to people playing the *roman à clef* game with your novels?

McCarthy: I suppose I really ask for it, in a way. I *do* rather object to it at the same time, insofar as it deflects attention from what I'm trying to do in the novel. What I really do is take real plums and put them in an imaginary cake. If you're interested in the cake, you get rather annoyed with people saying what species the real plum was. In *The Groves of Academe*, for instance. I had taught at Bard College and at Sarah Lawrence, but I didn't want to make a composite of those two places: I really wanted to make a weird imaginary college of my own. I even took a trip to the Mennonite country in Pennsylvania to try to find a perfect location for it, which I found—

now where was it? Somewhere near Ephrata—yes, it was Lititz, Pennsylvania, the home of the pretzel. There's a very charming old-fashioned sort of academy, a girls' college there—I'd never heard of it before and can't remember the name. It had the perfect setting, I thought, for this imaginary college of mine. Anyway, I would get terribly annoyed if people said it had to do with Sarah Lawrence, which it had almost no resemblance to. It was quite a bit like Bard. Sarah Lawrence is a much more *borné* and dull place than Bard, or than my college. And of course I was even more annoyed if they said it was Bennington. There was not supposed to be anything there of Bennington at all!

Interviewer: When were you at Bard?

McCarthy: '45 to '46.

Interviewer: And at Sarah Lawrence?

McCarthy: I was there just for one term, the winter of '48.

Interviewer: Did you enjoy teaching?

McCarthy: I adored teaching at Bard, yes. But the students were so poor at Sarah Lawrence that I didn't much enjoy it there. I don't think anyone I knew who was teaching there then did. But at Bard it was very exciting. It was all quite mad, crazy. I had never taught before, and I was staying up till two in the morning every night trying to keep a little bit behind my class. Joke.

Interviewer: Did they ask you to teach "Creative Writing"?

McCarthy: I've always refused to teach creative writing. Oh, I had in addition to two courses, about seven or eight tutorials, and some of those tutees wanted to study creative writing. I think I finally weakened and let one boy who was utterly ungifted for it study creative writing because he was so incapable of studying anything else.

Interviewer: But mostly it was these two courses.

McCarthy: Yes, and then you had to keep up with all these students. I had one boy doing all the works of James T. Farrell and a girl who was studying Marcus Aurelius and Dante. That was fun. That one I did the work for. And one girl was doing a thesis on Richard-son; that was just hopeless. I mean, I couldn't even try to keep up with teaching Russian novels, and, say, Jane Austen—who in my course came under the head of "Modern Novel"—*and* all the works of Richardson. So I could never tell, you know, whether she had read what she was supposed to have read, because I couldn't remember it! Everything was reversed! The student was in a position to see whether the professor was cheating, or had done her homework. Anyway, everybody ended up ill after this year—you know, various physical ailments. But it was exciting, it was fun. The students were fun. The bright ones were bright, and there wasn't much of a middle layer. They were either bright or they were just cretins. I must say, there are times when you welcome a B student.

I liked teaching because I loved this business of studying. I found it quite impossible to give a course unless I'd read the material the night before. I absolutely couldn't handle the material unless it was fresh in my mind. Unless you give canned lectures, it really has to be—though that leads, I think, to all sorts of very whimsical, perhaps, and capricious interpretations; that is, you see the whole book, say *Anna Karenina,* in terms that are perhaps dictated by the moment. One wonders afterwards whether one's interpretation of *Anna Karenina* that one had rammed down the throats of those poor students was really as true as it seemed to one at the time.

Interviewer: Which books did you teach in the "Modern Novel"?

McCarthy: Well, you had to call everything at Bard either modern or contemporary, or the students wouldn't register for it. Everyone thinks this is a joke, but it was true. I originally was going to teach a whole course on critical theory, from Aristotle to T. S. Eliot or something, and only three students registered for it, but if it had been called "Contemporary Criticism," then I think we would have had a regular class. So we called this course "The Modern Novel," and it began with Jane Austen, I think, and went up, well, certainly to Henry James. That was when I taught novels in pairs. I taught *Emma* and *Madame Bovary* together. Then *The Princess Casamassima,* with the anarchist plot in it and everything, with *The Possessed. The Red and the Black* with *Great Expectations.* And *Fontamara* with something. I only taught novels I liked.

Interviewer: Would it be roughly the same list, were you teaching the course now? Or do you have new favorites?

McCarthy: Oh I don't know, I might even add something like *Dr. Zhivago* at the end. I would probably do some different Dickens. I've read an awful lot of Dickens over again since then. Now I think I'd teach *Our Mutual Friend* or *Little Dorritt.*

Interviewer: Why did you start reading Dickens over again?

McCarthy: I don't know, I got interested in Dickens at Bard, and then at Sarah Lawrence. Another stimulus was a book done by a man called Edgar Johnson, a biographer of Dickens. Anthony West had attacked it in the *New Yorker,* and this made me so angry that I reviewed the book, and that set off another kind of chain reaction. I really *passionately* admire Dickens.

Interviewer: Could I go back for a moment to what you said about your early writing at college? I think you said that *The Company She Keeps* was the first fiction you ever wrote, but that was some years after you left Vassar, wasn't it?

McCarthy: Oh, yes. You know, I had been terribly discouraged when I was at Vassar, and later, by being told that I was really a critical mind, and that I had no creative talent. Who knows? They may have been right. This was done in a generous spirit, I don't mean that it was harsh. Anyway, I hadn't found any way at all, when I was in college, of expressing anything in the form of short stories. We had a rebel literary magazine that Elizabeth Bishop and Eleanor Clark were on, and Muriel Rukeyser and I. I wrote, not fiction, but sort of strange things for this publication.

Interviewer: A rebel magazine?

McCarthy: There was an official literary magazine, which we were all against. Our magazine was anonymous. It was called *Con Spirito*. It caused a great sort of scandal. I don't know why—it was one of these perfectly innocent undertakings. But people said, "How awful, it's anonymous." The idea of anonymity was of course to keep the judgment clear, especially the editorial board's judgment—to make people read these things absolutely on their merits. Well anyway, *Con Spirito* lasted for only a few numbers. Elizabeth Bishop wrote a wonderful story for it which I still remember, called "Then Came the Poor." It was about a revolution, a fantasy that took place in modern bourgeois society, when the poor invade, and take over a house.

Interviewer: When you left Vassar, what then?

McCarthy: Well, I went to New York, and I began reviewing for the *New Republic* and the *Nation*—right away. I wrote these little book reviews. Then there was a series about the critics. The *Nation* wanted a large-scale attack on critics and book-reviewers, chiefly those in the *Herald Tribune,* the *Times,* and the *Saturday Review,* and so on. I had been doing some rather harsh reviews, so they chose me as the person to do this. But I was so young, I think I was twenty-two, that they didn't *trust* me. So they got Margaret Marshall, who was the assistant literary editor then, to do it with me: actually we divided the work up and did separate pieces. But she was older and was supposed to be—I don't know—a restraining influence on me; anyway, someone more responsible. That series was a great sensation at the time, and it made people very mad. I continued just to do book reviews, maybe one other piece about the theater, something like the one on the literary critics. And then nothing more until *Partisan Review* started. That was when I tried to write the detective story—before *Partisan Review*. To be exact, *Partisan Review* had existed as a Stalinist magazine, and then it had died, gone to limbo. But after the Moscow trials, the PR boys, Rahv and Phillips, revived it, got a backer, merged with some other people— Dwight Macdonald and others—and started it again. As an anti- Stalinist magazine. I had been married to an actor, and was supposed to know something about the theater, so I began writing a theater column for them. I didn't have any other ambitions at all. Then I married Edmund Wilson, and after we'd been married about a week, he said, "I think you have a talent for writing fiction." And he put me in a little room. He didn't literally lock the door, but he said, "Stay in there!" And I did. I just sat down, and it just came. It was the first story I had ever written, really: the first story in *The Company She Keeps*. Robert Penn Warren published it in the *Southern Review*. And I found myself writing fiction to my great surprise.

Interviewer: This was when you became involved in politics, wasn't it?

McCarthy: No. Earlier. In 1936, at the time of the Moscow trials. That changed absolutely everything. I got swept into the whole Trotskyite movement. But by accident. I was at a party. I knew Jim Farrell—I'd reviewed one of his books, I think it was *Studs Lonigan*—in any case, I knew Jim Farrell, and I was asked to a party given by his publisher for Art Young, the old *Masses* cartoonist. There were a lot of Communists at this party. Anyway, Farrell went around asking people whether they thought Trotsky was entitled to a hearing and to the right of asylum. I said yes, and that was all. The next thing I discovered I was on the letterhead of something calling itself the American Committee for the Defense of Leon Trotsky. I was furious, of course, at this use of my name. Not that my name had any consequence, but still, it was mine. Just as I was about to make some sort of protest, I began to get all sorts of calls from Stalinists, telling me to get off the committee. I began to see that other people were falling off the committee, like Freda Kirchwey—she was the first to go, I think—and this cowardice impressed me so unfavorably that naturally I didn't say anything about my name having got on there by accident, or at least without my realizing. So I stayed.

I began to know all the people on the committee. We'd attend meetings. It was a completely different world. Serious, you know. Anyway, that's how I got to know the PR boys. They hadn't yet revived the *Partisan Review,* but they were both on the Trotsky committee, at least Philip was. We—the committee, that is—used to meet in Farrell's apartment. I remember once when we met on St. Valentine's Day and I thought, Oh, this is so strange, because I'm the only person in this room who realizes that it's Valentine's Day. It was true! I had a lot of rather rich Stalinist friends, and I was always on the defensive with them, about the Moscow Trial question, Trotsky, and so on. So I had to inform myself, really, in order to conduct the argument. I found that I was reading more and more, getting more and more involved in this business. At the same time I got a job at Covici Friede, a rather left-wing publishing house now out of business, also full of Stalinists. I began to see Philip Rahv again because Covici Friede needed some readers' opinions on Russian books, and I remembered that he read Russian, so he came around to the office, and we began to see each other. When *Partisan Review* was revived I appeared as a sort of fifth wheel—there may have been more than that—but in any case as a kind of appendage of *Partisan Review.*

Interviewer: Then you hadn't really been interested in politics before the Moscow trials?

McCarthy: No, not really. My first husband had worked at the Theater Union, which was a radical group downtown that put on proletarian plays, and there were lots of Communists in that. Very few Socialists. And so I knew all these people; I knew that kind of person. But I wasn't very sympathetic to them. We used to see each other, and there were a lot of jokes. I even marched in May Day parades. Things like that. But it was all . . . fun. It was all done in that spirit. And I remained, as the *Partisan Review* boys said, absolutely bourgeois throughout. They always said to me very sternly, "You're really a throwback. You're really a twenties figure."

Interviewer: How did you react to that?

McCarthy: Well, I suppose I was wounded. I was a sort of gay, good-time girl, from their point of view. And they were men of the thirties. Very serious. That's why my position was so insecure on *Partisan Review;* it wasn't exactly insecure, but . . . lowly. I mean, in *fact.* And that was why they let me write about the theater, because they thought the theater was of absolutely no consequence.

Interviewer: How did the outbreak of the war affect your political opinion? The *Partisan Review* group split apart, didn't it?

McCarthy: At the beginning of the war we were all isolationists, the whole group. Then I think the summer after the fall of France— certainly before Pearl Harbor—Philip Rahv wrote an article in which he said in a measured sentence, "In a certain sense, this is our war." The rest of us were deeply shocked by this, because we regarded it as a useless imperialist war. You couldn't beat Fascism that way: "Fight the enemy at home," and so on. In other words, we reacted to the war rather in the manner as if it had been World War I. This was after Munich, after the so-called "phony war." There was some reason for having certain doubts about the war, at least about the efficacy of the war. So when Philip wrote this article, a long controversy began on *Partisan Review.* It split between those who supported the war, and those who didn't. I was among those who didn't—Edmund Wilson also, though for slightly different reasons. Dwight Macdonald and Clement Greenberg split off, and Dwight founded his own magazine, *politics,* which started out as a Trotskyite magazine, and then became a libertarian, semi-anarchist one. Meyer Schapiro was in this group, and I forget who else. Edmund was really an unreconstructed isolationist. The others were either Marxist or libertarian. Of course there was a split in the Trotskyite movement at that period.

Toward the end of the war, I began to realize that there was something hypocritical about my position—that I was really supporting the war. I'd go to a movie—there was a marvelous documentary called *Desert Victory* about the British victory over Rommel's Africa Corps—and I'd find myself weeping madly when Montgomery's bagpipers went through to El Alamein. In other words, cheering the war, and on the other hand, being absolutely against Bundles for Britain, against Lend Lease—this was after Lend Lease, of course— against every practical thing. And suddenly, I remember—it must have been the summer of '45 that I first said this aloud—I remember it was on the Cape, at Truro. There were a lot of friends, Chiaro- monte, Lionel Abel, Dwight, et cetera, at my house—by this time I was divorced from Edmund, or separated, anyway. And I said, "You know, I think I, and all of us, are really *for* the war." This was the first time this had been said aloud by me. Dwight indignantly denied it. "I'm *not* for the war!" he said. But he was. Then I decided I wanted to give a blood transfusion. And I practically had to get cleared! Now no one was making me do this, but I felt I had to go and get cleared by my friends first. Was it wrong of me to support the war effort by giving a blood transfusion? It was agreed that it was all right. All this *fuss!* So I gave a blood transfusion, just one. Some other people were doing it too, I believe, independently, at the same time, people of more or less this tendency. That is the end of that story.

Years later, I realized I really thought that Philip had been right, and that the rest of us had been wrong. Of course we didn't know about the concentration camps: the death camps hadn't started at the beginning. All that news came in fairly late. But once this news was in, it became clear—at least to me, and I still believe it—that the only way to have stopped it was in a military way. That only the military defeat of Hitler could stop this, and it had to be stopped. But it took a long, long time to come to this view. You're always afraid of making the same mistake over again. But the trouble is you can always correct an earlier mistake like our taking the attitude to World War II as if it were World War I, but if you ever try to project the correction of a mistake into the future, you may make a different one. That is, many people now are talking about World War III as if it were World War II.

Interviewer: What I don't see, though, is how all this left you once the war was over.

McCarthy: Actually, as I remember, after the war was the very best period, politically, that I've been through. At that time, it seemed to me there was a lot of hope around. The war was over! Certain—

perhaps—mistakes had been recognized. The bomb had been
dropped on Hiroshima, and there was a kind of general repentance
of this fact. This was before the hydrogen bomb; and we never even
dreamed that the Russians were going to get the atomic bomb. The
political scene looked free. This was not only true for us—it seemed
a good moment. At least there was still the hope of small libertarian
movements. People like Dwight and Chiaromonte and I used to talk
about it a great deal, and even Koestler was writing at the period
about the possibility of founding oases—that's where I took the title
of that book from. It seemed possible still, utopian but possible, to
change the world on a small scale. Everyone was trying to live in a
very principled way, but with quite a lot of energy, the energy that
peace had brought, really. This was the period of the Marshall Plan,
too. It was a good period. Then of course the Russians got the atom
bomb, and the hydrogen bomb came. That was the end of *any* hope,
or at least any hope that I can see of anything being done except in a
massive way.

Interviewer: How do you characterize your political opinion now?

McCarthy: Dissident!

Interviewer: All the way round?

McCarthy: Yes! No, I still believe in what I believed in then—I still
believe in a kind of libertarian socialism, a decentralized socialism.
But I don't see any possibility of achieving it. That is, within the span
that I can see, which would be, say, to the end of my son's
generation, your generation. It really seems to me sometimes that the
only hope is space. That is to say, perhaps the most energetic—in a
bad sense—elements will move on to a new world in space. The
problems of mass society will be transported into space, leaving
behind this world as a kind of Europe, which then eventually tourists
will visit. The Old World. I'm only half joking. I don't think that the
problem of social equality has ever been solved. As soon as it looks
as if it were going to be solved, or even as if it were going to be
confronted,—say, as at the end of the eighteenth century—there's a
mass move to a new continent which defers this solution. After '48,
after the failure of the '48 revolutions in Europe, hope for an
egalitarian Europe really died, and the '48-ers, many of them, went
to California in the Gold Rush as '49-ers. My great-grandfather, from
central Europe, was one of them. The Gold Rush, the Frontier was a

substitute sort of equality. Think of Chaplin's film. And yet once the concept of equality had entered the world, life becomes intolerable without it; yet life continues without its being realized. So it may be that there will be another displacement, another migration. The problem, the solution, or the confrontation, will again be postponed.

Interviewer: Do you find that your critical work, whether it's political or literary, creates any problems in relation to your work as a novelist?

McCarthy: No, except that you have the perpetual problem, if somebody asks you to do a review, whether to interrupt what you're writing—if you're writing a novel—to do the review. You have to weigh whether the subject interests you enough, or whether you're tired at that moment, emotionally played out by the fiction you're writing. Whether it would be a good thing to stop and concentrate on something else. I just agreed to and did a review of Camus' collected fiction and journalism. That *was* in some way connected with my own work, with the question of the novel in general. I thought, yes, I will do this because I want to read all of Camus and decide what I think about him finally. (Actually, I ended up almost as baffled as when I started.) But in general, I don't take a review unless it's something like that. Or unless Anthony West attacks Dickens. You know. Either it has to be some sort of thing that I want very much to take sides on, or something I'd like to study a bit, that I want to find out about anyway. Or where there may, in the case of study, be some reference—very indirect—back to my own work.

Interviewer: This is quite a change from the time when you wrote criticism and never even thought of writing fiction. But now you consider yourself a novelist? Or don't you bother with these distinctions?

McCarthy: Well, I suppose I consider myself a novelist. Yes. Still, whatever way I write was really, I suppose, formed critically. That is, I learned to write reviews and criticism and then write novels so that however I wrote, it was formed that way. George Eliot, you know, began by translating Strauss, began by writing about German philosophy—though her philosophic passages are not at all good in *Middlemarch*. Nevertheless, I *think* that this kind of training really makes one more interested in the subject than in the style. Her work certainly doesn't suffer from any kind of stylistic frippery. There's certainly no voluminous drapery around. There is a kind of concision in it, at her best—that passage where she's describing the character of Lydgate—which shows, I think, the critical and philosophic training. I've never liked the conventional conception of "style." What's confusing is that style usually means some form of fancy writing—when people say, oh yes, so and so's such a "wonderful stylist." But if one means by style the voice, the irreducible and always recognizable and alive thing, then of course style is really everything. It's what you find in Stendhal, it's what you find in Pasternak. The same thing you find in a poet—the sound of, say, Donne's voice. In a sense, you can't go further in an analysis of Donne than to be able to place this voice, in the sense that you recognize Don Giovanni by the voice of Don Giovanni.

Interviewer: In speaking of your own writing, anyway, you attribute its "style" to your earlier critical work—then you don't feel the influence of other writers of fiction?

McCarthy: I don't think I have any influences. I think my first story, the first one in *The Company She Keeps,* definitely shows the Jamesian influence—James is so terribly catching. But beyond that, I can't find any influence. That is, I can't as a detached person—as detached as I can be—look at my work and see where it came from from the point of view of literary sources.

Interviewer: There must be certain writers, though, that you are *drawn* to more than others.

McCarthy: Oh, yes! But I don't think I write like them. The writer I really like best is Tolstoi, and I *know* I don't write like Tolstoi. I wish I did! Perhaps the best English prose is Thomas Nash. I don't write at all like Thomas Nash.

Interviewer: It would seem also, from hints you give us in your books, that you like Roman writers as well.

McCarthy: I did when I was young, very much. At least, I adored Catullus, and Juvenal; those were the two I really passionately loved. And Caesar, when I was a girl. But you couldn't say that I had been influenced by *Catullus!* No! And Stendhal I like very, very much. Again, I would be happy to write like Stendhal, but I don't. There are certain sentences in Stendhal that come to mind as how to do it if one could. I can't. A certain kind of clarity and brevity—the author's attitude summed up in a sentence, and done so simply, done without patronizing. Some sort of joy.

Interviewer: It's a dangerous game to play, the influence one.

McCarthy: Well in some cases it's easy to see, and people themselves acknowledge it, and are interested in it, as people are interested in their genealogy. I simply can't find my ancestors. I was talking to somebody about John Updike, and he's another one I would say I can't find any sources for.

Interviewer: Do you like his writing?

McCarthy: Yes. I've not quite finished *Rabbit, Run*—I must get it back from the person I lent it to and finish it. I thought it was very good, and so stupidly reviewed. I'd read *Poorhouse Fair,* which I thought was really remarkable. Perhaps it suffered from the point-of-view problem, the whole virtuosity of doing it through the eyes of this old man sitting on the veranda of the poorhouse, through his eyes with their refraction, very old eyes, and so on. I think, in a way, this trick prevents him saying a good deal in the book. Nevertheless, it's quite a remarkable book. But anyway, I nearly didn't read *Rabbit, Run* because I thought, Oh my God! from reading those reviews. The reviewers seemed to be under the impression that the hero was a terrible character. It's incredible! No, I think it's the most interesting American novel I've read in quite a long time.

Interviewer: What about others? Did you like *Henderson the Rain King?*

McCarthy: Well, yes, the first part of *Henderson* I think is marvelous. The vitality! I still think it's an amusing novel right through the lions, almost like a French eighteenth-century novel, or *conte,* very charming. But it doesn't have this tremendous blast of vitality that the first part has, and it doesn't have the density.

Interviewer: What other recent American novels have you been interested by?

McCarthy: Well, name one. There really aren't any! I mean, are there? I can't think of any. I don't like Salinger, not at all. That last thing isn't a novel anyway, whatever it is. I don't like it. Not at all. It suffers from this terrible sort of metropolitan sentimentality and it's *so* narcissistic. And to me, also, it seemed so false, so calculated. Combining the plain man with an absolutely megalomaniac egoism. I simply can't stand it.

Interviewer: What do you think of women writers, or do you think the category "woman writer" should not be made?

McCarthy: Some women writers make it. I mean, there's a

certain kind of woman writer who's a capital W, capital W. Virginia
Woolf certainly was one, and Katherine Mansfield was one, and
Elizabeth Bowen is one. Katherine Anne Porter? Don't think she
really is—I mean, her writing is certainly very feminine, but I would
say that there wasn't this "WW" business in Katherine Anne Porter.
Who else? There's Eudora Welty, who's certainly not a "Woman
Writer." Though she's become one lately.

Interviewer: What is it that happens to make this change?

McCarthy: I think they become interested in décor. You notice the
change in Elizabeth Bowen. Her early work is much more masculine.
Her later work has much more drapery in it. Who else? Jane Austen
was never a "Woman Writer," I don't think. The cult of Jane Austen
pretends that she was, but I don't think she was. George Eliot
certainly wasn't, and George Eliot is the kind of woman writer I
admire. I was going to write a piece at some point about this called
"Sense and Sensibility," dividing women writers into these two. I *am*
for the ones who represent sense, and so was Jane Austen.

Interviewer: Getting away from novels for a moment, I'd like to
ask you about *Memories of a Catholic Girlhood* if I might. Will you
write any more autobiography?

McCarthy: I was just reading—oh God, actually I *was* just starting
to read Simone de Beauvoir's second volume, *La Force de l'Age,* and
she announces in the preface that she can't write about her later self
with the same candor that she wrote about her girlhood.

Interviewer: You feel that too?

McCarthy: On this one point I agree with her. One has to be
really old, I think, really quite an old person—and by that time I
don't know what sort of shape one's memory would be in.

Interviewer: You don't agree with her on other points?

McCarthy: I had an interview with *L'Express* the other day, and I
gave Simone de Beauvoir the works. Let's not do it twice. I think
she's pathetic, that's all. This book is supposed to be better, more
interesting anyway, than the first one because it's about the thirties,
and everyone wants to read about the thirties. And her love affair
with Sartre, which is just about the whole substance of this book, is
supposed to be very touching. The book *is* more interesting than the
first one. But I think she's odious. A mind totally bourgeois turned
inside out.

Interviewer: I have something else to ask, apropos of *Memories of a Catholic Girlhood*. There are certain points, important points and moments in your novels, where you deepen or enlarge the description of the predicament in which a character may be by reference to a liturgical or ecclesiastical or theological parallel or equivalence. What I want to know is, is this simply a strict use of analogy, a technical literary device, or does it indicate any conviction that these are valid and important ways of judging a human being?

McCarthy: I suppose it's a reference to a way of thinking about a human being. But I think at their worst they're rather just literary references. That is, slightly show-off literary references. I have a terrible compulsion to make them—really a dreadful compulsion. The first sentence of *The Stones of Florence* begins, "How can you stand it? This is the first thing, and the last thing, the eschatological question that the visitor leaves echoing in the air behind him." Something of that sort. Well, everybody was after me to take out that word. I left it out when I published that chapter in the *New Yorker*, but I put it back in the book. No, I do have this great compulsion to make those references. I think I do it as a sort of secret signal, a sort of looking over the heads of the readers who don't recognize them to the readers who do understand them.

Interviewer: If these references *are* only literary ones, secret signals, then they are blasphemous.

McCarthy: Yes, I see what you mean. I suppose they are. Yes, they are secret jokes, they are blasphemies. But—I think I said something of this in the introduction of *Catholic Girlhood*—I think that religion offers to Americans (I mean the Roman Catholic religion) very often the only history and philosophy they ever get. A reference to it somehow opens up that historical vista. In that sense it is a device for deepening the passage.

Interviewer: Could we go back to your novels for a moment? I'd like to ask you about how you begin on them. Do you start with the characters, the situation, the plot? What comes first? Perhaps that's too hard a question, too general.

McCarthy: Very hard, and I'm awfully specific. I can really only think in specific terms, at least about myself. *The Groves of Academe* started with the plot. The plot and this figure: there can't be the plot without this figure of the impossible individual, the unemployable

professor and his campaign for justice. Justice, both in quotes, you
know, and serious in a way. What *is* justice for the unemployable
person? That was conceived from the beginning as a plot: the whole
idea of the reversal at the end, when Mulcahy is triumphant and the
President is about to lose his job or quit, when the worm turns and is
triumphant. I didn't see exactly what would happen in between; the
more minute details weren't worked out. But I did see that there
would be his campaign for reinstatement and then his secret would
be discovered. In this case that he had *not* been a Communist. *A
Charmed Life* began with a short story; the first chapter was written
as a short story. When I conceived the idea of its being a novel, I
think about all I knew was that the heroine would have to die in the
end. Everybody objected to that ending, and said that it was terrible
have her killed in an automobile accident in the last paragraph—
utterly unprepared for, and so on. But the one thing I knew
absolutely certainly was that the heroine had to die in the end. At first
I was going to have her have an abortion, and have her die in the
abortion. But that seemed to me so trite. Then I conceived the idea
of having her drive on the correct side of the road and get killed,
because in this weird place everyone is always on the wrong side of
the road. But all that is really implicit in the first chapter.

Interviewer: So the charge that readers are unprepared for the
last paragraph you feel is unfair?

McCarthy: There may be something wrong with the novel, I don't
know. But it was always supposed to have a fairy tale element in it.
New Leeds is *haunted!* Therefore nobody should be surprised if
something unexpected happens, or something catastrophic, for the
place is also pregnant with catastrophe. But it may be that the
treatment in between was too realistic, so that the reader was led to
expect a realistic continuation of everything going on in a rather
moderate way. It was, to some extent, a symbolic story. The novel is
supposed to be about doubt. All the characters in different ways
represent doubt, whether it is philosophical or ontological doubt as in
the case of the strange painter who questions everything—"Why
don't I murder my grandmother?" and so on. Or the girl's rather
nineteenth-century self-doubt, doubt of the truth, of what she
perceives. In any case, everyone is supposed to represent one or
another form of doubt. When the girl finally admits to herself that

she's pregnant, and also recognizes that she must do something about it, in other words, that she has to put up a real stake—and she does put up a real stake—at that moment she becomes mortal. All the other characters are immortal. They have dozens of terrible accidents, and they're all crippled in one way or another, and yet they have this marvelous power of survival. All those drunks and human odds and ends. Anyway, the girl makes the decision—which from the point of view of conventional morality is a wicked decision—to have an abortion, to kill life. Once she makes this decision, she becomes mortal, and doesn't belong to the charmed circle any more. As soon as she makes it, she gets killed—to get killed is simply a symbol of the fact that she's mortal.

Interviewer: You say that her decision makes her mortal. But her decision has also included someone else, the painter.

McCarthy: Yes, yes. I see what you mean. I hadn't thought of that, that when she asks somebody to help her it implies some sort of social bond, some sort of mutual bond between people in society, while the rest of these people are still a community of isolates.

Interviewer: His joining her in this mortal, social bond, that doesn't make him mortal as well? He is still a part of the charmed circle?

McCarthy: He's too sweet to be mortal! Well, he's a comic figure, and I have this belief that all comic characters are immortal. They're eternal. I believe this is Bergson's theory too. He has something, I'm told, about comic characters being *figé*. Like Mr. and Mrs. Micawber: they all have to go on forever and be invulnerable. Almost all Dickens' characters have this peculiar existence of eternity, except the heroes, except Pip, or Nicholas Nickleby, or David Copperfield.

Interviewer: What other characters in your novels do you consider—

McCarthy: The comic ones? Who knows whether they're immortal! As far as I'm concerned, they're immortal!

Interviewer: Then you haven't thought of this distinction between "mortal" and "immortal" in relation to characters in other of your novels besides *A Charmed Life?*

McCarthy: I didn't think of this distinction until just recently, and not in connection with myself. It's just at this very moment—*now* talking with you—that I'm thinking of it in connection with myself. I would say that it is a law that applies to *all* novels: that the comic characters are *figé,* are immortal, and that the hero or heroine exists in time, because the hero or heroine is always in some sense equipped with purpose.

The man in *The Groves of Academe.* Well, he's immortal, yes. He is a comic villain, and villains too always—I think—partake in this comic immortality. I *think* so. I'm not sure that you couldn't find an example, though, of a villain it wasn't true of. In Dickens again. In the late novels, somebody like Bradley Headstone, the schoolmaster, he's a mixed case. He's certainly not a villain in the sense of, say, the villain in *Little Dorritt,* who belongs to the old-fashioned melo-dramatic immortal type of villain. Headstone is really half a hero, Steerforth is half a hero, and therefore they don't conform to this.

This all came to me last year, this distinction, when I was thinking about the novel. Not my novel: The Novel.

But maybe that's really part of the trouble I'm having with *my* novel! These girls are all essentially comic figures, and it's awfully hard to make anything happen to them. Maybe this is really the trouble! Maybe I'm going to find out something in this interview! That the whole problem is *time!* I mean for me, in this novel. The passage of time, to show development. I think maybe my trouble is that these girls are comic figures, and that therefore they really can't develop! You see what I mean? They're not all so terribly comic, but most of them are.

How're they ever going to progress through the twenty years between the inauguration of Roosevelt and the inauguration of Eisenhower? This has been the great problem, and here I haven't had a form for it. I mean, all I know is that they're supposed to be middle-aged at the end.

Yes, I think maybe that *is* the trouble. One possibility would be . . . I've been introducing them one by one, chapter by chapter. They all appear at the beginning, you know, like the beginning of an opera, or a musical comedy. And then I take them one by one, chapter by chapter. I have been bringing each one on a little later on in time. But perhaps I can make bigger and bigger jumps so that you could meet, say, the last one when she is already middle-aged. You see what I mean. Maybe this would solve the problem. One five years later, another eight years later, and so on. I could manage the time problem that way. This has been very fruitful! Thank you!

Interviewer: I want to ask you about the problem of time in the novel. You have written that a novel's action cannot take place in the future. But you have said that the action described in *The Oasis* all takes place in the future.

McCarthy: *The Oasis* is not a novel. I don't classify it as such. It was terribly criticized, you know, on that ground; people objected, said it wasn't a novel. But I never meant it to be. It's a *conte,* a *conte philosophique.*

Interviewer: And *A Charmed Life* you say has fairy-tale elements.

McCarthy: I'm not sure any of my books are novels. Maybe none of them are. Something happens in my writing—I don't mean it to— a sort of distortion, a sort of writing on the bias, seeing things with a sort of swerve and swoop. *A Charmed Life,* for instance. You know, at the beginning I make a sort of inventory of all the town characters, just telling who they are. Now I did this with the intention of describing, well, this nice, ordinary, old-fashioned New England town. But it ended up differently. Something is distorted, the description takes on a sort of extravagance—I don't know exactly how it happens. I know I don't mean it to happen.

Interviewer: You say in one of your articles that perhaps the fault lies simply in the material which the modern world affords, that it itself lacks—

McCarthy: Credibility? Yes. It's a difficulty I think all modern writers have.

Interviewer: Other than the problem of arrangement of time, are there other specific technical difficulties about the novel you find yourself particularly concerned with?

McCarthy: Well, the whole question of the point of view, which tortures everybody. It's the problem that everybody's been up against since Joyce, if not before. Of course James really began it, and Flaubert even. You find it as early as *Madame Bovary.* The problem of the point of view, and the voice: *style indirect libre*—the author's voice, by a kind of ventriloquism, disappearing in and completely limited by the voices of his characters. What it has meant is the complete banishment of the author. I would like to restore the author!

I haven't tried yet, but I'd like to try after this book, which is as far as I can go in ventriloquism. I would like to try to restore the author. Because you find that if you obey this Jamesian injunction of "Dramatize, dramatize," and especially if you deal with comic characters, as in my case, there is so much you can't say because you're limited by these mentalities. It's just that a certain kind of intelligence—I'm not only speaking of myself, but of anybody, Saul Bellow, for example—is more or less absent from the novel, and has to be, in accordance with these laws which the novel has made for itself. I think one reason that everyone—at least I—welcomed *Dr. Zhivago* was that you had the author in the form of the hero. And this beautiful tenor voice, the hero's voice and the author's—this marvelous voice, and this clear sound of intelligence. The Russians have never gone through the whole development of the novel you find in Joyce, Faulkner, et cetera, so that Pasternak was slightly unaware of the problem! But I think this technical development has become absolutely killing to the novel.

Interviewer: You say that after this novel about the Vassar girls, you—

McCarthy: I don't know what I'm going to do, but I want to try something that will introduce, at least back into my work, my own voice. And not in the disguise of a heroine. I'm awfully sick of my heroine. I don't mean in this novel: my heroine of the past. Because the sensibility in each novel got more and more localized with this heroine, who became an agent of perception, et cetera.

Let me make a jump now. The reason that I enjoyed doing those books on Italy, the Venice and Florence books, was that I was writing *in my own voice*. One book was in the first person, and one was completely objective, but it doesn't make any difference. I felt, you know, now I can talk freely! The books were written very fast, the Venice one faster. Even the Florence book, with masses of research in it, was written very fast, with a great deal of energy, with a kind of liberated energy. And without the peculiar kind of painstakingness that's involved in the dramatization that one does in a novel, that is, when nothing can come in that hasn't been perceived through a character. The technical difficulties are so great, in projecting yourself, in feigning an alien consciousness, that too much energy gets lost, I think, in the masquerade. And I think this is not only true of me.

Interviewer: How did you come to write those books about Florence and Venice?

McCarthy: By chance. I was in Paris, just about to go home to America, and somebody called up and asked if I would come and have a drink at the Ritz before lunch, that he wanted to ask me something. It was an intermediary from the Berniers, who edit *L'Oeil*. They were in Lausanne, and this man wanted to know whether I would write a book on Venice for them. I had been in Venice once for ten days, years ago, but it seemed somehow adventurous. And there were other reasons too. So I said yes. I went out to meet the Berniers in Lausanne. I had absolutely no money left, about twenty dollars, and I thought, what if all this is a terrible practical joke? You know. I'll get to Lausanne and there won't be any of these people! There'll be nobody! I ran into Jay Laughlin that night, and he said that his aunt was in Lausanne at the moment, so that if anything happened to me, I could call on her! But in any case, I went to Lausanne, and they were real, they were there. And we drove to Venice together.

I knew nothing about the subject—maybe I exaggerate my ignorance now—but I was *appalled*. I was afraid to ask any questions—whenever I'd ask a question Georges Bernier would shudder because it revealed such absolutely terrifying depths of ignorance. So I tried to be silent. I'd never heard before that there was more than one Tiepolo, or more than one Tintoretto, that there was a son. I vaguely knew Bellini, but didn't have any idea there were three Bellinis. Things like that. I couldn't have been expected to know Venetian history, but actually Venetian history is very easy to bone up on, and there isn't much. But the art history! And I considered myself a reasonably cultivated person! My art history was of the most fragmentary nature!

But it was fun, and then that led me into doing the Florence book. I didn't want to, at first. But everything in Venice, in Italy for that matter, really points to Florence, everything in the Renaissance anyway, like signposts on a road. Whenever you're near discovery, you're near Florence. So I felt that this was all incomplete; I thought I had to go to Florence. It was far from my mind to write a book. Then various events happened, and slowly I decided, all right, I would do the book on Florence. After that I went back to Venice and studied the Florentines in Venice, just for a few days. It was *so* strange to come back to Venice after being immersed in Florence. It looked so terrible! From an architectural point of view, *so* scrappy and nondescript, if you'd been living with the Florentine substance and monumentality, and intellectuality of architecture. At first coming back was a real shock. Oh, and I discovered I liked history! And I thought, my God, maybe I've made a mistake. Maybe I should have been an historian.

Interviewer: It would also appear that you discovered you loved Brunelleschi.

McCarthy: Oh, yes! Yes! Also, I felt a great, great congeniality—I don't mean with Brunelleschi personally, I would flatter myself if I said that—but with the history of Florence, the Florentine temperament. I felt that through the medium of writing about this city I could set forth what I believed in, what I was for; that through this city, its history, its architects and painters—more its sculptors than its painters—it was possible for me to say what I believed in. And say it very affirmatively, even though this all ended in 1529, you know, long before the birth of Shakespeare.

Interviewer: In reading the Florence book, I remember being very moved by the passage where you talk of Brunelleschi, about his "absolute integrity and essence," that solidity of his, both real and ideal. When you write about Brunelleschi, you write about this sureness, this "being-itself," and yet as a novelist—in *The Company She Keeps* for instance—you speak of something so very different, and you take almost as a theme this fragmented unplaceability of the human personality.

McCarthy: But I was very young then. I think I'm really not interested in the quest for the self any more. Oh, I suppose everyone continues to be interested in the quest for the self, but what you feel when you're older, I think, is that—how to express this—that you really must *make* the self. It's absolutely useless to look for it, you won't find it, but it's possible in some sense to make it. I don't mean in the sense of making a mask, a Yeatsian mask. But you finally begin in some sense to make and to choose the self you want.

Interviewer: Can you write novels about that?

McCarthy: I never have. I never have, I've never even thought of it. That is, I've never thought of writing a developmental novel in which a self of some kind is discovered or is made, is forged, as they say. No. I suppose in a sense I don't know any more today than I did in 1941 about what my identity is. But I've stopped looking for it. I must say, I believe much more in truth now than I did. I do believe in the solidity of truth much more. Yes. I believe there is a truth, and that it's knowable.

Mary McCarthyism

Brock Brower/1962

From *Esquire*, 58 (July 1962), 62-67. Reprinted by permission of the Hearst Corp. Copyright © 1962 by Hearst Corp.

Mary McCarthy has the Nicest Smile. At the slightest social pressure, it springs open and automatically catches. She can hold it there— flicking its long, white upper blade of handsome, emphatic teeth this way, that way at every threatening conversational turn—for some- times five, ten minutes at a stretch. Nothing cows it. She can smoke through it, argue through it, spill the beans through it, even *smile* through it. It has gotten way beyond being anything quite so straightforward as her Best Feature. As a child, she remembers resorting to it, as such, regularly, snapping it down protectively on her face like a rubber band, the orphan's sweet guise of lovableness. But that early defensiveness—like her Faith, or her worry over bowleg- gedness—is something she long ago left behind in Seattle with the Sisters of the Sacred Heart. Since then, whether framed under the large hats, the "terrific hats" she was famous for during her more Bohemian days in the Village, or enaureoled by the severe, yet somewhat wispy bunning of the greying hair she favors now in the quieter days of her fourth husband, that smile has become a subtle emanation of the mind: the poised cutting edge on one of the most knifelike female intelligences that Vassar, the Trotskyite movement, *Partisan Review,* the authorship of ten books, or eight years of marriage to Edmund Wilson ever tempered. "When most people smile at you, you feel cheered up," one of the maimed once told Dwight Macdonald, "but when *Mary McCarthy* smiles at you . . . !" It comes out of nowhere seemingly, like a concealed weapon, and the only difference now over the old days is that while she still carries it on her, she doesn't use it *quite* so often, *quite* so outrageously. "Mary," they all say, "has mellowed."

For whom, after all, has she *recently* left for dead in the blood- stained alley behind *Partisan Review,* his intellect cut from ear to ear? Nobody really, unless you count England's leading dramatic critic,

Kenneth Tynan—that "somewhat adenoidal spokesman-for-those-under-thirty" (?!)—caught naked and alone in the pages of his own newspaper, *The Observer,* such as Marat was caught by Charlotte Corday in his own bathtub. She began her recent review of selections from Tynan's critical output, a volume entitled *Curtains,* by asking, "Is the title of this collection a pun ('It's curtains for me, pal')? " and, quite typically, she pinked him mortally on his "positive" side. "On his 'positive' side, Tynan tends to write advertising copy. . . . The worst I can say of Tynan is that I thought better of him when I began this book than when I finished it." (?!!!) Who would've thought the young man had so much blood in him?

It was so like her old self, that review, precisely the kind of outrage that has made the name Mary McCarthy feared throughout the intellectual badlands ever since she began her literary career back in the late Thirties as a dramatic critic herself, for *Partisan Review.* She has since gone on to win acclaim as a short-story writer, a novelist, a really superb essayist, and "quite possibly the cleverest woman America has ever produced" (according to *Time*'s latest distribution of superlatives for book-jacket copy), but from the beginning, her most individual gift has clearly been for the quick wit and fell decision of a hanging judge supported by a devastating female scorn. "You don't so much review a play as draw up a crushing brief against it," Edmund Wilson once told her while he was courting her, and the same could be said for all things mortal—bad writing, weak principle, political error, moral or mental lapse, the pandering of modern communications, or just the rather shaggy beast in men— that have fallen under her basilisk eye. Even in her famous short stories, such as "The Man in the Brooks Brothers Shirt" or "Portrait of the Intellectual as a Yale Man," or in her three novels, *The Oasis, The Groves of Academe,* and *A Charmed Life,* she is still really the advocate drawing up a harsh brief against something or, more likely, somebody reprehensible. Her fiction, according to Macdonald, is really "a series of views of people's performances," and sometimes these "reviews" have been so crushing as to make life itself smart. When Philip Rahv, editor of *Partisan Review* and her old friend, discovered what she'd done to him as "Will Taub" in her first novel, *The Oasis,* he all but sued Mary. "That book! *That book!*" he used to moan to his compatriots, and Tynan—now harrowed as a living man, not as a mere fiction—must be all the more anguished. She has undoubtedly one of the most dread critical minds around, and this— combined with her substantial literary talent, her Amazonian courage in battle, her independence, and that smile—have placed her at the head of a train of intellectually rebellious young women, who, a little like the maenads, follow her more than she perhaps realizes, or ever wished.

In fact, there is some hint—from her friend Elizabeth Hardwick, a much gentler lady with a book review—that, at age fifty and much past her own Village days, Mary finds a certain sadness now accompanies the unpleasant duty of ripping up a bright young man like Tynan in his intellectual prime. "I once said to Mary, thinking more of myself really, 'Isn't it *awful* to be in your forties and still find yourself attacking people? Wouldn't you rather just write nice things about people you enjoy reading?' And Mary said, 'Oh Lord yes, I know just what you mean. I don't want to do it. It's something for young people to do. *But they don't do it!*' "

And so *she* must—smiling through—though what was once a pleasure has now become a duty. Not long ago, while she was waiting to tape an *Open End,* David Susskind walked up to her and, out of the blue, with a certain foreseeable male vanity, asked bluntly, "Why are you always so *bitter?* That's what I don't understand." Mary looked truly surprised. "But I don't think I'm bitter!" She smiled hopefully in all directions. "Do *you?*"—asking anybody. She really could not understand how someone could mistake high standards for personal bitterness, and she struggled with the problem, almost fidgeting, just as another woman might struggle with the awkward situation of being far too tall for her escort. It's embarrassing, but a woman of intellect can't very well walk around mentally stooped over all the time. It's just too bad if some people are frightened off.

And indeed they are. A not uncommon reaction among many who read her is to count up the bodies in that alley behind *Partisan Review*—the Man in That Shirt ("No, he was *not* Wendell Willkie! "); the Yale Man (an ex-liberal, who, in real life, has now gone all the way over to William F. Buckley, Jr.'s *National Review*); Dottie Who Made an Honest Woman of Herself, by following in the stony path of *volte-face* virtue and getting herself fitted for a diaphragm; several husbands, or pieces thereof, crammed into her novels like dismembered limbs into a Grand Central baggage locker; Simone de Beauvoir, inflated and punctured as "Mlle. Gulliver en Amérique" in *On the Contrary*; even old friends and lovers from *Partisan Review* itself—and then to conclude in horror, "But she's so *nasty!*"

But no, *not* nasty, insist her very loyal friends. Only incredibly honest. "Mary is almost physically incapable of saying anything she doesn't mean," says Miss Hardwick. "Almost *bodily.*" Macdonald— who incidentally makes his own battered appearance in *The Oasis* as his former pacifist self, "Macdougal Macdermott"—says it's in fact an amusing sight to watch Mary straining *not* to say what she really thinks. "She's always going to be goring somebody's ox, and when she knows she shouldn't, she gets kind of fussed," he notes. "She's a lot like what the Bloomsbury Group must have been like. Woolf, Forster, Keynes, Strachey, they all put personal friendship very high up on the scale, but, above all else, they put telling the truth. Mary has this same aristocratic attitude. She's extremely loyal, but, at the same time, extremely scrupulous about the truth."

Either way, nasty or honest, this intense scrupulosity, even in the most incredible fixes—such as the one her heroine, Margaret Sargent, gets into with the Man in the Brooks Brothers Shirt, waking up in a Pullman Compartment, convinced Nothing Has Happened, and suddenly brushing against his naked, unfamiliar body—has become her personal celebrity. "Lots of women had taken up with a man on the train before—or at least they'd *thought* about doing it— but this was the first time anybody ever *wrote* about it," recalls Miss Hardwick. "I was absolutely bowled over by it." So were a great many others (though there was actually some sentiment among the *Partisan* editors against publishing the story on the grounds it was *journalism,* not fiction), and ever since it has been a case of Mary's influence reaching a little further outward with each new literary "shocker." No one book or story has ever done it for her as much as the cumulative effect of a scene here—the outlandish seduction in *A Charmed Life*—a character there—the anti-Semitic colonel in her story, *Artists in Uniform*—and an outrageous statement somewhere in between—that John Hersey's *Hiroshima* "made [the atom bomb] familiar and safe, and so, in the final sense, boring." Taken all together, they display a candor that might slip from any honest

woman occasionally but never from one honest woman so often. The
shock, in the end, is the constancy of her candor.

Yet she always manages to carry it off—the most scathing critical
attack, or the most clinical sexual scene—with an uncanny ladylike
primness. She would not seem so audacious were she not also so
fastidious. Her style, for instance; if there is such a thing as dainty,
Ciceronian English, that is what she writes. Even during her school
days, "writing with a Latinate turn, compressed, analytic, and yet
having a certain extravagance or oratorical flourish sounded in my
ears like a natural, spoken language." On the other hand, what most
people consider the "natural, spoken language" often woolies her. "I
have a horror of slang," she says. "I couldn't say somebody was
'loaded,' for instance—unless I put it in quotation marks." Yet she
can have her distrait Margaret Sargent wake up the morning after—
hung-over, mortified, in need of a bath, undoubtedly bruised in
(quote) places (unquote)—and respond to her Pullman lover's "Kiss
me" by frankly confessing, "I have to throw up."

What saves Margaret Sargent from being really besmirched by this
experience is her *inexperience*. Margaret—like all the thinly disguised
Mary McCarthy *personae*—is the innocent at the nadir. She is
"absolutely bowled over by it" herself—*surely nothing worse than
this could ever happen to her*—yet it does, continually, teaching the
always humiliating but never learned lesson to the wide-eyed,
Pollyannish Girl with the Safety Pin in her Panties that "a Fall is only
a pratfall after all."

In fact, there is a kind of hidden lesson hook in the scandal of her
better stories. Here (O Mistress Mary!), here's how a girl takes up with
a steel man on a train, keeps the Young Man and the Husband civil
to each other, seduces a fellow left-wing editor, goes for a "fitting,"
acts the gay divorcee at a genial party, goes to an analyst, seduces
her own ex-husband, decides on an abortion, and finally suffers
remorse for all these things, great or small. Nor have these lessons
been lost upon youth—any number of bright young things, edging
closer to defloration and beyond, imagine they have learned about
the world from her, cf., Radcliffe's turnout for "An Evening with Mary
McCarthy"—and Philip Roth probably paid this uncanny didacticism
its ultimate left-handed compliment in *Goodbye, Columbus*. When
Neil Klugman tries to encourage his girl, Brenda Patimkin, to get

herself "fitted." Brenda glowers accusingly at him for his seemingly
firsthand knowledge of the Margaret Sanger clinic:

"You've done this before?"

"No," I said. "I just know. I read Mary McCarthy."

"That's exactly right. That's just what I'd feel like, somebody out of
her."

The reference is to Dottie in a much scandalmongered 1954 story
that does for contraception what *Moby Dick* did for whaling, but that
feeling—like "somebody out of *her*"—is much more universal. It
applies broadly to any number of emotional predicaments in which
young women, tripped up by their own shaky modernity, often find
themselves, or fear to find themselves. Many an intelligent young
lady has declared fiercely for her sexual freedom, for her right to her
own mind, even for the challenge of a heads-on competition with
men, no quarter asked or given, in bed or out—just like "somebody
out of *her*"—only to find herself disastrously undermined by
feminine self-doubt, foolish shame, and a desperate need to be Told
What To Do—equally like "somebody out of *her*." Mary has defined
these contradictions almost too well, so exactly, in fact, that her
hostile critics claim that what she has really defined, for all men to
know, is the Modern American Bitch. But bitchiness is hardly a fair
estimate of her critical, imperious, yet highly feminine sensibility.
What she is actually writing—when she's supposedly being "just
bitchy"—is her own true and faithful account of the sexual politics of
certain modern women (what other "lady politician" has dared?),
and one wag has described the upshot of this side of her work as
Mary-McCarthyism.

Perhaps it's even worse to call Mary an -ism, but she has given
such a detailed record of her affairs, marriages, political leanings, and
other follies—and, incidentally, arrogated to her own use so many of
the trials she has caused others—that she really has become her own
central idea. In that sense, despite her intellectualism, she really *does*
think like a woman. In her early stories, and in her mock-heroic *My
Confession,* for instance, she reduces the entire radical movement of
the Thirties to a vaguely amorous aspect of her own personality.
Defend Trotsky! was the insistent sweet-nothing she whispered at
assignations in Webster Hall, and "out dancing in a nightclub, tall,
collegiate young Party members would press me to their shirt

bosoms and tell me not to be silly, honey." As passionately involved
as she once was in the old anti-Stalinist Left, she just can't help
treating it as long-dead gossip of a slightly personal nature. Actually,
she loves intellectual gossip—"Did you *hear* what Stravinsky did
when he was at the White House for dinner?"—and she is constantly
getting herself intellectually gossiped about. "Why is everybody
always talking about her?" pleads one disgruntled listener. "Do you
know I once knew more about Mary McCarthy and Philip Rahv than
I knew about *myself?*"

Her novels and stories—her "reviews of people's performances"—
are an extension of this gossip. "She's always writing *romans à clef,*"
complains one unfriendly critic, "and then handing you the *clef.*" In
The Oasis, she might as *well* have used the real names, her Utopian
colony was so patently inhabited by all her old soul mates from the
Europe-American Groups (organized to help refugee intellectuals in
the Forties) and so raucous with their chivvying, backbiting quarrels.
It took years for some of the "characters" in *The Oasis* to speak to
her again. In her later novels—*The Groves of Academe, A Charmed
Life*—her tracings from life have been a little less exact, but then
again, this only starts up an egregious guessing game about the
composite figures. How much did she make up, and how much really
is Edmund Wilson? By now, she has also begun to pop up in other
people's novels. Certainly nothing she ever "did" to anybody in one
of her books is quite as satirical as what Randall Jarrell, according to
literary gossip, "did" to her in his book, *Pictures from an Institution.*
How much did *he* make up, and how much is really Mary and her
third husband, Bowden Broadwater?

But, despite all these recriminations, Mary believes this is how
novels are. "Most novels are that way—filled with real people. Very
little is invented," she says, and in a recent essay, *The Fact in Fiction,*
she has written, "Even when it is most serious, the novel's
characteristic tone is one of gossip and tittle-tattle . . . if the breath of
scandal has not touched it, the book is not a novel. That is the trouble
with the art-novel (most of Virginia Woolf, for instance); it does not
stoop to gossip." She readily stoops to gossip herself—or rather, as
she puts it, "I am guilty of over-exuberant analysis,"—tattling on her
"characters" as if they had a half-life somewhere between fact and
fiction, which they do. Dottie, for instance, whom she left all alone

on a park bench outside the birth-control clinic in 1954. Dottie is to
be part of a novel called *The Group* about eight Vassar girls in search
of Progress. But Mary became "too depressed by it." "The fates of
these girls were going to be just too cruel for me to go on. I mean, to
humanity—not just to the girls. I only took it up again this year." Yet,
in real life, "Dottie isn't like that at all. That never happened to her.
The incident is entirely fictional. I saw Dottie recently, and she hasn't
changed a bit." Then who is Dottie? What is she? And Mary can
contrive the most dreamlike exculpations to show that a "character"
isn't really "somebody" after all. As she told Macdonald, the former
husband in *A Charmed Life* "can't be" Edmund Wilson, because (1)
the former husband is tall, and Wilson is short, and (2) the former
husband writes *successful* plays, and even though Wilson has been a
playwright, "everybody knows that Edmund never had a successful
play in his life!" True, true, we must be reading things into it. . . .

The qualifying breath of scandal then has touched her own books
and "made them novels"—some would even say it's Mary herself
who breathes into them the magic fire, like a she-dragon lying back
in the lair of Invaded Privacies—but in all fairness, she has easily
survived as much scandal as she has published. She would not make
a very good subject for an art-novel; her life has been far too
calamitous and outrageous. Orphaned at six, when an influenza
epidemic took both her parents in 1918, she grew up in Minneapolis
and Seattle with various grandparents and relatives, a bright,
deprived, rebellious girl stifled by all the usual petty tyrannies,
described in her most sensitive book, *Memories of a Catholic
Girlhood.* First the Cruel Uncle—Uncle Myers, a pinchpenny
household dictator, whose one book was *Uncle Remus,* and who
beat her for such grave offenses as winning first prize in a statewide
essay contest on "The Irish in American History." Then the
Church—her spiritual heritage from her Irish father, eked out in the
loneliness of convent schools. One day she decided to Lose Her Faith
in an exhibitionistic bid for attention—her first *scandal*—but though
fully prepared to Regain It at the dramatic moment, she suddenly
found, after listening unconvinced to all five grey proofs of God's
existence, that she really *had* lost it. It was typical of the kind of
apostasy that has overtaken her at her worst moments. Like objects
jump at some people, lapses fall upon her. Her one big moment in

convent school, for instance, came when a Sister snapped at her in class, "You're just like Lord Byron, brilliant but unsound." Thrilled by this sinister tribute, she ran home to tell her Seattle grandfather, and he promptly telephoned the Mother Superior to demand, scandalized, "what right one of her Sisters had to associate his innocent granddaughter with that degenerate blackguard, Lord Byron." To her mortification, the remark was coldly withdrawn on Monday, but it remains the classic example of the kind of dubious accolade that has been thrust upon her all her life, as if she simply could not win praise without having to take part of it in scandal.

Her four marriages, for instance. The scandal falls so patly against her, and she gets no sympathy, only excellent notices. She reacts by claiming—as she once did to her brother, the actor Kevin McCarthy, in a moment of marital despair—that no two people should be *allowed* to stay married for more than seven years, unless they could prove in court that they *should*. Her own marriages have lasted three years (1933-1936) to the late Harold Johnsrud, an actor, who "too young for character parts and too bald for juveniles," was suited only to play blind men in "the portentous and equivocal atmosphere of left-wing drama"; eight years (1938-1946) to Wilson, the impediment apparently being that "my mind was so totally different from Edmund's"; fifteen years (1946-1961) to Bowden Broadwater, a quiet reading period that has been aptly described as "a rest for Mary"; and more than a year now (1961-) to her present husband, James West, a State Department official, whom she met in Poland on a lecture tour and married after mutual divorces, much bad press, and considerable coolness issuing from the American Embassy. It has been an emotional collision course, no question, but Mary has survived it with her dignity intact because, as her close friend and intellectual companion, Hannah Arendt, points out, "it has by no means been calculated. . . . With Mary, it happens like a thunderbolt. She's not at all reflective about it." She just—as past husbands have sadly discovered—ups and walks out.

Yet, during the time she *has* been married, she has tried very hard to be the good wife. She really is a determined homemaker, to such an elaborate extent that some of her more jaded dinner guests—looking around at the embroidered samplers hanging on the walls of the Broadwater apartment in praise of Our Home—have thought she *must* be kidding. But no, she does everything well, except sweep. "I cannot sweep. I hate sweeping. And I don't know how to use a vacuum cleaner." She is also an excellent French cook. "I know you hear that about a lot of women," her brother says, "but Mary really *is*." Hannah thinks there is "something of a peasant" in Mary, but there is much more likely something still of the orphan. Mary has never been any good at being alone, and she instinctively nests as a hedge against that anxiety. "Mary must feel she can come home, *always*," Hannah notes, "and there must always be somebody there to tell *all* about it."

She has sometimes had to establish a home for herself under very trying circumstances. The tumult and the shouting from her marriage to Wilson has yet to subside completely in the gentle dells of Stamford, Connecticut. Its one totally happy issue is their son, Reuel Kimball Wilson, Mary's only child, "a marvelous boy," who, according to Hannah, has discovered "he can have the best of *both* worlds." "I tried to make him a lawyer," says Mary. "But I see now—though he would have made an admirable judge—he would've made a poor lawyer. He always had such a balanced mind." (Mary still remembers some of the Rhadamanthine judgments he passed as a schoolboy on Man & Ideas, e.g., "I think slavery is a good idea, but quite mean," or on Macdonald's postwar struggle with his political conscience, "I think Dwight is trying to give up progressiveness, but it's too late.") Reuel, now twenty-three and still much his father's son, has chosen instead the study of language. "He's really brilliant at it, too," says Mary. "Of course his father was a whiz at languages, but Reuel can actually *speak* them."

Despite the eventual rupture, however, she owes Wilson a large literary debt and freely admits it. It was not so much a question of influence—Mary stubbornly denies anybody's influence, including Wilson's, on her own thinking, though "I believe he *did* cure me of liking Aldous Huxley, if I wasn't over it already"—as a matter of encouragement. "He's extremely generous toward any young talent he believes is really there." He originally asked to meet her when she was only twenty-eight, because he very much admired the Theater Chronicle she was writing for *Partisan,* now part of her book, *Sights and Spectacles.* He very soon, however, started her off on an entirely new literary direction. "We'd been married about a week, and he said, 'I think you've got a talent for writing short stories.' So he put me off in the one free room we had at Stamford with a typewriter and shut the door. I wrote *Cruel and Barbarous Treatment* straight off, almost without blotting a line." This was the first of Margaret Sargent's misadventures—and pretty much a candid recounting of the prelude to one of her own divorces. She wrote five more of these stories—including briefs against the Yale Man, and the Man in That Shirt—and in 1942 they were loosely collected as *The Company She Keeps,* a book that has since become the *vade mecum* of Mary McCarthyism.

"Edmund always tried to make things easy for me—getting me help during the war when we had Reuel, and when help was really hard to find—so that I could go on with the writing." But at the same time, his own work naturally dominated. "Edmund gets his whole household involved in whatever he's doing. He tends to lecture rather than to converse, and he'll lecture all through dinner—even all through lunch, if he happens to come out for lunch." Mary overlapped mainly with Wilson's Marxist-Pacifist period, though, since she was something of a sympathizer herself, this wasn't half as trying on her patience as a briefer but more intense Walt Disney period. "I nearly went out of my mind. I can't stand Walt Disney, and he couldn't get enough of it." Obviously they split over much more than the Seven Dwarfs, but it does give some idea of how abruptly they could come to loggerheads. In fact, Mary's final exit from Wilson's domicile was another of those pratfall Falls that later appeared in one of her novelizations of life. But in her own words before the judge:

"We had about eighteen people at the party. Everybody had gone home and I was washing dishes. I asked him if he would empty the garbage. He said, 'Empty it yourself.' I started carrying out two large cans of garbage.

"As I went through the screen door, he made an ironical bow, repeating, 'Empty it yourself.' I slapped him—not terribly hard— went out and emptied the cans, then went upstairs. He called me and I came down. He got up from the sofa and took a terrible swing and hit me in the face and all over. He said: 'You think you're unhappy with me. Well, I'll give you something to be unhappy about.' I ran out of the house and jumped into my car."

But if that is Mary seen at nadir, she must also be seen at zenith,

where, truly, she appears as the handsome, nervously controlled,
various woman of intellect who has had the courage to make all her
gifts answer in the absence of any one single compelling talent. "With
Mary, work is constant," says a friend. Despite all her tergiversations,
"she will always come back to the typewriter." In the last twelve
years, she has published eight books—two novels, a brilliant
collection of essays that speak out, *On the Contrary*, a retrospective
volume of theatre criticism, a book of short stories, the touching and
widely read memoir of her Catholic girlhood, and two noble if
somewhat *Les Guides Bleus* attempts at art history, *The Stones of
Florence* and *Venice Observed*. This would be an impressive enough
output for any writer, but during the same period, and with equal
flair, Mary started several other ventures that make her seem only the
more indomitable for all their feminine muddle and quixotic failure.
During the McCarthy period, specifically, she was so personally
disturbed over the course things were taking that she tried (1) to
become a lawyer, and (2) to start a national magazine.

"It began with the defeat of Stevenson in 1952. I was terribly
worked up about the Constitutional aspects of the McCarthy
business, and it seemed that the judiciary—not even the lawyers,
really—were the only ones who stood firm. The legal profession
obviously needed some reforestation. Lawyers had gotten to be
people who had a license to practice hairdressing. So I thought
maybe I ought to know more about it, and in 1952 I conceived the
ridiculous idea of going to Harvard Law School. I was all set to take
the tests (but really I was too old, I couldn't have retained the
material) when it occurred to me it *was* ridiculous, I could do just as
well at C.C.N.Y. or N.Y.U. I was just being snobbish about Harvard.

"So I finally called an old friend, Judge Biggs, of the Pennsylvania
Circuit Court, and he told me, don't do anything until I'd talked to
him. So he came down in his white Jaguar, with his wife and a box of
cigars, for a weekend, and I'm afraid he talked me out of it.

"But the press and the magazines were so terrible that then I felt
maybe the thing to do was to start a new magazine. It was to be
Dwight, and Dick Rovere, and Hannah, and myself, but I was the
one who really wanted to do it. I was the one who was going to be
editor, the one who got out the magazine. It was going to be more
middle-of-the-road than *politics*"—Macdonald's defunct pacifist "little

magazine"—"with a reasonable circulation." It had a terrible name. *Critic.* Which is bad.

"I had a fantastic time. I learned more about politics, trying to raise money for that magazine, than I ever . . . *all* the Democrats, *all* of them were interested in *bigness.* Which, of course, was just what we were fighting. The only people who were really willing to put up the money were all *Republicans,* people who were interested in the arts. I'd gotten myself stuck with the idea of a $100,000 budget, and I got it up to $55,000 and *I* ran out of money. By June, I was destitute."

So it all came to naught and yet it is so very much the sort of thing—the Intellectual Fray, the Exploded Hope, the Niggardliness of Political Virtue, the Hypocrisy of Commitment—upon which her own literary imagination turns, that it's as if she'd been aware precisely of the point at which her own literary imagination turns. It's as if she'd been aware precisely of the point at which the book had to stop. "I probably *could* have raised all that money. I was impatient, partly," she says. "On the one hand, I have a desire to be an activist, and on the other hand, *I don't.*" And it seems only just that the one good deed to come out of all this activity should be the settling of an old literary quarrel that really began in one of her earlier books.

"Hannah convinced me that the magazine had to have Philip Rahv. So I finally got up my courage and telephoned him. He still wanted me to say I was sorry, and I still wasn't going to say I was, but I finally invited him to a long peace luncheon at the Charles. When we came out of the restaurant, all smiles, one of the *PR* gang saw us and actually *blanched.*"

So *that* at least was over, and indeed many of her old antagonists speak of Mary with a much more forgiving air these days. Her fast friendship with Hannah Arendt, for instance, is built over the buried ruins of one of Mary's worst outrages. They first met during the early Forties, at Rahv's insistence, and as a result of that one evening alone, "I cut Mary for six years." It all started when Mary, indulging the full frivolity of her *enfant-terrible* role, said she really felt sorry for Hitler, he didn't know what was happening to him, he expected the Jews to love him. "She was being so deliberately naughty," recalls Hannah. "I counted to one hundred and twenty to let Rahv—who is not the greatest hero of the age—say something to her, and when he didn't, it was just too much. I had to do something about it." Mary remembers "a sense of explosion in the room," and Hannah was gone. "I was horror-struck. I continued to admire her—on the principle that you must not adjust your attitude toward someone on the basis of his or her attitude toward you. But I didn't *dare* speak to her." Then, slowly over the next six years, they found that on any number of public questions they always ended up on the same side, and "usually alone." Gradually, they drew closer, both actually in need of each other's comradeship. "It is very difficult for women intellectuals to have women friends," says Hannah. "You need someone to face the problem with you of how to be regarded as a woman." By now, they've traveled several times in Europe together, Hannah very much in the lead, and done such things as invade the predominantly male Christian Gauss Seminars in Princeton "like two troopers." "Mary is someone I could ask to give my seminar on Machiavelli, for instance, when I couldn't." Like many others, she seems willing to accept a certain eternal childishness in Mary, now that Mary has grown more serious-minded. "But she will always be getting into impossible situations. She is always the child who sees no emperor's clothes, and of course this means she is expecting the most gorgeous clothes. In the sophisticated circles Mary travels, this is dynamite."

But, in Mary's case, it's easy to make too much of the child playing with dynamite, and miss the womanly dignity with which she *chooses* to be outspoken. "You know what my favorite quotation is?" says Margaret Sargent, just before her Fall. "It's from Chaucer. Criseyde says it, 'I am myn owene woman, well at ese.'" Mary, at fifty, is a lot wiser than her *persona* at twenty-and-some, but that doesn't mean that she has ever left off being her own woman. If anything, maturity has deepened her sense of intellectual independence, her bravado, her penchant for risk. "I am myn owene woman, well at ese"—and one startling aspect of her present fame, a mark of her rather special position among other famous and intellectual women—is that she has accomplished it all *without a man*.

Not that there haven't been men in her life. But as her own woman, she has never been bracketed with a man in the way that most other outstanding women have been, even in their eminence. Eleanor Roosevelt is *Mrs.* Roosevelt, Clare Boothe Luce may be playwright, Congresswoman, and ambassador, but she is still very much regarded as *Mrs.* Luce. Jackie Kennedy is charming, intelligent, and lovely, but really as the President's wife. And even Simone de Beauvoir, despite her own outspoken championship of the Second Sex, is still the unwed existentialist bride of Jean Paul Sartre. But Mary is definitely *Miss* McCarthy, even though she may be in private life Mrs. Bowden Broadwater, or Mrs. James West. Even looking back on her most famous marriage, it's absurd to think of her as the ex-Mrs. Edmund Wilson. She simply cannot be bracketed, in her own particular excellence, with even that overawing presence in American letters.

Yet she is still, as the publisher, Roger Straus, points out, "a real dame." A difficult dame perhaps, but still a real one. In fact, she has an insistent femininity, and claims "a horror of career girls. The girls who are theatrical agents, or in publishing, or the kind of woman who tells anecdotes, or who uses slang." She has all a woman's foibles. She loves clothes—"too much," she says—and shops Hattie Carnegie's for those "young" outfits that are expensively "right" for a cocktail party or a dressy afternoon. One of her prized possessions is a lovely diamond-and-silver brooch, given to her by her present husband as a wedding present: an intricate piece of Polish jewelry that she likes because it is "so old-fashioned." She loves to entertain in style—and to take charge of the party. Recently, for an occasion at Kevin's house in Dobbs Ferry, she cooked up a *cassoulet Toulouse* that took three geese, fifteen pounds of beans, three days, an eleven-page recipe, every pot in the house in the absence of a medieval cauldron, and served eighty-five people. After dinner, there was a program of theatricals, scenes written by such guests as Robert Lowell and Niccolo Tucci, and enacted by such guests as E. G. Marshall and Zero Mostel. "I said to Kevin, 'Don't you think we ought to build a stage?' but Kevin didn't think we ought to build a stage."

"She's very gay," says Miss Hardwick. "She doesn't believe in dreariness." And eternally, exasperatingly, despite her own caustic intellect, "she believes in Love." Macdonald is positively awed by it. "Anybody can see—and I don't mean she's offensive about—that she's *madly* in love with this new husband."

Perhaps this is what makes her, among intellectual women today, finally a unique case. For the tensions she creates around herself, it's necessary to go back to Madame de Staël and Récamier; no woman, in our complex, yet businesslike society, is supposed to consider them worth her while any longer. They may have been fine for George Sand, but nobody wants to get *that* involved, what with just normal female anxiety being what it is today. Have an affair, make a marriage, raise a child, write a novel, marry again, study art history, join the bar, start a magazine, join intellectual discussions, cook well, Attack the Center, Attack Tynan, entertain, gossip. Smile—do any several of these things, but for pity's sake don't try to be the Renaissance Woman!

Yet, despite all the criticism of her conduct—the many slurs on her femininity and the attacks on her work—there is a secret admiration for her candor, her audacity, and her stupendous try for the woman's moon. "She's one of the few people who never backs away," says her brother. "When I'm outspoken, I manage to make enemies. But when Mary's outspoken, people are convinced." *I am myn owene woman, wel at ese.* And once the Man in That Shirt understood the Middle English, he looked at her with "bald admiration."

"Golly," he said, "you are, at that!"

Contrary Mary—Vassar '33
Newsweek/1963

From *Newsweek Magazine*, 2 September 1963, 80-83. Reprinted by permission of *Newsweek* (September 1983). Copyright © 1983 by Newsweek Inc.

For the Greeks of antiquity, Athena was the personification of the clear upper air and the unclouded intellect. She was a war goddess also, and the lightning shaft was her weapon. For Americans of today, the female presence most nearly like her is Mary McCarthy. In this country, Mary McCarthy is the she-intellect supreme. Critic, novelist, essayist, thinker, author of *Stones of Florence* and *Venice Observed,* she is the First Lady of American letters. In her most daunting role—that of critic—she hurls a harpoon of electric destructiveness. Like Athena, she is—or has been—the adored of a cult.

Formerly, her public consisted typically of brainy undergraduates in the progressive colleges for girls and egghead subscribers to the *Partisan Review.* But now the vista widens. Thanks to the publication this week of her new novel, *The Group (Harcourt, Brace & World. 378 pages. $5.95),* the nation's No. 1 bluestocking is threatened with popularity, nay, money. Already Otto Preminger is ringing her up at night to dangle $250,000 movie offers before her astonished fancy. Her publishers, scenting a boom, have run off a first printing of 75,000 copies, and these were being ordered up by booksellers at the rate of 5,000 a day.

In the old days at the *Partisan Review*—Mary McCarthy's literary alma mater—success on this scale would have black-balled the winner. The governing critical principle of the PR brain trust was that anything successful was no good. On holiday at Bocca di Magra in Italy last week, Mary McCarthy was uneasy in spirit. "It's all a bit stupefying," she said. Into the bayside town that she loves (she has a story on it in the *New Yorker* next month), long-haul buses were pouring hordes of tourists, like reminders of the public that will shortly be reading her book. Characteristically, one of the first things she plans to do with her forthcoming wealth is buy a motorboat which will transport her away from Bocca di Magra's crowded beach and across the blue bay to a swimming hole in the white marble that pours down the flanks of the Carrara Mountains.

Since her marriage to her fourth husband, James West— information officer for a U.S. Government agency—Seattle-born Mary McCarthy has lived in Europe. She writhes at sight of her compatriots. "It's getting to the point," she said last week, "where any American who isn't slack-bodied, dim-witted, adenoidal suddenly finds himself being singled out as 'an exceptional American.' It's like telling a Jew he's a good Jew. If you don't have one of those fur-bearing accents, they think you're English. The ordinary American has deteriorated terribly."

One of the gifts that has made Mary McCarthy a powerful and piercing essayist is her vehement concern with the way the world goes, and this was in full working order last week even while she was treading water with an interviewer 300 yards offshore. "The Kennedy Administration," she scolded, "think they know something about culture, but they haven't a clue. At least in Roosevelt's time there was some concern for beauty—a desire not to allow progress to root out the natural and beautiful in America. The private car was perhaps the New Deal's equivalent of the TV set. When the New Deal built superhighways, there was some effort to make them beautiful. Since the war, America has become ugly at a frightening pace."

Giving the world the rough of her tongue in smoothly turned English is the unexcelled specialty on which Mary McCarthy's narrow fame has rested hitherto. As a literary critic, she leaves her victims shrunken as though by the art of the Jivaro head-hunter. The reputation of J.D. Salinger is probably maimed for good since she found him to be " 'sincere' in the style of an advertising man's necktie." Reviewing *Curtains* by Kenneth Tynan—the cleverest drama critic to inspect the stage since Miss McCarthy quit that job on the *Partisan Review*—she demanded to know: "Is the title of this collection a pun ('It's curtains for me, pal')?" Possibly next on her extermination list is Leon Edel, author of a massive biographical study of Henry James. Deeming this work "abysmal," Mary McCarthy suffers intellectual heartburn every time a time a new

volume of the incomplete study comes out to a new set of
complimentary reviews.

She falls upon her victims from a sense of duty like an inquisitor
giving a heretic to the flames. Her own simile is milder: "It's as if
you're in a hall and they say, 'Any questions?' after a speech has
been made, and then you feel, all right, if nobody else will, I will."
One acquaintance explains of her: "For all her brilliance as a writer,
there's a piece missing in Mary, she doesn't actually know when she
is being brutal—just as she doesn't realize how objectionable she is
being in the 'dirty' chapter of her new book."

As a sure-shot best-seller, Mary McCarthy's new novel, *The Group*,
carries its insurance in chapter two. The novel as a whole is a loosely
managed narrative of seven years in the lives of eight upper-middle-
class girls, graduates of Vassar in the class of '33 (to which the author
belonged also). In the second chapter, one of these misses partakes
of a seduction so prolonged and so microscopic in detail that the
author seems to have written it for burial in a time capsule against the
day when sex is a forgotten activity. At the moment it is a superfluous
document. Even more so is a succeeding episode detailing the lore of
the pessary. Published nine years ago as a short story called "Dottie
Makes an Honest Woman of Herself," this fragment was saluted by
one ironical commentator as an ambitious attempt to do for the
female contraceptive what Herman Melville did for the whale.

By the author's say-so, *The Group* has behind it an elaborate
theoretical apparatus which gives depth to the feminine trivia
cluttering the foreground. Shaded from the Italian sun by a floppy
hat from Lanvin's, Mary McCarthy explained this last week at an
outdoor café table furnished with a Campari and soda. The book,
she said, is actually about technology and the mirage of political and
social progress which misled the young in the 1930s. The novel's
many heroines live by the fashionable recipes of the time—"so that's
the whole idea—to see the tails of these ideas disappearing down
these little ratholes." In the execution, however, the ratholes are more
apparent than the ideas, and the reader who approaches the book
without benefit of the author's indoctrination lecture gets the uneasy
feeling that this is the kind of thing Rona Jaffe might have written with
a better education.

The shock which the scenes of mattress-play will provoke in the club ladies may not equal the shock of intellectual readers at the book's heavy cargo of womanish inconsequence. Downwind from the highbrows, murmurs can already be heard, and Norman Podhoretz—a Partisan Review confrere—is slicing *The Group* to tatters in the October issue of *Show* magazine.

There are spots in the new novel—e.g., a character who perpetuates the cliché of the charming, enchanted madman—where Mary McCarthy strays close to the one fault not to be expected of her, namely, sentimentality. Robert Elliott Fitch, a critic of standing who is also a Unitarian Minister, has called her earlier fiction "cerebrogenital" in that it addresses the head and the groin, leaving out the heart and the guts. Critics who employ a cruder idiom have classified her criticism as an exercise in the art of pure bitchery. The thought of a Mary McCarthy gone soft is bound to embolden her enemies.

It will take a bigger assault, however, than anything now foreseeable to put a dent in Mary McCarthy. "I am content to believe," she says, "that I can take care of myself"—and she can, although the intensity of her toil on this novel would have left anybody else too spent for combat. She has worked on the book since 1952—in Newport, R.I., Tripoli, Libya, the Grand Hotel in Warsaw. The major effort took place last winter in her Paris apartment on the rue de Rennes when she at last joined struggle with a rigorous deadline; her publisher had printed up the first ten chapters, salesmen were already out taking orders. Even so, some of the pages went through her Hermes for dozens of rewritings in her endless hunt for precision of thought and language. The job done, she flew to Rome to relax— and dropped in bed with hepatitis. Back to Paris in a wheelchair, she had to be paroled from the American Hospital in Neuilly to check her proofs.

In Bocca di Magra last week, her eyes were still marked by the strain of writing and illness. Mary McCarthy is now 51, and hues of white and gray dominate the Irish colleen's once black hair, parted in the middle and drawn back in a bun. If Mary McCarthy were describing Mary McCarthy, she would pitilessly note that her upper lip now displays the mustache of middle age. She is, nonetheless, a handsome woman still, as she floats down the Italian street, chin high, beach bag held primly to her side as they taught her to do in the Sacred Heart Convent in Seattle. Although she can write

sentences that would make a top sergeant gasp, it is a rare "damn"
that escapes her lips. In the serenely classical figure she cuts, there is
no hint of her tempestuous past in the hurly-burly of Bohemian
amour and avant-garde politics.

Part of her fascination for the world of double-dome gossip is that
most of her history is open for scrutiny under the disguise of fiction. It
bothers her not at all to acknowledge that her most famous story,
"The Man in the Brooks Brothers Shirt"—about an impromptu
shack-up aboard a transcontinental train—is an episode of autobiography. The book that is generally held to be her best, *Memories of a
Catholic Girlhood,* is outright self-history, the story of her ghastly
upbringing after her parents died in the influenza plague of 1918.

Mary and her brother, Kevin—who made his own fame as an
actor—were put in the care of a great aunt married to a lout who
resented brains. "She was bright," Kevin reminisced in Hollywood
last week where he is making TV films, "and there's that well-known
story about her winning first prize in a national essay contest when
she was 11 or 12. When she came home our guardian beat her with a
razor strop, so she wouldn't get snotty. So she wouldn't get uppity.
That big, fat bastard beating her! Something must have congealed
right there within her breast against life as it is and as it has been."

At Vassar, a real-life member of the class of '33 remembers that
Mary—later to be far too beautiful for a brain—"looked just like the
girl in the Charles Addams cartoons" and behaved accordingly:
"She's extremely intolerant; in class, her criticisms were merciless." In
senior year, she was courted by an actor named Harold Johnsrud
who appeared in *Winterset* and became her first husband. One of the
husbands in "The Group"—painted as an effigy of dishonesty—is
modeled upon Johnsrud who died in a hotel fire.

After a marriage-like affair with Philip Rahv, co-editor of *Partisan
Review*—whom she fictionally flayed in her novel *The Oasis*—she
married the most imposing personage among U.S. critics, Edmund
Wilson. She was already famous among eggheads for her own
critical pieces and her vocal performances as a parlor Trotskyite, but
Wilson set her to writing fiction. He lived to repent this when—after
their divorce—she drew a poisonous portrait of him in *A Charmed
Life.* Wilson, says her friend and Vassar contemporary Eunice Jessup,
"treated her like a schoolgirl. Tyrannical. Then she got pregnant and

realized the corner she was in. She had a real breakdown and was in Payne Whitney. Some people wondered if she should have the child, but he's been a wonderful success." (Last week in Italy, Mary McCarthy was fretting about sending a $500 money order to son Reuel, 24, a Slavic-language scholar about to be married in Mexico City to a girl his mother has never seen.)

For fifteen years after Wilson, Mary McCarthy was married to Bowden Broadwater, a Manhattan prep-school administrator who washed the dishes and looked after her son. Friends say Broad-water—who took it unkindly when she ran off with her present husband on a lecture tour in Poland—is writing a novel, paying her back in the McCarthy style. Her brother, Kevin, thinks the new marriage is the right one: "Her husband now is bright and he's handsome. He's somebody who might have been out of a picture book of our childhood—an image of our parents, as we remember them."

Throughout much of her history of domestic tempest, the American Athena has further enlivened her days and nights by eager combat in unnumbered salon skirmishes centering upon politics and literature. If something needs showing up, it is Mary McCarthy who has the courage to take on the obligation. None of the consequent embroilments has kept her from steadily gathering weight as a literary personality. If the new novel provokes critical displeasure, this is no great matter because no single one of her works expresses the peak of her achievement. It is the totality which entitles her to be called our only real woman of letters. Her fiction—with the possible exception of the new novel—has concerned itself with showing what mentally alive people think and feel. In a country where even the greatest writers have tended to be, not only unintellectual, but stupid, she—with her wakeful cerebrum and her insistence on the value of knowing and judging—stands out like the female brainy one for whom the Greeks built the Parthenon.

Mary McCarthy Said: "Men Have More Feeling, Women Have More Intelligence"

Peter Duval Smith/1963

From *Vogue*, 149 (October 1963) 98, 99, 142, 143, 144, 149.
Reprinted by permission of *Vogue* (October 1963). Copyright ©
1963 by The Condé Nast Publications Inc.

McCarthy: Well, you know, I've always thought that women—
women novelists at any rate—could be divided into the sense
women and the sensibility women. It's one of Jane Austen's titles,
Sense and Sensibility, and there's the sensible heroine who is the
sensibility girl. And I don't really mean by that an opposition between
the intelligence and the heart. In fact, at least in Jane Austen, the
sensibility girl often is quite unfeeling and selfish and even heartless,
whereas the sense girl has a good deal of discipline of the will, self-
control, and so on.

Some people would say that the sensibility girls were the only ones
capable of powerful feeling, but I'd rather say they're mostly just
interested in their own perceptions—they're rather flighty, perhaps a
bit weak. And the sense women—I'm still talking about Jane
Austen—the sense women are strong with a kind of robust mind,
with common sense, a certain knowledge of the world and the way
things work, and with humour.

Smith: Doesn't the label apply to writers as well as their
characters? Which is Jane Austen, sense writer or sensibility writer?

McCarthy: Well, she's obviously, I think, a sense writer. She's
always striving a bit to overcome her sensibility, but she's a sense
writer, with a certain romantic tendency maybe, but she remains a
woman of sense.

Smith: What other women of sense have been good novelists?

McCarthy: Oh, George Eliot certainly is a sense writer, and
among the Americans . . . well, Edith Wharton certainly was a sense
writer.

Smith: And among contemporaries?

McCarthy: We don't seem to be so strong on the sense anymore.
Among American women writers today I'd say Eudora Welty. Even

though she writes in a kind of fanciful vein, she has an extremely robust sense of humour—a strange kind of humour. I would say she was a sense writer.

Smith: Carson McCullers, for instance, is not a sense writer?

McCarthy: No, definitely not—she's a sensibility writer. They tend, as I say, to be interested in their own feelings, and—what shall we say—in the interior décor of the emotions.

Smith: You are a sense writer definitely?

McCarthy: I wish I were. Yes, I'd like to be.

Smith: You know the way that women novelists hate so much to be called women novelists—why is this?

McCarthy: Do you think so? I don't mind being called a woman novelist. After all, I am one. But I know what you mean. I think it's just a piece of feminism. Mind you, I hate the endings in "ess"—I'd hate to be called an authoress, or a sculptress—and I suppose, in that sense, to call a woman novelist a woman novelist, instead of just calling her a novelist, is like putting an "ess" on the end.

Smith: This self-consciousness isn't a new thing. Remember the Brontës played at being men: their books were first published under male pseudonyms. Were they sensibility writers or sense ones?

McCarthy: Well, let's see . . . Charlotte Brontë had a touch of both, I would say, but Emily was certainly a pure sensibility writer.

Smith: And why were they ashamed of being women novelists?

McCarthy: I don't think it was that they were ashamed. It's a question of the reading public. George Eliot wrote under the pseudonym of a person purporting to be a young clergyman because had she written under her own name her novels wouldn't have sold. It was a purely practical matter, I think.

Smith: You've got a passion for George Eliot. Why, and for which of her books especially?

McCarthy: Well, chiefly *Middlemarch* which I think is really one of the great novels; and I like the first part of *Daniel Deronda* very much, and I like *The Mill on the Floss.* I know it's a rather different kind of book, and there's certainly more picture-painting, more delicate watercolour stuff, but it's still, I would say, a sense book rather than a sensibility one. It's very touching, I like it very much.

Smith: Is it because George Eliot is a woman writer that you like her? Does she say something to you as from woman to woman?

McCarthy: I wouldn't think so. . . .

Smith: You like her in just the same way as you like Dickens or Henry James?

McCarthy: Yes—or Tolstoy. . . . I think so. . . . I think that the women sense writers usually have a certain amount of moral strictness—moral rigour, severity. But you also find that in Tolstoy in the strongest way. You might say that there was a feminine streak in Tolstoy; I don't think so, but I don't see any difference in the way he looks at people. Perhaps George Eliot understands her women characters better than some women novelists do, but I don't read her as a woman, I read her as a reader.

Smith: You say you like the first part of *Daniel Deronda* very much, but some of that is practically propaganda for feminism, isn't it?

McCarthy: Yes, but I don't like that bit.

Smith: Do you think there are specifically masculine and feminine qualities in intellect?

McCarthy: In general I would say that men actually have more feeling, and women perhaps more intelligence. I know this isn't the usual way round to put it. I think men are more available for feeling, but that women have quicker minds—perhaps not so powerful, perhaps not such powerful intellects; they perhaps aren't able to go so deep or with such breadth into things—there are no great women philosophers, for example. But for sheer quick intelligence and reason women are better, I think. Women are extremely reasonable.

Smith: Why are there no great women poets?

McCarthy: There are some.

Smith: I'm thinking of Dante and Goethe and Shakespeare, people who produced a pretty immense range of great work.

McCarthy: Well, I don't know. I'd almost agree, but Virginia Woolf you know. . . . It's probably a question of having the time to do it. And also conventions play some part, and lack of experience. It would have been extremely difficult for a woman to become a Goethe or a Dante. Perhaps in the future. . . .

Smith: There aren't great women playwrights either.

McCarthy: No, there aren't, and that I think is maybe because a play after all is really a contest, and action is the essential of a drama. And I think it's a little bit true that women tend to view things either as passive creatures who are acted upon rather than who act, or as observers. There's the aunt who's the observer, you know, and the pretty niece to whom things happen, but who seldom causes anything to happen.

Smith: Yes, but isn't it ideal for a playwright to be an observer? He's presumed to have more detachment than any other kind of writer, in that he mustn't take sides in his play or he's liable to mess it up.

McCarthy: That is true enough. But the main thing is the action, and I think that if this world perhaps becomes more feminized that's one reason why there'll be fewer plays written. Mind you, it is very hard for any of us, men or women, to imagine an action anymore because we've all become more and more passive in the contemporary world.

Smith: If women do have more detachment than men, why do the heroes produced by some women novelists have this quality of wild exaggeration about them that doesn't fit in with the men we know at all? I mean characters like Mr. Rochester in *Jane Eyre* or Heathcliff in *Wuthering Heights.*

McCarthy: Well, those are sensibility novels, and I think *one* virtue that the sensibility women writers have—they've others—is that they are able to create male heroes. Granted that you don't, you know, meet Mr. Rochester in a normal post as a governess, but these are dream men. The sensibility writers are very good at creating dream men—people like Rhett Butler in *Gone With the Wind* or even Mr. Darcy in *Pride and Prejudice.* Jane Austen tried to be more detached than the other ladies in doing Mr. Darcy, but in fact he's another of these Byronic heroes, these dream men that one can fall in love with.

Smith: But if novels are supposed to be like real life, these people can't be characters in good novels?

McCarthy: Well, they belong to a part of life that dreams and imagines. That kind of man is going to come and lift you out of being a governess, or whatever your fate is—so these men certainly belong to the life of a young girl. They're the imaginings of a young girl.

Smith: How is it then that the women sense novelists, like George Eliot, often have male characters who are also too good to be true, but this time in a gentle and endlessly considerate way rather than a violent, passionate way? I'm thinking of Will Ladislaw in *Middlemarch,* for one.

McCarthy: Yes, that's true. Will Ladislaw is supposed to have been based on her husband—like him he's absolutely a vulnerable character. In general, I think the women sense novelists are not very good at creating heroes. They're extremely good at social observation, and the men characters who are peripheral or even semi-central but who are not heroes are extraordinarily well done: Lydgate the doctor in *Middlemarch,* for instance. And sense women are extremely good. I think, at doing cads—like Frank Churchill in *Emma* and the Willoughbys and the Wickhams, all those weak attractive young men that you find in Jane Austen. All the women sense novelists are extremely good at catching these particular kinds of rotters. No, "rotter" is too strong . . . charming, weak men.

Smith: And plainly the sort of men that they are themselves attracted to?

McCarthy: Yes, have a fatal weakness for. Dear me, yes.

Smith: What's your own recipe, in your novels, for a conquering hero?

McCarthy: I haven't got any heroes in my novels. I've got—well, I've got one, who's the protagonist of *The Groves of Academe*—but no, he's not a hero.

Smith: You've got mainly heroines in fact.

McCarthy: Oh dear! Yes.

Smith: Certainly in *The Company She Keeps, The Oasis.* . . .

McCarthy: There's always that heroine. I know. I would dearly love to get rid of her, to scrap her. She's always thinking about herself, and doubting herself, she's partly observing and partly doubting herself, and this is rather the conventional heroine of the woman novelist. Women novelists incarnate the principle of doubt in this kind of heroine, and I'm so sick of her. She doesn't exist in the book I'm working on now. [Editor's note: *The Group.*] I've banished her.

Smith: Is it because she's too autobiographical that you hate her so?

McCarthy: Well, I think so. I think that's true. I always try to make her different from myself—to make her a White Russian, or almost anything—but as soon as she begins questioning her motives and representing, let's say, the conscience, at that moment she's too close to me and I don't like her.

Smith: Do you remember that essay by Virginia Woolf where she said that what she wanted was the androgynous state where she'd be half a man and half a woman and so be in the ideal position to write about both sexes? I think she thought Shakespeare had been in that condition.

McCarthy: The prospect doesn't interest me. I mean, after all, it would be to be a monster. And it also shows. I think, that Virginia Woolf, like so many of the women writers of sensibility, tended to be extremely conceited.

Smith: Don't you sometimes feel irritated, though, that you are a woman and there are various things you can't know?

McCarthy: Yes. I'm sure I couldn't write a successful scene that took place in the smoking room of the United States Senate. However, I have tried at least once to do something from a man's point of view—that is, to be inside the mind of a man, though he's not following wholly masculine pursuits, granted. There is that difficulty: simply not knowing, never having been present.

Smith: Does being a woman inhibit you from writing about sex? Haven't you repeated the frankness of your famous early story, "The Man in the Brooks Brothers Shirt"—about a wild scene in a train compartment?

McCarthy: Oh yes I have. At least in *A Charmed Life* there is a sexual scene that's rather apropos of what I was just saying. It's something between a seduction and a wake, a scene in which the heroine starts to be with her former husband, semi against her will, and then she thinks, "Well, after all I've done it so many times with this man, why stop now?" You know, why protest now? And I wrote it first from her point of view and the scene was just a disaster—it brought out this unpleasant quality I was talking about in the heroine. So I decided to try to do it from the man's point of view, and I thought it came out very well as a great comedy.

Smith: Is there any other aspect of emotional life that you find tricky to write about because you're a woman? I suppose women are a little more sensitive to the undercurrents of life than men are. . . .

McCarthy: I'm afraid I'm not sufficiently inhibited about the things that other women are inhibited about for me. They feel that you've sort of let the side down, you know, that you've given away trade secrets, if you write very candidly about certain things.

Smith: There are awfully few good autobiographies by women.

Your own *Memories of a Catholic Girlhood* must be one of not more than half a dozen.

McCarthy: That stops when I'm about seventeen though, so that I haven't given away too much. I don't know why women haven't written their autobiographies. Simone de Beauvoir's done it, but I don't like her.

Smith: What about the limitations of men writing about women?

McCarthy: I think that in general men write better about women than women write about men. The best men writers—the great ones like Tolstoy, for example, or Stendhal—I think they know women perhaps as well as women know themselves. I think that they surpass women in this respect. I can't imagine that a woman novelist could become as intimate with a male hero as Tolstoy is with Anna Karenina or Flaubert with Emma Bovary. You can imagine a woman novelist hitting off a male character for a short stretch; but living intimately with him through a whole novel—I can't imagine this.

Smith: You don't find with Madame Bovary or Anna that there's a tiny bit missing that a man could never get?

McCarthy: I'm completely satisfied. I wonder what the reason is for this. It might be that women talk much more about their feelings to their husbands, lovers, and so on. Therefore the husband has gotten an intimate perception from his wife of what it's like to be a woman. But men do not sit around talking to women about what it's like to be a man, they're not nearly so talkative about their so-called inner life.

Smith: But women talk to each other a lot, don't they, and their men only get an occasional, rather horrifying hint of what's said?

McCarthy: I think that's a thing of the past, really. It depends on the country. In Europe I think women still exchange confidences that no man would ever be allowed to be privy to, but I think American women and Englishwomen talk quite as freely to men as they would to their girl friends.

Smith: Perhaps women are becoming more like men psychologically?

McCarthy: Well, I can't be sure . . . I don't know. . . .

Smith: You've been a lot in the masculine world, haven't you? For instance, when you came down from college in the mid-thirties you went straight into left-wing politics in New York.

McCarthy: Well, I was very much a woman, a girl rather, in that way. I never took a very active part. I was really more or less passive, I got involved with politics because the men I was with were involved in politics, and I was just there. You know. I didn't talk nearly as much in those days. I went to meetings and so on, but I usually remained silent. Maybe I argued at parties, and with young Stalinist men who took me out dancing, and I participated in May Day parades, but that's different.

Smith: Yes, but you're a very intellectual person—you're truly interested in ideas.

McCarthy: Yes, but I was less interested in ideas at that time. I think I was much more of a sort of literary girl. I was very apolitical in college, and it was only the Moscow trials I think, that put my mind to work.

Smith: How did that happen?

McCarthy: Oh, well, I got involved through going to a party in signing something—a petition for Trotsky to have the right of asylum in Mexico. I really knew nothing about the subject, but in general I was for the right of asylum. And so I found myself quite by chance a member of a Committee for the Defense of Leon Trotsky. And once I was on this Committee I began to be attacked by a lot of Stalinists who were trying to prize me off it, so I had to defend myself, and defend Trotsky, so I began to read books and so on, and moved into a quite different world.

Smith: And you've been involved in politics continuously since then?

McCarthy: Well, yes. I don't mean that I've been running for office! Though during the McCarthy period I did have one flurry of wanting to become a lawyer. The men in my family had all been lawyers, and it seemed to me that the legal position in America was being weakened, that the old jurists were extremely good, but the younger ones who were replacing them were not of the same quality at all, and that the country needed a very strong legal system to protect itself against such things as Senator McCarthy. So I had this dream of going to law school and becoming a practicing lawyer, you know, a Portia. Of course I was much too old, and I was deterred, fortunately, I suppose.

Smith: Do you think that you've got any special role to play in society as a woman, or would this just be as an intelligent person?

McCarthy: I feel it's just as a person and not as a woman. I really don't have much suffragette side. I think of myself as a person, not as a woman; belonging, you know, to the world, not to a lot of other women. I can't stand people who hold themselves together, in pressure groups and interest groups, and are motivated usually by envy of other people. I can't stand feminine envy—envy of men. I can't stand any kind of envy, I think it's one of the great vices of the modern world. It's grown because of the idea of equality, which is with us to stay, certainly. I am for equality, but, at the same time, with the idea of equality envy inevitably quickens and can become absolutely ferocious. I'm sure envy and self-pity are the great sins of our particular period, and are companion sins to each other.

Smith: We hear a lot about equality but we don't see too much of it, and little as you want to talk about the sex war, that squalid little phrase, the fact is that now that women have more or less equal rights with men they seem to be just as discontented.

McCarthy: I think on the whole they're more discontented. If you're nearer having some great big prize, you're more discontented than if it's as far away as the moon. I think American women particularly are extremely discontented and this antagonism on the part of women towards men is stronger today in America than it's ever been.

Smith: What do the women want?

McCarthy: They want everything. That's the trouble—they can't have everything, they can't possibly have all the prerogatives of being a woman and the privileges of being a man at the same time, and you get these awful career girls who want to be able to talk like men and go in for telling long boring anecdotes—a purely male prerogative, thank God.

Smith: Are you going to write about this new American woman, one day?

McCarthy: Well, I am rather doing that now. I've been working on a novel for years, it's about eight Vassar girls, called *The Group*. It's about the idea of progress. There are these eight girls who go through the book and who are subjected to all the progressive ideas of their period, in architecture, design, child-bearing, home-making, con-traception, and so on. It's a kind of technological novel about woman's sphere. There are men in it, but not really. They appear at parties and so on, and they talk, but their sensibilities aren't there, they're only heard. The novel's told from the point of view of these eight individual girls—though of course their mothers are all there too, large figures from the past, and the girls are sitting on their ample laps like little dolls on the lap of a great big madonna.

Smith: You sound as if you preferred the mothers to the daughters.

McCarthy: Well, I'm afraid I do think the mothers are better than the daughters. The mothers sort of belong to the full suffragette period with its great amplitude—you know, women smoking cigarettes in holders and dancing the cha-cha—and the girls are rather tinny in comparison with the mothers, I'm afraid. This wasn't my intention to start with, but that's what does seem to have emerged.

Smith: How did you begin as a writer?

McCarthy: I began by writing little poems when I was about eight.

Smith: Then your writing never had anything to do with wanting to make a mark for yourself in a male world, if I may put it like that?

McCarthy: No, you may not. I don't think of the world that way, I don't think of it as a male world, I think of it as the world, and I've never wanted to be a man. I much prefer being a woman, probably for very bad reasons like liking clothes and so on, but I love being a woman.

Smith: Have you ever felt that by your writing you've missed things that you would have had if you'd done something else?

McCarthy: I don't know, except I would have had more leisure if I hadn't been a writer. But, no, I don't think so. I'm married and I have a grown-up child, and I don't think that writing has cut anything out of my life. Actually, though, I wanted originally to be an actress—up to, oh, twenty-one—from eighteen to twenty-one I was very passionate about becoming an actress. But I didn't have any talent and so, you know, I had to give it up. My tragedy was that I became a writer instead.

Meeting Mary McCarthy

Katharine Whitehorn/1965

From The *Observer*, 29 August 1965, 6-9. Reprinted by permission of The *Observer.*

I knew Mary McCarthy by sight, I thought, as I waited for her in the Lanvin boutique: a severe-looking woman with a bun as she appears in the book-jacket photographs. Her appearance seemed to go well with the incisive writing, the ruthless criticism, the devastating analysis of female experience.

So when a great gawky American with loose grey curls under a large straw hat advanced towards me with a friendly, uncertain smile I simply didn't recognize her. It took me a long time to recover from the shock and fit the woman and the authoress together: to come to terms with this alarming youthfulness and re-assemble my enormous admiration for her along different lines. That first morning all I could do was yammer.

At Lanvin's, she was asking them to make up a piece of tribal cloth given her by an Underdeveloped friend; and on the whole they were taking it well. She was wearing a discreet navy dress they had made for her—with the success of *The Group* she bought couture for a season, but mostly she gets her clothes from the slightly less expensive boutique. It could not, however, be said that the effect was French: "I hate the French uniform," she said—and added such et ceteras as two-tone American shoes, a spotted scarf, a country hat.

Leaving Lanvin's, we dripped our way through the rain to Hermès next door: it's the world's most expensive leather shop, but surprisingly sells bathing dresses as well, and she bought one for a price that worked out at about a pound an inch. The bell rang; the shop shut for lunch; we were out on the street. "That's it about the French," she said as we climbed into a taxi. "They *aren't* mercenary—they don't really want to sell you things at all. My son Reuel had the phrase for it: he said 'Mummy, the French *grudge* gipping you.' " She leant forward to give directions to the driver, and went on "And what I hate about it is that you become so abject, you get so grateful to the one taxidriver in a hundred that actually knows the way to where you want to go—and *he's* probably a foreigner."

In a television programme some time ago she complained that the French never invite you to their homes; after which she received a number of sudden invitations. But she still maintains that most of the French people she likes have foreign wives or connections. Her husband, James West, with whom we lunched in the administrative château of O.E.C.D., where he works, thinks she overstates it; but they both prefer Poland to Paris. It was in Poland, where he was a diplomat and she was lecturing, that they originally met: one catches faint nuances of "Darling, they're playing our country" whenever the place is mentioned.

I felt this later in the day when we climbed up the dark stairway to the studio of a Polish painter, Lebenstein, from whom they were to buy a gouache. He provided champagne, but it did little to counter-act the compelling melancholy of his paintings, each of which showed a more hopeless picture of life than the one before. When we finally tottered out I felt that the logical thing to do next would be to throw ourselves into the Seine, but the Wests cheered up at once. We whisked home through the rain to supper in their flat in the rue de Rennes; it was an admirable supper, cooked from Elizabeth David, but it was not fattening. As she is a woman, and as she is an American, she was dieting.

A day so spent is not, apparently, typical: "Mostly I don't do anything much except work," she said. But the homes of those who really don't, look it—and hers didn't. It was pretty, very feminine: pale pink curtains she made herself, flowered wallpaper; lots of white paint against deep green, a pattern of hearts on the breeze curtains. The details were careful: a tiny rose in a minute bottle, a big butterfly in the disc of a glass, a Florentine miniature. In contrast, the kitchen was a spartan workroom: a stove specially got from Germany, and a big iron Spanish coffee-grinder: "I found the electric grinder heats the coffee up; it isn't so good."

She told me that Kay's flat in *The Group*—pillow ticking chair covers and red cushions—was one she had had in the thirties: "It depresses me to see young people nowadays having exactly the same fads as we had, like absolute belief in psychoanalysis and absolute insistence on modern furniture."

Her study was neat—Kenneth Tynan's denunciation of her article on Osborne was filed under Controversy—and her antique desk was dominated by a terrifying bird given her by the poet Robert Lowell; she works with it staring at her from a bare eight inches away, but says she hardly looks at it. She types all her own work—"I hate to lose contact with the prime materials"—and uses the typewriter as a creative device: if she's stuck she starts typing out a bit she's sure of in the hope that the momentum will carry her over the sticky bit.

She usually works from nine till four, then goes out to shop for food. Her own lunch is something light—consommé or eggs, but never, I gathered, sloppy. "I don't believe you should behave differently when you're alone and when you're with people," she said. "I suppose it's part of believing in singleness, not just double-ness."

This shipshape discipline of her working life has been built up and maintained through some pretty fair private tempests. When she left Vassar, the New York women's college, and married her first husband she wasn't sure whether she wanted to be a writer or an actress. Her teachers at Vassar told her she'd never be any good at creative writing, "and my husband saw me in a play and told me to forget about acting."

For some time she wrote criticisms for small leftish magazines such as the *Partisan Review*—she was a Trotskyite and parted company with the Communists over the Moscow Trials of 1936. (Her anarchist sympathies could still be construed as leftish, but she has avoided the political arthritis you get if you try to maintain the same attitude for 30 years.) Then her extraordinary second husband, Edmund Wilson, "put me in this little room and he didn't actually lock me in but it was clear I couldn't come out until I had written some fiction"—the first story in *The Company She Keeps.*

It took her seven years of steady trying to get free of Wilson, and she then married for 13 to Bowden Broadwater, a New York teacher who protected her and arranged their New York life around her "as if I was a sort of precious writing machine." She would show him each chapter as it was finished—not before, though she suspected he used to look; and now shows them to James West: "Why *do* women writers have to show their work to someone?" She is now working on a book about a 19-year-old boy; one wonders if it will owe

anything to her own son by Edmund Wilson, Reuel; but she isn't
keen on talking about things before she has written them.

It was when she was sitting on a sofa with her feet under her,
smoking continuously and talking about books, husbands, politics,
people that the woman and the writer finally jelled, and I saw that the
girlishness that had unnerved me at first was a vital part of the writer.
I had always had the same feeling about her books: a horrified blend
of "This is so good everyone should read it" and "Oh God, this is me
all over—I hope *nobody* reads it." I had never stopped to think that,
if she had been as forbidding as I imagined; she could never have
attracted the emotional experiences she dissects so devastatingly. Or,
of course, the confidences: the books are not autobiographical. She
said she *impersonated* each person she wrote about: "The Danish
translator was the only one who spotted that *The Group* was written
from the point of view of each girl in turn, like a pastiche."

She confirmed, to my relief, my theory that the title is almost
always the clue to her books: *The Company She Keeps* stresses the
difficulty a woman on her own has in having any identity that is not
just a reflection of each person she meets in turn; *The Group* is not
just a random sample, but an exploration of the effect on these girls
of thinking of themselves as a group of special people; *A Charmed
Life* is what the intellectuals of New Leeds live, a life on special terms,
out of all contact with reality: the girl loses it when she makes an
actual real-life decision to take any sort of action, and is killed in a car
crash.

Of her two great strengths as writer, one is certainly that she has
opened up so many hitherto unmentioned areas of feminine experience. The contraception sequence in *The Group* is well known—
"That woman," said Sonnenberg, "has done for the pessary what
Herman Melville did for the whale"; since that book, too, people
having trouble with breast-feeding can just say, "Like Pris Hartshorn-
Crockett," where before they could only blush. It is she who has
admitted that a woman can feel loving towards a man *because* she is
leaving him, and that she can get seduced by accident—not from
vice or romanticism but simply by failing to spot the moment
between "I can't say no *yet*" and "I can't say no *now*."

Her other enormous strength, it seems to me, is detachment: the
ability, while one eye is closed in a swoon, to keep the other one

open, noticing. *Cast a Cold Eye* is the title of one of her books—it could be the clue title to her whole life. She has too good a head not to see what a dance her emotions are leading her—never mind, on with the dance. She observes herself and, which is a lot more dangerous, her lovers and friends; and a good deal of the venom she inspires is a result of just this. Men don't mind being denounced by a woman, but they can't stand her making a witty thing out of them. My own guess is that she is not, actually, especially malicious, even in public controversy: I get rather the impression that she says these devastating things with the immunity of a child who doesn't really believe the grown-ups can be hurt.

Quite a number of grown-ups, it must be admitted, have been sent reeling one way and another. Mary McCarthy has emotional integrity of the most disruptive kind: she says she never thinks very far ahead, and her loyalty is always to the present commitment.

It is clear from what she says that she has not married so often in a search for a never-never happiness: on the contrary. "I'm an extremely happy person," she said. "Until recently I never knew what people meant when they said they were depressed." Her recent divorce and re-marriage were not, it seems, a question of what was wrong with Bowden Broadwater but what was right with James West.

When you say that someone's new husband is an international civil servant, ex-diplomat, ex-Air Force major, who has the pink and white aspect of the conventional Senator, you tend to assume that she has simply settled down at last. But it would be a great mistake to think that, in West, Mary has found no more than a little grey home. The impulses that cause a father of three to leave a pretty housewife in her thirties for a fiftyish authoress are not standard, and nor is he. As amusing to talk to as she is, he has a Past—a cultural past, a theatre-managing past; and the force that swept Mary McCarthy off her feet was clearly the explosion of that stored charge. "He kept saying 'You remind me of the thirties', " she said; and the reawakening was symbolised for her by his books: "His shelves were covered with books on international finance, politics, things like that; then one day they were all gone: he'd brought up his old books from the cellar and the shelves were filled with philosophy and Henry James.

"I have this dream of us sitting in the winter in Vermont by a vast stove—I'm reading Hegel, he's reading philosophy, and it's snowing outside." Perhaps this is a mellower dream than she might have had 20 years ago; perhaps it is more realistic; but, as a romantic, she is plainly still going strong.

A romantic who can cast a cold eye on her romanticism: it is an interesting combination. I have a friend who thinks that everyone has an emotional age—not a mental age—towards which they hurry, for which they yearn. He attributes his own troubles to being emotionally 18, and points with amazement to management types who have apparently longed since birth to be 50. Mary McCarthy, I should say, has a mental age of about 200 and an emotional age of 24; and what novelist would ask more?

A Conversation with Mary McCarthy
Edwin Newman/1966

This is a transcript of a televised interview with Mary McCarthy broadcast on WNBC-TV, New York, filmed and recorded in Paris, 4 December 1966. Reprinted by permission of WNBC.

For many decades, American writers and artists have been attracted to Paris. The attraction was keenest after World War I and blossomed again after World War II and it persists today.

On this typical Paris street with the busy traffic purring through and mixture of shops and homes, lives and works the American novelist and critic Mary McCarthy.

Miss McCarthy shares this apartment with her husband, an American official in an international organization. It reflects her style.

She's never been an overwhelmingly prolific writer. She's always been an extremely careful and precise one, with a style and with a view of the world very much her own and with a reputation for clinical and even heartless observation.

I went to her Paris apartment to talk to her about her life and work.

Newman: Hello, I'm Edwin Newman. This is A Conversation With Mary McCarthy, novelist, critic, essayist, one of the first ladies— perhaps the first lady of American letters.

Miss McCarthy, your novel, *The Group,* was made into a movie. I think it was the first work of yours to be made into a movie.

McCarthy: Well, not exactly.

Newman: It wasn't?

McCarthy: Yes, really, yes, but years ago my first book, *The Company She Keeps,* the title was bought only—just the title. And there was a movie made about a girl's reform school under that name. (LAUGHS)

Newman: I remember. That was not what you had in mind. The fact that *The Group* was turned into a movie—could be turned into a movie—or let us say that Hollywood could do it, is that a sign, may I ask, of some mellowing on your part?

McCarthy: I hope not. I don't think it really proves much of anything about a book. But I just was trying to think whether any of my earlier books—no, they couldn't have been—like say, *A Charmed Life,* could have been made into a film. But it would have been harder.

I think that the whole structure of *The Group* is unified, perhaps, in a more conventional way—that is with its collective heroine and so on and episodes. And I gather that there are a lot of complaints that the movie is too episodic. But anyway, it has more of that kind of conventional form.

I don't think the others were so very unconventional, but they— they didn't have that kind of limited and conventional form, I'm not expressing this well, but anyway, that *The Group* has.

Newman: So, it doesn't prove anything about you?

McCarthy: Well, I think not. I (LAUGHS) I mean—I think it might prove something very nice or—such as, you know, War and Peace can be made into many, many movies and so on.

Newman: What I really had in mind, Mary, of course I don't know what view you have of yourself, but if one reads the critics about you, the words one most often comes across are words like acid, pitiless, satirical, and corrosive, and say you have a killer instinct.

McCarthy: I don't agree with . . .

Newman: Do you . . .

McCarthy: Oh, I'll accept satirical.

Newman: But you don't—you won't accept corrosive or pitiless?

McCarthy: No, I don't think so. I think I made the fatal mistake of calling one book, *Cast A Cold Eye.*

Newman: *Cast A Cold Eye.*

McCarthy: And I was warned by a friend—by Robert Lowell, the poet, before I did it that I—that I would never hear the last of that. That reviewers were so lazy . . .

Newman: Well, I'm not. As a matter of fact, when I framed my question I—about all these words that are applied to you, I tagged on the end of it, 'and, of course, you yourself called one of your books, *Cast A Cold Eye.*'

McCarthy: That was meant as a sort of—for one thing Yeats didn't mean what the reviewers mean—meant at that time by things like calling reviews dry ice in this book and so on. Yeats meant a kind of—kind of passionate dispassion or detachment.

Newman: An unblinking eye?

McCarthy: Yes, yes. He didn't mean, I don't think, coldness of heart.

Newman: Not the fishy eye?

McCarthy: Yes, yes.

Newman: Well, how do you see yourself then? Do you think critics have been unfair to you when they ascribe these qualities to you?

McCarthy: Well, I think that's vulgar. That's all. I don't know whether it's—I don't know whether it's unfair. I might be worse, you know, but different. But I think it is—I think also it does show a lack of imagination and a lack of—I mean a lack of interest in looking at the object itself. And instead of seeing—instead of that, seeing the object in terms of some preconception about what it's like.

Newman: Well, that's—it's undoubtedly true, isn't it then, the name Mary McCarthy has a certain connotation?

McCarthy: Maybe that's partly being a woman too. That if you aren't—it seems to me that women writers if they're at all satirical or partly satirical can do—be identified with cats. And that a man writer can be infinitely more savage, ruthless, et cetera and not be classified under—under these epithets.

Newman: That applies not only to writers, of course.

McCarthy: It's true, yes.

Newman: Let me give you an example of something along these lines. Incidentally, I want to turn later to your own work as a critic. In one of your works—I think it's "The Man In The Brooks Brothers Shirt," in the course of what I will call a love scene, you mention the safety pin, do you not?

McCarthy: Yes, yes.

Newman: That is holding up an article—an article of apparel, let us say.

McCarthy: Underpants, yes.

Newman: That the girl was wearing. And because you did that—I've got notes on that in here somewhere—you were described as clinical, spectatorial, antiseptic. Now when you included that item, that detail, did you think about it a long time before?

McCarthy: Well, it was a detail against myself, really. It's funny, I was just talking yesterday to a friend in some quite different context—a French friend—a woman, younger than I. And she began to describe how her clothes were put together when she was about that age. And that somehow you cannot bear to sew on a button and—so, the result is that you're just tacked together (LAUGHS) with safety pins.

And it was made as—obviously, as some very damaging detail about the heroine of that story. That nowadays people don't have buttons on underpants anyway, but in those days they did have little buttons on the side, that I hadn't bothered on to sew this on. I'm admitting right now that this story is autobiographical. And that it was also the kind of detail that—that a worldly man would regard as sloppy, bohemian, and so on.

Newman: And particularly a successful businessman?

McCarthy: Exactly. Exactly. Maybe—yes. An actor probably would take it calmly.

Newman: Well, I think that sort of thing is perhaps the reason that you're thought to be so pitiless, that you look at things and try to see them exactly as they are. Which I take it, you would accept as the job of a novelist, would you not, or a short story writer?

McCarthy: Yes, yes. But I mean one can never really succeed, but you can try. I mean it would be—I mean perhaps monstrous vanity to think that you had succeeded in seeing things absolutely as they are. But I do—it is, at least, my effort to try as hard as possible to tell—to tell—to see and tell things as they are.

Newman: Leaving aside, for the moment, your own work as a critic which has been primarily in the field of drama but also, of course, in other fields—in the field of the novel. As a novelist, and as a short story writer, how much attention do you pay to critics?

McCarthy: Well—do you mean do I change my work? No, not at all.

Newman: Do you mind—do you mind what they say? Does it matter to you apart from the effect it has on, of course, income?

McCarthy: Well, I don't think about the effect it has on income.

Newman: You do not?

McCarthy: No, not at all. And I doubt whether it has much effect on income really. That is *The Group* got a terribly bad press on the whole—let's say two-thirds bad and, you know, was this kind of runaway best-seller. But, anyway, I never think about the effect of criticism on income.

I don't know. I suppose one is hurt sometimes or infuriated—often infuriated. And sometimes one is more infuriated by favorable reviews than by unfavorable ones. You're always looking—and it's very foolish, it really would be better not to read the reviews—but you're always looking for some reviewer who will tell to you something about your book that you didn't know yourself and at the same time that you think is true. And that very, very rarely happens.

Newman: You have not learned anything just from reviewers. Are you distinguishing, by the way, between reviewers and critics?

McCarthy: Well, I think I mostly only had reviewers. (LAUGHS)

Newman: But you are—you have not learned anything about yourself that is usable from—from criticism?

McCarthy: Criticism of friends. That is in conversation or letters. But very, very rarely—I can't offhand think of an example, although there must be some examples—very, very rarely from a book review. I mean I can remember being struck by some review that appeared in an obscure journal in Naples that said—that she never uses the countryside at all, there's absolutely no nature in her books. And it isn't quite true, but it's true enough to be striking. And it set me wondering.

Because as it happens, I like the countryside. But that's one re-mark, offhand, that I can think of. And there must be others.

Newman: You're in no doubt that the critic has a legitimate func-tion?

McCarthy: Well, I do it myself.

Newman: You do it yourself, yes.

McCarthy: Yes, yes.

Newman: So . . .

McCarthy: No, I don't mean to—as if I sound as if I were airing grievances against reviewers—I don't mean to. I think every author, whether he practices criticism or not, does tend to have this exper-ience of being terribly—of being such a fool as to anticipate reading the reviews and then to be let down afterwards. And as I say, equally by the favorable, if not more.

Newman: Reviews, after all, are not written for the people who wrote the thing being reviewed, they're written for those who might read them.

McCarthy: Maybe you've got hold of something essential. That the author would like to have the criticism addressed to him. That is to his particular kind of interest in what he's done. And, of course, some reviews are written to the author. I think I tend to do that. Rather that if the author is living to think about what this person will think about what I'm saying—agree or disagree—and I do keep that in mind.

I'm now thinking of things that are favorable, but that are analytic. Let's say I've just done a long thing on Ivy Compton Burnett. And I'm very much aware that Ivy Compton Burnett is alive, that I want her to read this review. And I am anxious as to what she'd think of it.

Newman: She's old.

McCarthy: I think she's 82 or 83.

Newman: Does that affect you—inhibit you at all when you write?

McCarthy: Well I like her work so much that it didn't (LAUGHS) create any problem.

Newman: You have been said to be—and you said yourself when we were discussing the safety pin—an autobiographical writer. Are you entirely autobiographical in fiction?

McCarthy: No, no. No, not at all. Perhaps—certainly more in my first book. And I think that tends to be true of all novelists. Even Kafka (LAUGHS) perhaps,—no, his first book was America which wasn't autobiographical at all.

Newman: He'd never been in America when he wrote it?

McCarthy: No. But it generally is true. In *The Company She Keeps,* a lot of things have changed, but that's much closer to my own life than anything I've done since. Though, of course, I've used a lot of things.

Newman: Some of the American writers are said—particularly by European critics and British critics—to be one-book writers. They produce one good book and never again produce anything to equal it, apparently because their first book was so heavily autobiographical.

McCarthy: Yes.

Newman: Is that a fair statement about American novelists?

McCarthy: I don't think so. I'm trying to think of an example.

Newman: Well Mailer, himself, I think.

McCarthy: Well, I don't like Mailer's novels. And I didn't like *The Naked and the Dead*. But I think on the whole he's improved. I like the sort of half-reportage that he does very much. And I think that he's at his best in those. And I didn't read *The Deer Park*. Without having read it, my impression is that it's his best work. (LAUGHS)

Other people say it of Jim Jones—*From Here to Eternity*. And it certainly had some kind of high pitch of feeling like—what was that instrument the hero Pruitt played?

Newman: Oh, yes, bugle.

McCarthy: The bugle did have some high—some pitch of feeling that, say, his last book, *Thin Red Line* doesn't have. But I think *The Thin Red Line* is quite a good book and in some ways better than *From Here to Eternity*. But it doesn't have that charge.

And I think it is true that early novels do tend to have this thing that people lose. And there's also the whole business of becoming a writer. As soon as you become a writer, you lose contact with ordinary experience or tend to. And you become a professional writer. I've written about this subject myself. And that the worst fate of a writer is to become a writer.

Newman: Is it because he associates only with other writers?

McCarthy: Yes, I mean at best he might have a painter friend or so. You know, he's very well developed, well rounded, if he has a painter friend.

Newman: Does this have some connection with something else you've written which is that in the state of a novel today, nobody is writing about very rich characters, who exist in American life, like the psychoanalyst and the social worker and the foundation executive and so forth?

McCarthy: Yes. Yes, I have written that. Yes, well, I think that he probably is still in touch with the analyst and perhaps with the foundation worker.

Newman: Yes, rest assured that many of them get in touch with the foundation.

McCarthy: Yes, but in general the whole tendancy of all branches of modern life is to become specialized. And it isn't very good for an author's work.

I think, of course, Faulkner who refused this specialization, refused to become a writer and always insisted on describing himself as a farmer—I think that perhaps his work is as good or as great as it is partly because of this.

Newman: You, I gather from what you've written think that the novel is in a pretty poor state in the moment.

McCarthy: Well, I'm not unique in thinking that. I think everybody thinks that. But I still have hope for the novel. And since I wrote that I have read a number of good novels. That was at sort of a low point, I think.

Newman: Yes, I think at that point you said nobody had written a great novel since Thomas Mann except, perhaps, Faulkner.

McCarthy: Did I say that? Something like that anyway. Yes, all right.

Newman: That was written about five or six years ago. Would you alter that view now?

McCarthy: Well, I could name—yes, I think Nabakov—I may have mentioned *Lolita.* But I thought *Pale Fire*—this strange book of Nabakov's—whether it's a novel or not, but whatever it is, was a marvelous work.

I'm on record endorsing *The Naked Lunch.* I liked very much— let's see, what else. I liked Herzog and I think Bellow came forward with—with Herzog, especially in the actual writing of it.

Newman: You have a view of the novel that goes back to the original meaning of the word which is news.

McCarthy: Yes.

Newman: Isn't that so? And one of your objections, of one of your complaints against the contemporary novel is that it has lost touch with that, it doesn't deal in matters of information, in what I think you call social matters.

McCarthy: With fact. Yes. Well, I do think that the novel gets its life from doing that. And that the more it turns into an art form, the art novel, the more it sort of vaporizes. And I don't know how—I would like to be able—I don't write a fact novel either. I would like to find some way of getting back to it. Well, Jim Jones, I would say, at least in *The Thin Red Line* was doing it. But that's quite rare.

I would like to find some way of getting back to it. But you sort of get yourself painted into a corner.

Newman: Well, may I ask you in that connection about *The Group* which has pretty large chunks in it of description of contemporary American life in a particular class—what people eat, what people wear, how meals are prepared, how babies are fed, that sort of thing. And so much of it that some people objected, I think . . .

McCarthy: Yes, yes, yes.

Newman: Wasn't that a fact novel then? Did that have some connection with this belief of yours?

McCarthy: Well—the reviewers thought so. That was something that surprised me, because to me I would have wished it had more. That is to me these lists of what they wore and the grotesque things they ate and so on in this period—these catalogs of mine—were not at all close to, say, the documentation of Balzac or DeFoe which I admire. But they were almost fantasy. That is, it's true people did dress this way and eat this way. But the very question of—the very fact of the lapse of time turns these things into grotesque catalogs. Just as if you see a movie in period costume, you can't take so much interest in this thing as a story in some ways. There's always sort of the bloomer joke in it, if you see what I mean.

I would like to write like Tolstoy. That would be my ideal. Not to imitate Tolstoy, but to be able to see. And in some ways I think I can see what he saw. But the result isn't the same. And I would say—my impression is that my books never exactly start out to be funny, at least here. And they're like somebody who makes a remark and discovers it's funny in the middle of making it. And I think this is true of my books—something like that happens.

They all have these distortions, these comic or hopefully sometimes epic distortions. And I suppose that—and I'm not comparing myself to Stendhal—but you do find something like that in Stendhal. That is these marvelous things like the description of Napoleon's entry into Milan or the Battle of Waterloo that they're both factual and—and a kind of comic epic.

Newman: Well, does this perhaps have something to do with that unblinking eye that so many people have said you have?

McCarthy: Yes.

Newman: That is you and there's really nothing you can do about it?

McCarthy: Except that—you see, this isn't a straight vision. It always turns out astigmatic, let's say. And it may be that the very nature of American life which is, after all, what I write about has gotten to be—the whole thing has got to be such a circus that it inadvertently turns into comedy no matter how you try to handle it. At least for me.

And, of course, if you were living in some rural area like Reynolds Price or like Faulkner before his death, you might get something quite different.

But I think the metropolitan novelist tends to be rather struck with this grotesquerie.

Newman: You have tended to—if one were to speak of a painting—you've used a small canvas.

McCarthy: Yes.

Newman: Or perhaps small strokes.

McCarthy: Well, I've mostly written about intellectuals. Maybe that's what he means. Though *The Group* was different because it's the only thing I've done that wasn't about intellectuals.

Newman: Yes.

McCarthy: That the only intellectual girl, really, in it was off stage throughout the whole book—almost the whole book. I was trying to not deal with bohemians and intellectuals in this particular thing. But I couldn't write a large political novel like Trollope. I don't know anything about the practice of politics in Washington, let's say.

And the war novel is out for a woman, unless—I don't know a WASP or something. No, no not a WASP, what do I mean?

Newman: A WAC.

McCarthy: A WAC.

Newman: I just thought—maybe there were WASP's. I think they had to do something to do with flying aircrafts.

McCarthy: I think there were, but now you can't use the word because it means something different. But . . .

Newman: Let me carry this a step further. You have said that a novel must have a bit of scandal, a bit of gossip about it.

McCarthy: Yes.

Newman: But that it must be small enough for that to be grasped—the scandal. In other words you couldn't write a novel about the hydrogen bomb which you regard as a scandal.

McCarthy: Yes.

Newman: Because it's too large a scandal.

McCarthy: Yes.

Newman: It's a worldwide scandal.

McCarthy: No, no. Scandal sort of in the theological sense. Scandal before God, let's say.

Newman: So your feeling is in the first place you have to write about something you know.

McCarthy: Yes.

Newman: Which any writer ought to do. But it has to be something manageable, something that is adapted to your own style. You don't think in these grand terms—in these ethic terms?

McCarthy: Well, I think about the hydrogen bomb probably more than the next person. And I can see worrying about it in an essay. I have even written a few words on the subject here and there. Or the subject of nuclear war.

But I couldn't conceive a novel that I would write that would deal with such a question.

Newman: And you wouldn't venture to write a book that went across different periods of time, for example. You wouldn't carry it across centuries?

McCarthy: Well, I was going to do that once. I had a novel that I discarded that was going to do that. And I never got it out of the New York Public Library, because that was where the first scene was. And it never got beyond the New York Public Library.

I do think that this tends to be a limitation on all women writers. George Eliot was certainly the best among women writers in this respect of getting beyond this. In *Middlemarch* she does take a whole community and deal with it on all levels. But the community in the English Midlands, I imagine, or in Warwickshire where she came from wasn't so big. And furthermore a community was more of a community at that time than it is now.

Newman: Don't you also feel that the novel is handicapped, sort of overpowered by the size of world events, world powers?

McCarthy: I think most novelists feel this, yes. That they feel that what they're doing is not worthwhile. Or they wonder if they have a doubt about it, considering the events that are happening outside the room that they're writing in. And I think one can't yield to this feeling. But it is there. And I think sometimes it leads people to write a lot of pretentious novels and poems in order to match these events.

Newman: There's just nothing to be done about it really, you just keep going in your own way?

McCarthy: Well, you don't sort of patent a style and then keep writing what your style tells you to say. You try to keep—at least I try as much as possible to rid myself of this corset that I've made for myself. That is to be able to say something different and see some-thing different.

If you don't learn something from what you write, you might as well not write. There's no point in it.

Newman: We've been talking about the novel so much and you have said that the staple ingredient in the novel is fact. I would like to ask you whether there can be such a thing as that celebrated invention, the non-fiction novel?

McCarthy: You mean Truman Capote's invention?

Newman: Yes.

McCarthy: Well, I think that's a publicity gimmick that Truman sold himself first and then the public. There isn't such a thing. I agree with the critic Stanley Kaufman who summed it up by saying to talk about a non-fiction novel is the same as saying hard-topped conver-tible or fresh frozen food.

More seriously, I think that he exemplifies a tendency, though it hasn't worn that label before, which is first that you tot up the novel and make it a kind of art form. And then you start doing the same damned thing to reality.

Newman: About you, Miss McCarthy, and here I go a bit into your own biography, people have often spoken of your having left the confessional booth for the psychiatrist's couch. I'm sure you know that that has been said about you. As a writer you of course had a Catholic girlhood and you wrote about that. Yet do you see an affinity there? Has that been in your mind at all in your career?

McCarthy: Well, I do think that I've suspected that. I don't think the remark about the psychiatrist's couch has any bearing at all. It figures in one short story at a point when I was going to a psychoan-

alyst, but I don't believe in psychoanalysis. In fact I regard this as
fraud, especially as practiced.

But I do seem to have some confessional impulse, and a lot of my
work I think does come out of this confessional impulse, and it may
have to do with my Catholic training.

However, of course, there are other authors who had this confessional impulse who didn't have Catholic training. After all there was
Rousseau who was trained as a Calvinist. It may be even more
Calvinistic, but, of course, American Catholicism has that sort of
Calvinistic flavor. That is in examination of conscience added to the
ritual of confession. I suspect that American Catholics are
impressionable ones, take the whole business of examination of
conscience more seriously than say Italian Catholics.

Newman: Is that by the way one of the things that attracts you to
Italy?

McCarthy: I don't think so. I don't like the Catholic side of Italy at
all. I did rather like Pope John like everyone else.

Newman: I meant the fact that they take it less seriously than
American Catholics.

McCarthy: I think that Italy is full of ex-Catholics like me, and it
does make some sort of bond between people. I don't know,
perhaps like the bond between ex-Communists. But a great many of
my close friends are ex-Catholics, and we have this thing in common
that we have so many points of reference that we understand each
other through.

Newman: Since you mentioned ex-Communists, let me speak
about your political life and your work as a critic and let me specify
that when you were on the left in American politics you were of the
anti-Communist left.

McCarthy: Yes.

Newman: I think that you were only 21 when you were already
writing book reviews, weren't you?

McCarthy: Yes.

Newman: In *The Nation* and *New Republic*.

McCarthy: Yes. I think I might have been one day short of 21
when I did the first one.

Newman: How did you get from Vassar to Greenwich Village or
wherever it was?

McCarthy: Well, I got to the *New Republic*. That was where I first went. When I was in college, until my senior year, I was archconservative in politics and I was a monarchist—positively practical . . .

Newman: Were you a monarchist for the United States?

McCarthy: No. But I would have been happy to have all clocks turned back. And then suddenly in my senior year—it happened through reading Dos Passos and that led me to Sacco-Vanzetti. I looked up everything which we had in the library about the Sacco-Vanzetti case, and that in turn let me to the *New Republic, The Nation* and so on, until I finally went and interviewed Malcolm Cowley, who was then the literary editor of the *New Republic* and asked him for a book to review. He finally gave me a little tiny book to do a little tiny review of. In the meantime just as soon as I graduated I got married and lived in New York. I didn't live in Greenwich Village then; I lived in Greenwich Village later.

Newman: Well, in those days you had a pretty firm political outlook, did you not, in the early days, *The Nation, New Republic?*

McCarthy: No, in those days I didn't.

Newman: You did not?

McCarthy: In those days I was just vaguely on the left. I didn't really become seriously interested in politics, I think, until the time of the Moscow Trials, and then I found myself on the Trotsky Defense Committee, which obliged me to be able to argue with all these Stalinists that I was surrounded by, including many respected figures today.

And at that point I became much more seriously interested in politics but still in a very amateurish way. But I find that I have grown in the course of the years much more political, that I care much more about politics than I would have dreamed possible when I was young.

Newman: Well, if you care about politics now, you have, I think, described yourself as a libertarian socialist.

McCarthy: Yes.

Newman: A believer in decentralized socialism?

McCarthy: It's just like being a monarchist in America.

Newman: Perhaps some people would suggest it's like writing a non-fiction novel.

McCarthy: No.

Newman: Is this something that you have developed and expanded?

McCarthy: No, it isn't something that I've patented. It is a view that many people hold; it's one of the tendencies of anarchism, libertarian socialism. And one of the teachers of it in America now is Paul Goodman.

Newman: Let me ask you this. You are said to have been asked by a friend of yours whether you would not enjoy saying nice things about writers, playwrights instead of attacking them and you are alleged to have said that you had to attack them because the young people who should have been attacking them were not doing so. Do you remember saying that?

McCarthy: Yes, but it wasn't quite that way. Yes, I think it was a question of perhaps, say, of attacking J. D. Salinger. I think that was what it turned on. Well, I think I said something like this: I've been sitting around for five years or more watching this Salinger thing, and hearing among all my friends that my opinion of Salinger was shared and yet no one spoke, and I do feel that this kind of review that explodes a reputation, or publicizes a hidden secret, the 'Emperor's Clothes' and so on, that that should be done by young people. It's a lot of fun, and they enjoy it, and also they're not engaged in long works, that sort of thing. And I noticed my friends and I both agreed on this, but that the young people weren't doing this at all, were in fact pretending to write a rather academic criticism. So that we who were veterans were sort of mustered back in service, and it's always rather fun, it wasn't that I didn't enjoy it, but one was a bit too old for it.

Newman: As twenty years as a drama critic, does one get tired of the theatre?

McCarthy: Well, I didn't go that often, and there were years when I didn't go at all. It depended partly on whether I was living in New York, and if I wasn't, I might go once or twice a year. No, I love the theatre; I don't like movies very much, and I would rather see a bad play than a good movie. There's something about the experience. Do you feel that way?

Newman: No. I don't. I'd rather see the movie.

McCarthy: Well, I like the business of the intermissions, and I feel that going to the theatre is a kind of communal event. It has some connection with politics, a kind of civilized political atmosphere. And in fact in New York, many of the most regular theatre goers were those old New York socialists, mostly, Jewish socialists from the old world. And it was part of their atmosphere that they brought with them. And I think that if you find a country with a weak theatre, you find a country that's in rather bad shape politically.

Newman: Miss McCarthy, you said quite recently that since the war the United States has been getting ugly at a frightening rate. Is that another reason you feel somewhat estranged from it?

McCarthy: Yes. Well, not so much. In fact, Europe is uglier at a frightening pace.

Newman: Is that traceable to what we call the "population explosion?"

McCarthy: Yes, these developments have begun with the industrial revolution, and I think that France is getting uglier faster, especially the whole belt around Paris. It has become absolutely monstrous, and much worse than anything in America. It makes you almost yearn for the Jersey Turnpike—these satellite cities that are growing up now around all the chief cities, at least in central France, huge apartment buildings, very surrealistic looking, extremely ugly, and housing mainly workers, working class housing developments.

But you have the inside of the city all old and beautiful. And then as if there were a wall, a Berlin Wall, or something around, you've got outside the working class in these wretched high apartment buildings, with nothing around at all, no gardens. A split-level ranch house is preferable, I think, to these gloomy skyscrapers, and it shows, I think, such contempt for the people who work. Anyway, you see the same thing, not quite as bad, in Italy. But, France is just notorious for its cynicism.

Newman: Are you affected by that? Are you affected by your surroundings when you work? Of course, you live here in Paris because Paris is your home, this is where your husband works. But, are you affected by your surroundings when you work, are you affected by the absence of old friends, or as you say, a milieu?

McCarthy: Yes, very much. I miss the language, I miss the American language, and I think it's a serious problem for any writer. Yes, and especially, it's a serious problem for me now because I'm writing something about a nineteen-year-old American boy, though you do get a certain number of them here—junior-year abroaders, and so on. And I miss friends. I have really very few close friends. But that's not true everywhere in Europe. It wouldn't be true in London or Rome. But it is true in France. Everybody is outside.

Newman: Let me make a personal observation, if I may. We've been sitting here for about an hour, and most of the time, you've been smiling very pleasantly, and, of course, I had met you before, but I've been trying to reconcile this picture of you with what so many critics have said about you and the words I've used before, corrosive, acid. And it has been said of you that to you intelligent people are people who refuse to harbor illusions, somebody who strips away legends, who strips away fantasies, strips away fiction, you show us people as they are.

And, suppose you walk into a dinner party. Are people disturbed, do they say, "here comes that terrible woman who . . .

McCarthy: I don't know what they say to each other.

Newman: . . . and takes notes on us," and . . .

McCarthy: Well, I have noticed that if I come as Mrs. West, the atmosphere is slightly different. And people have very naive ideas about what writers do. They think they go home and immediately write things down in their notebook about them. My experience is that if you use something of a real person, it takes about five years before it gets into a novel, before any part of the experience gets into a novel, it usually takes about five years maturation. The things that simple people say, "My life would make a wonderful story. Why don't you write it?" It doesn't happen that way.

And in the same way, other people imagine that they would be good character or even objects of satire in fiction. Their idea is usually wrong. They can be there for years and you wouldn't use them, especially if they're rather banal, because other people have used them before.

Newman: Do people volunteer themselves as subjects? Have you had that happen?

McCarthy: Sidney Hook once said to me, "why don't you write about somebody really big," and I think he meant, "like me."

Newman: What work may we expect from you now, Miss McCarthy? What shall we look forward to?

McCarthy: Well, I'm working on a novel that's going to take quite a long time to finish, I don't know how long. I would optimistically say another year, or maybe less. Maybe nine months, maybe two years, I don't know.

Newman: Miss McCarthy, is this a comfortable time for an American living in Europe, or in France?

McCarthy: I don't think anytime was ever a comfortable time for an American living in France, that is, if he was in contact with the French, and not simply at Harry's Bar or the Ritz Bar, and so on. But, however, this particular moment, the combination of the Vietnamese War, and racial violence in the United States put an American in a rather uncomfortable position. You're sometimes put on the defensive, and begin to defend America in a way that you might not do in the United States. You might on the other hand feel, I think, more distant and objective about it, perhaps more like a European. I think my friends, my European friends, have been very kind about it. That is, they treat me as the exceptional American.

But, their view of America is really very dark, and, I must say, I rather share it. I share their feelings about Vietnam, and I think everyone, except people in the South, or, some people in the South, share their feelings about such things as Meredith's being shot in that march. What they don't know, and what I don't know much about either anymore, is the whole movement that supposedly is taking place on the campuses, the whole change in American youth. And there is one reason that I should like to go back to America, to find out something more about that, or have some connection with it.

Newman: Of course, the attitude of the French is often described as anti-American, which is an over-simplification, since it is certain American attitudes that they dislike, just as we dislike certain French attitudes without being anti-French. But, are those French feelings confined to the United States, or do they have the same attitudes towards other countries?

McCarthy: I think the French dislike all foreigners, including other Parisians. By the way, the Parisians are much worse in this respect, I've found, than people elsewhere in France. I think all foreigners in France have observed this. But, they're terribly anti-English. I think they really dislike the English much more than they dislike the Americans. And that when America is not showing its worst side, they have certain sympathies with Americans. And that they are jealous of the English. And, much more really deeply, I think they dislike the English more than they dislike the Germans. But I may have talked to the wrong sampling.

Newman: I am sure that the English dislike the Germans more than the French dislike the Germans. I'm sure that's true. What about the American political scene? You said you'd like to go back and see what's happening on the campuses, is there anything else you miss?

McCarthy: Oh, I would like to play some part, of my Portia, it's an impulse coming to the fore. I would like to have some sort of political effectiveness, now, and, of course, it's always possible to write something, and perhaps eventually I will write something on the subject. But it is the kind of thing that you feel happier about doing if you're doing it in combination with some sort of solidarity with other people. I would like to do something to make even further demands than are being made by the intellectual community in America to get out of Vietnam, because I think that the moment is past for signing manifestos, that that was okay, a month ago, or whatever, but the moment is past, it no longer means anything. I think you have to put another chip down, and I'm not sure what that chip is, and I think I would feel surer about it if I were in the United States.

But, I think, if we don't do anything, more than sign our names, which is sort of not hard to do, it doesn't take any courage in the intellectual community in America now to sign, because everybody's doing it, it's popular, it's fashionable. But, I think if we don't do something more serious and this whole thing continues on its course, unarrested, if somehow we aren't able to reach the political conscience of Washington, that we will really not be much better off than the German people under the Nazis whose excuse was, "Well, we didn't know about it," or, "what could we do, we were just one person." I think that the whole question raised by the Eichmann case and by the horrors that obviously went before it has become a permanent question in politics for everybody all over the world. It is impossible to condemn the German people in retrospect for passivity, while behaving in the same way yourself. At least, you have a bad conscience about it. And this bad conscience, on my part, would inspire me to want to be on the scene.

Newman: But, you want to be there because you think it is a bad scene, an unpleasant scene, an improper scene?

McCarthy: Yes.

Newman: You don't want to be there because you think you would *enjoy* being?

McCarthy: No, I want to be there because I think maybe I could do something. There's two things to be said. There has to come some point where you feel something has to be done, and nobody else does it, you think you have to do it by yourself. On the other hand, it's really better to do things—and I don't mean safer, I mean more effective, and more fruitful—to do things with other people.

A single political impulse of one person, especially one person far away, may be completely wrong in this situation, in any actual situation. Some sort of group decision might be more worthwhile. I mean, I'm not in favor of going home and burning myself up. But, I think something should be done.

Newman: Thank you very much, Miss McCarthy.

Mary McCarthy Talks to James Mossman about the Vietnam War

James Mossman/1968

From *The Listener,* 79 (18 January 1968) 78, 79, 80. Reprinted by permission of *The Listener* (January 1968). Copyright © 1968 by *The Listener.*

Mary McCarthy, you open your recent book by saying that you went to Vietnam hoping to find information damaging to the American cause. Now what caused you to make up your mind in advance so completely, if you didn't know the facts on the spot?

I don't think one really needs to go to Vietnam to have an opinion about Vietnam. After all, we have been in this war, basically, since 1954. I thought it was a good idea to say that I was prejudiced to begin with, to lead with my chin.

Didn't the fantastic situation you found make you slightly pause in your crusade?

No. But I was surprised for other reasons. I admit you simply cannot visualise until you are actually in Vietnam how overpowering the American presence is. You feel like a grain of sand, and all the time I was there I felt like a protesting grain of sand.

Did you feel, vicariously, excitement at the power of your country?

No: horror rather—incredulity—something like that. I had promised my husband not to go into combat or out on patrol; but I was strongly counselled by Bernard Fall, the late (alas) expert on Vietnam, that I ought to go up in a bomber. And I said that I would not trust myself, being in a bomber, if we were shot at from below, not to begin to empathise with the crew and that I didn't want to empathise. He said you had to be able to go up in that bomber and be with the crew and to feel nothing. But if you see a wounded man, it doesn't matter really who this wounded man is, you can't help but feel a sort of anguished sympathy, not with his war aims, but with him.

*Were you ever in a position in Vietnam to find out if GI's—
wounded or otherwise—have got war aims or views?*

I didn't really talk much to anybody below the level of captain: it
was impossible. I think it is partly: no 1 my age, compared to theirs;
no 2 my sex, compared to theirs; and no 3 educational level. At one
point I was stuck in Pleiku Airport for four or five hours; I happened
to be with the *Newsweek* Pentagon correspondent, a man called
Lloyd Norman, and there were lots of GI's there, just out of combat.
And we were trying pathetically to start up these little conversations
with them; and we couldn't get anywhere. We ended up talking to
each other: we discussed things like the Moscow trials, the Thirties,
while the GI's would be reading their comics.

*Would you have found it equally impossible to bridge the gap
between you and them in America? Say they'd been serving in a
shop in New York?*

Well, New Yorkers are something rather special; they have this
special New York humour, and awareness, and wised-upness. The
only actual GI that I had any kind of real conversation with was from
the east, a Jewish boy, from Connecticut. He sounder rather
browned off.

*My impression, when I was there last, certainly, was that the troops
were very uneducated and that there is a certain tendency for the
brighter people to stay at university if they can make the grade; and
for the uneducated—including the Negroes—to go to the draft.*

Yes, the war is the answer to automation. This is one thing that has
made it tremendously difficult to mobilise the Negroes in America
against Vietnam. Many Negroes would face unemployment after high
school. They go to Vietnam; they are relatively well paid and if they
rise to master sergeant they are really doing, from the point of view of
what they would be doing in the United States, very, very well.

*Leroi Jones, the Negro writer, once told me that he thought it was
deliberate policy to draft Negroes and get them off the streets, to get
the Black Power people away and hope that is the end of them.*

Actually, I don't think those people are in Vietnam. I believe the
last I heard of Stokely Carmichael was that he was in Paris. I doubt
very much whether the Black Power people are in Vietnam, though

some may be there. But the majority of the Negroes, you get the impression, are rather non-political or, if anything, support the war effort.

Do you think there is a chance that they would feel that this was a way of making it, of equalising with whites?
I don't know about that. Of course, the one good thing I saw in Vietnam was that at least in the daytime, on the field, there was real integration. At night there is segregation. The Negroes go to their own bars and restaurants in Saigon. We didn't have desegregation in World War II—it was Truman who introduced that in the armed forces.

Can you tell me, Mary McCarthy, what is your fundamental objection to your country's involvement in Vietnam?
The application of a technology and a superior power to a political situation that will not yield to this.

That means you are accusing your people of stupidity and not wickedness.
I think they are wicked too, but sometimes those things seem to be somewhat equivalent.

Why do you think they are wicked?
The absolute indifference to the cost in human lives of the pursuit of US foreign policy—that I consider wicked.

I gather that your name is absolute mud out there and CIA men actually spit when your name is mentioned.
I am delighted to hear it. I didn't think that I had made so much of an impression.

What did you find the Americans were saying was the justification for their war now?
'To punish aggression'.

Do you think that they believed what they were saying?
No, I think they learned it. They couldn't really pursue this thought more than a sentence further. You'd say: 'Why didn't we punish aggression in Goa?' And they'd say: 'Well, this is different.' The level of argument was very low.

What would you say was the quality of the people running the war—the civilians and the soldiers?

I felt the soldiers were much more competent; the civilians were extremely fugged up. The military were quite competent in terms of the job that they had to do, insofar as I could judge. There was more double-thinking on the part of the civilians who were not in danger than among the military. The military didn't particularly want to discuss such questions as war aims. The whole thing is, of course, run in a sense very efficiently in that they don't keep anybody out there very long. There is not much hot water, but aside from that there is almost every other conceivable convenience, so that except when they are in combat it really doesn't feel much like war. They really do profoundly believe in the superiority of the American way of life; and the American way of life in the long run—in a sense they are right— is menaced by communism, let's say. I think it'd be a good thing for the American way of life to be menaced; but these people believe in it.

What is the American way of life?

Technology—plenty of milk—God knows. Nothing to do, I think, with freedom. I think it is to do with technology, know-how and comfort. Free enterprise produces all these objects, so that they believe that they owe these objects to free enterprise. At this moment in world history, it is true that free enterprise is giving more Cadillacs and stimulants than socialism is giving to people. I don't think this is an eternal and necessary thing, and perhaps it isn't a good thing that people should have all these perquisites.

The line they were always plugging when I was there was that they were fighting to give the Vietnamese in the south the right to choose their own way of life.

They weren't talking that way so much in February. It was really more on the lines of: we are trying to teach these goddamned people something that they won't learn.

Did you get any impression that they respected the Vietnamese in any sense?

I think that the real feeling, except for a very, very few, was a complete contempt for the whole Vietnamese people, and less contempt for the Vietcong than for the others.

Is that a racialist feeling?

I didn't feel that it was racism. Exactly the same sentiments could be entertained by, for instance, an occupying army in Hungary. Say we had moved in in 1956 at the time of the Hungarian Revolution, and we saw all those Hungarian peasants who weren't able to use American tools, fix cars, and so on: I think we could have begun calling them the equivalent of apes. They call the Vietnamese apes. It is the contempt of the rich for the poor.

Or the man of a proud destiny and choice and the man . . .
And the man without: yes.

Do you feel that they are using indiscriminate tactics militarily now? One hears stories of terrorism and absolute carte blanche *violence. Can you believe your fellow countrymen would torture people?*

It was our fellow countrymen who were standing by watching while South Vietnamese tortured other South Vietnamese.

What about all the aid one hears about? One sees on the television marine doctors looking after kids in hospitals, suffering from malnutrition and so on.

The number of kids they treat is infinitesimal compared to the population, and compared to the malnutrition in the population. But it is done, and this is what salves the American conscience. It isn't a fake; they are really concerned. They feel happy when they cure a child of malnutrition and send it home. The fact is that the whole effort of the United States is to make everyone, including the people who are fighting the war, feel as if they were still civilians and that the war was not happening except, say, on a two-hour-day basis.

But if they feed a child for a while because it is suffering from malnutrition and then when it is all right they send it back home again, presumably it suffers from malnutrition again.

I didn't ask. I hate to ask questions that it is going to be embarrassing for people to answer. I wouldn't be a good interviewer.

Your book sounds as if you were angry all the time. If you were that angry, how could you be embarrassed with asking questions about it?

I don't know; I seem to sympathise with the person I am talking to.

I don't mind quarrelling with somebody, but I don't like to embarrass some decent man who thinks he is in good faith. Nevertheless I did ask quite a few embarrassing questions.

You said that as an intellectual your basic objection to the war was that they are trying to put power to bear on a situation that isn't amenable to it. What would you do?

I would withdraw, quickly. I don't know physically how long it would take to disengage. The French disengaged quite rapidly after Dien Bien Phu, and indeed they performed an extraordinary evacuation. I couldn't spell out the terms, or the whole way in which an evacuation would take place. The South Vietnamese would be left to make a deal with the NLF. I think that this is already somewhat brewing.

They would presumably then go communist.

I don't know exactly how communist they would go. The September programme at the front offered some sort of mixed political situation, a mixed economy, with free elections, secret ballots, some free enterprice, plus agrarian reform.

But your feeling is that it is their business?

Yes. I think we should have a very bad conscience in respect of the Vietnamese, not the political leadership, but the people who have worked for us—cooks, cleaning women, interpreters, drivers—who are not political people, who couldn't form part of a political exodus but who nevertheless may suffer. Something probably should be done about getting these people out.

What is your feeling about your President at the moment? He is often presented as a Machiavelli and a wicked man, and equally strongly as a man in a hell of a dilemma.

I think he is in a dilemma that he has created himself and he is perfectly free to exit from at any time. And if he digs himself into this imaginary dilemma deeper, it may be that his motivations are evil. One hypothesis is that his purpose is not even winning the war but simply prolonging the war with more and more blood-letting. Perhaps the United States does not want to get out of Vietnam. Perhaps it wants to stay indefinitely occupying this territory, even invading

North Vietnam eventually. This is only a hypothesis. It would make a little sense of what otherwise seems to be an insane policy.

But when you are in America, there is an extraordinary number of people who don't seem to care about the war. There's very little said about it outside of Washington and New York. Does that surprise you?
Yes: when I was there last summer, in the State of Maine, in the country, people had become distinctly uneasy, uncomfortable and harried about the war.

Are you surprised that liberals in general are not being more uncompromising about it?
I am certainly not the only one that says: 'Get out.' There is a sort of middle group of people, like Schlesinger and Galbraith. Galbraith has come up with a new thing that I believe appeared in *Playboy*. It is now a little pamphlet called 'How to Get Out of Vietnam', and he offers Johnson a series of recipes for getting out, all of which involve in the end unilateral withdrawal, though he doesn't say it that way.
I am in favour of all kinds of efforts: to march on the Pentagon and destroy the draft card, or refuse to pay taxes. There are also things like boycotts. I think there is a new group that is working on boycotts, not only of the Dow Company that manufactures napalm but of practically every American product.

Do you feel happy in Paris, or do you wish you were back in the States committed to the scene, to your own people? You live in Paris; you criticise America from a well known anti-American camp; you are safe.
I am not an expatriate. And I am not pro-French. I live in Paris because my husband works there. But we did have some such idea in mind when we went back to America last summer: we bought a house in Maine, feeling that if we are going to attack this country we have got to be there.

A Discourse on Nature

Eric Rhode/1970

From *The Listener,* 83 (11 June 1970) 785, 786. This is a transcription of a radio interview. Reprinted by permission of *The
Listener* (June 1970). Copyright © 1970 by *The Listener.*

*There's one theme which runs through these essays: the theme of
nature. You're uneasy about nature and where we stand in relation
to it. And you lament that nature has vanished from the novel.*

I do lament it. But it seems obvious why it's gone. People
themselves are in so much less contact with nature—why should it
appear in novels? Since most novelists now are city people and their
ordinary experiences are far removed from nature except for
holidays, nature just becomes stage scenery in the novel as in life. Of
course, this is not true of Yugoslav fiction or even of Soviet fiction. It's
not true, by the way, of Japanese fiction—of Kawabata's *Snow
Country,* for instance. But it *is* true of the Western novel. And if we
lose nature, in the form of trees and farms and animals, then it seems
we also lose some criterion of the natural, which is a moral criterion,
which was very evident in Shakespeare, say: what is natural is good
and what is willed is bad. But then if you don't have any real nature,
what is the human criterion of the natural? If you don't have a tree,
or some everlasting form of nature—or at least more lasting than
man—and if you're not in contact with that, nor with the seasons, but
only with frozen food, how can you hold onto a concept of the
natural as a moral value in human life?

*In your essay on 'Macbeth' you say at the end it is a poem about
nature to satisfy rather conventional minds, like myself, but the whole
point of the essay is that you have dropped the poem aspect of the
play and see it as though it were a play by Arthur Miller.*

Better.

*So that you can talk about Macbeth as a literal-minded business-
man. Were you conscious here of kicking against the traditional
notion of nature?*

What I say there is that nature is ambivalent, which of course is true, and that it's the evil and destructive forces of nature that are being invoked in *Macbeth*. The natural atmosphere of storms, birds of prey, with the marvelous line about the rain, 'Let it come down' — all this side of nature is being invoked. And the whole problem of nature is this problem of nature's ambivalence.

Don't you think that there's an inclination in Macbeth towards the natural, with the notion of pity, the new-born babe; that, in a sense, he is a bigger figure than you make out because he is to some extent drawn to what he's destroying?
I think he's a very boring figure until he's absolutely steeped in crime and completely isolated. At that moment he becomes real and, let's say, natural.

You say he becomes real in the sense that he perverts poetry into rhetoric.
This doesn't seem so true at the end: then you feel that he's finally speaking at least from his own nature and speaking out of a tyrant's solitude amid the elements.

Someone from the old standpoint of the natural, talking in terms of norms and nature, as they used to do, would say that three of your essays showed that you had aligned yourself with the perverse. Now this is using the old language, as I say, and you'd want to redefine this in terms of the new language. I'm thinking of the essays on 'Pale Fire' and 'The Naked Lunch', and your two essays on Ivy Compton-Burnett. You would claim, in fact, that the norms have changed and that these writers are signposting to something quite new?
I think it is odd that in that large group of essays there are so many essays on what conventional people would call decadent writers. And you could even perhaps throw in Flaubert as a decadent writer.

Compton-Burnett, for instance: why does her world fascinate you in the way it does? I feel that with her and with Nabokov, and perhaps to a lesser extent with Burroughs, you are drawn to them as though to a strange mirror or strange lights.
Certainly there's the ingeniousness of the workmanship in the case of Compton-Burnett and Nabokov. By the way, both of those writers are very much concerned with nature, though there is no nature in

the form of the outdoors. Nabokov, after all, is a scientist, a lepidop-
terist. There are also a lot of birds, by the way, in *Pale Fire*. It's a
curious kind of interest in nature.

It's a kind of stuffed nature, though.
Well, there is that element in *Pale Fire,* but also there's astronomy.
It's like an 18th-century collector's interest in the natural world.

*Your essay on George Orwell starts off in a very admiring way
about Orwell and then, half-way through, switches to a catalogue of
his eccentricities. Finally, you make him out to be a sort of whole-
hearted crank. Did you find while you were writing the essay that
your views on Orwell changed?*
I think they changed while I was reading that collection of letters
and journalism. I still can't quite make up my mind what I think
about Orwell. On the one hand, I admire him, and I also think that
what he did with poverty in his early works—and he occasionally
comes back to it in an essay like 'How the Poor Die'—is not only
quite marvelous but extremely unusual in modern literature, or
modern politics for that matter. In this kind of inquiry he himself was
the subject and the guinea pig, and he really died of it, in my opinion.
The only other example I can think of off-hand is Simone Weil, who
went to work in a factory, wrote an interesting book about factory
work, and died here in England because she had tuberculosis and
refused to eat more than the diet of the occupied countries in
Europe. All this I admire intensely. What I don't like about Orwell—
I don't think he was exactly a crank, he hated cranks—is his
belligerent decency, his dislike of homosexuals. There is a kind of
belligerent philistinism which surprised me in Orwell. I hadn't known
it was there, or hadn't noticed it. I discovered that he not only hated
but heresy-hunted writers I'm extremely fond of, such as Tolstoy,
trying to find, you know, the hidden flaw in Tolstoy.

*What is curious is that up to ten years ago you yourself were
writing essays on the same model as Orwell: you were concerned
with the sociological and the political. Now you've abandoned this,
and you're looking at Orwell from the standpoint of the new
morality—the morality implied, for example, in your discussion of
Burroughs. But you aren't really explicit about the new morality: you*

aren't aligned to it. You are playing with it, but you daren't commit yourself to it.

Though I'm not at all like Orwell personally, I recognise this kind of belligerent Anglo-Saxon empiricism and I think it is inadequate. I look back on this period of my own mental life without absolute joy and admiration, and perhaps I was rather hard on Orwell. But I don't think this essay was an attack. It was some kind of attempt at under-standing Orwell and included some attempt at self-understanding. It's true I haven't gone forward from that point, but there was some sort of exploration . . . People seem to think that I said in that essay that Orwell would support the war in Vietnam. What I said was I didn't know what his position would be. I said that the only people who seem to be his followers in terms of that blunt, no-nonsense English style—Kingsley Amis and so on—do support the war in Vietnam. I said that I couldn't imagine Orwell sympathising with a protest march. On the other hand, I said that there was his fundamental decency, and that he probably would have had to find some weird way of opposing the war in Vietnam while separating himself from Hippies and other pacifist-type protesters.

Someone from the traditional morality might say: 'We are now entering an age of decadence where people follow will-o'-the-wisps. Superstition reigns. This is the age of darkness indeed.' How would you counter them? In the arts the anti-novel in a journalistic entity has faded out. There are very fine writers who wrote within the framework of the anti-novel.

Who survive like islands.

Like Natalie Sarraute. Where are we? What's happening? If we throw out the old morality, what are we going to have instead?

I'm not for throwing out nature. Somebody is throwing it out, not me. I'm against those people who are throwing it out—not out of the novel but out of life.

But you're drawn to the other side aren't you? You're drawn to the explanation of chaos.

That's part of nature, too. I am writing a novel that in some way deals with these questions now—it's almost finished. It has a 19-year-old hero who is a Kantian. I would say I was a Kantian myself. In any

case I'm writing a novel about this. God knows how it'll be judged.
The boy seems very old-fashioned, though it only takes place about
four years ago. I think as far as writing goes I agree with Orwell that
there is one absolute principle—it would be the principle of
Solzhenitsyn, who is, I think, another great current writer, and much
more to my taste than George Orwell in his fiction—and that is the
obligation to tell the truth. Orwell had this belief and there I agree
with him.

*You've always been a warm supporter of vanguard writing. Could I
ask if this novel is your first attempt at an experimental book?*
No. It's rather traditional. None of my books are as much like
Tolstoy as I would like them to be. And it isn't Tolstoyan, of course.
But it *is* traditional. I can't seem to write any other way.

*And do you find this a paradox? That you should be drawn to the
experimental as a critic?*
Why do you have to admire yourself? That would be awful. Surely
the aim of love is not to find one's similar. One should be able to
admire and love one's opposite.

The Editor Interviews Mary McCarthy

Philip Rahv/1970

From *Modern Occasions*, 1 (Fall 1970), 14-25. Copyright © 1970 by *Modern Occasions*.

What do you think President Nixon is up to? Is he really trying to extricate us from Vietnam; or, as some say, is his main intent somehow to "pacify" anti-war sentiment at home while devising new methods of shoring up the Saigon government? Is "Vietnamization" a code-word, or does it stand for something actual?

I don't know what President Nixon is up to. Does he? In thinking about Vietnam (now Indochina, and this shift in vocabulary has taken place almost unnoticeably, by slow stages, like our original insertion of troops into Vietnam), it seems to me that we should not be too much interested in the Chief Executive's state of mind, his avowed aims and concealed aims, and all the rest of it. The president is an instrument of American interests more wide-ranging than his personal choices. I am perfectly willing to believe that Johnson meant it when he said during the Goldwater campaign that he did not want to send American boys to die for Asian boys or whatever were his exact words. The fact that in practically the same breath he was urging the passage of the Tonkin Gulf resolution on the Senate does not prove to me that he had already resolved on the troop landings that took place the following March. Johnson's sincerity or insincerity in his campaign oratory and in his later pictures of himself as a peace-seeker was beside the point politically. Such questions of innocence and depravity concern God or Shakespeare, but whether the man in office is a naive bungler or a crafty villain does not seem to affect very much the political actions he or, rather, his office undertakes. Had Bobby Kennedy been nominated and elected, I am not at all sure we would be out of Vietnam now.

My guess is that Johnson had depths of craft and guile unknown to President Nixon but by the same token had a capacity for emotional sincerity (not incompatible with lying) unknown to Nixon too. Nixon appears to be too shallow, to use Huntley's word, even to be a hypocrite, which requires at least two layers of reality. In any case, again I am willing to believe that when he took up the presidency he badly wanted to get out of Vietnam, much more badly in fact than his predecessor had, since (a) it was not his pigeon and (b) he saw where it had led the adversary party—to humiliation, division, and defeat at the polls.

That Nixon's motive for wanting to extricate himself from the war may have been of a low, expedient sort—a desire to see himself and his party reelected—did not detract from its sincerity and even seemed to guarantee it. The word "Vietnamization," in my opinion, started out as a code; it meant in plain English "withdrawal," phased so as not to look like a rout. Nixon was in a position to carry out this policy; the Democratic leadership could hardly slur him for lack of patriotism, a charge that could only come from extreme rightists of both parties who were and are in a minority. And the Wallace movement did not regard the war as "its" issue; Wallace, it is said, realized too late that the presence of General LeMay on the ticket had frightened off voters.

All this seemed obvious in the early months of 1969, and as late as May, Kissinger was pleading with militant Quakers to hold their fire because Nixon would have us out of the war in plenty of time for the Congressional elections of November, 1970. It even looked as if the White House would welcome the fall of the Saigon government, as proof of the failure of "Vietnamization" (here used in its literal rather than its code sense), which would provide an immediate excuse for departure from the scene, and it did not seem excluded that we might give a quiet little push to help topple Thieu and Ky; after all, we had done it with Diem. In fact, "Vietnamization" could be interpreted as such a push and maybe was by Saigon. If the Saigon government collapsed, like a game of jackstraws, the ensuing chaos would endanger U.S. lives and property. And anti-gook sentiment, already rampant in the U.S. Armed Forces, might have been mustered in the home population, which had already heard a good deal from the anti-war movement about Saigon corruption, ineffi- ciency, the ARVN stealing chickens, large fortunes stashed away in Switzerland. . . . We might have gone home from Vietnam in a white blaze of moral indignation and thwarted Yankee idealism: we had been much too good to those slopes. And when the inevitable

inquest was conducted, it would have been the Democrats—
Kennedy, Johnson, Humphrey—who would have been held responsible for the whole ill-fated adventure. So real did these possibilities
seem that warnings began to be heard about the dangers of a retreat
into a new isolationism.

When the Saigon government did not in fact fall, and Washington
continued to sustain it with a certain degree of abjection (based
perhaps on a guilty conscience), this was the first clear sign that
Nixon's subjective intentions, even his private interest, no longer had
any relevance to what he was "up to." Richard M. Nixon as a man
and office-seeker might honestly want to be shut of this Asian war,
but the presidency was exercising a counter-pull: stay there and win.
The word "victory" is not currently mentioned but is understood
from the insistent refusal of its opposite: "defeat." What has
happened, I think, is nothing so simple as a deliberate policy shift
based on rational analysis, right or wrong. The American so-called
free-enterprise system, highly competitive, investment-conscious,
expansionist, repels a loser policy by instinctive defense movements
centering in the ganglia of the presidency. No matter what direction
the incumbent, as candidate, was pointing in, he slowly pivots once
he assumes office. To reverse direction, as Johnson seemed to be
doing when he announced a partial bombing halt, is to feel called
upon to step out of the picture, as he dramatically did a few
paragraphs later. And among ex-presidents, there has been perfect
concord on the desirability of staying in Vietnam; retired generals and
ambassadors and State Department officials are free to dissent but
not ex-presidents. That would be treason.

Certainly Nixon and his advisers must be justifying their slow
turnabout by rational arguments. First they started persuading
themselves that Vietnamization was working, i.e., that what had
started out as a deception or cover-up was changing into a wondrous
reality as the pacification figures zoomed. Then they got reassurance
from the polls. More and more, probably, they let themselves be
convinced by body counts, captured documents, intelligence reports
of war weariness in Hanoi. Now they appear to be trusting to time: if
we will only hold out a little longer, slow down the rate of withdrawals, play it by ear, Vietnam will straighten itself out. The
President's susceptibility to these arguments is made all the greater by

the insulation of his office from the outside world. Any information that reaches him has been pre-filtered to remove noxious elements, and he is left mainly with the old bottled laughing-gas from the Saigon agencies.

That was why he was so startled by the reaction to Cambodia. He apparently had not noticed that the invasion was widening the war rather than scaling it down, as he had promised. His shock and surprise at the outcry were probably genuine. In his own mind, he is only implementing the policy he announced from the first: Vietnamization. And that is true, but the word now denotes something different, something tough. In the same way, it is hard to be sure what, if anything, he means by the threatening tone he takes toward Hanoi in his televised speeches, warning the Communists of punishment if they foolishly seek to take "advantage" of American troop withdrawals. At the beginning, this could be taken as mere belligerent rhetoric masking a weak position; as time passed, and he became more confident, the threats sounded more genuine and were underscored by a half-covert resumption of the bombing north of the DMZ. Yet there is always a wobble, a vacillation, in his minatory pronouncements; he reserves the "right" to do something vague and unstated. I feel myself that he would be very reluctant to resume full-scale "limited" bombing of the North; to return to a strategy already proven by his predecessor's experience to be both unpopular and ineffectual would be a sort of defeat.

He must be haunted by the ghosts of LBJ's speechwriters, who visit him at night and try to tamper with his brand-new script. But watching and listening to him in his Indochinese telecasts, inevitably one is struck by having seen the show before, with the original cast featuring Lady Bird, Rusk, and Rostow. One is reminded of the saying that a person who does not understand history is doomed to repeat it. But really the drama is much older than the Lyndon B. Johnson starring vehicle. We saw it with Roosevelt ("I hate war"), with Woodrow Wilson ("He kept us out of war"). American presidents, not excepting Lincoln, have a tradition of pulling out the rug on their own pacific campaign promises which seemed at the time to have been heartfelt. Of course politicians in general tend to betray those who brought them to power, e.g., De Gaulle in Algeria, and this is not always a matter of bad faith. But with the American presidency, something more than ordinary speciousness or a mistaken assessment of reality seems to be involved: a basic self-deception which is in the American character itself.

Whether the Americans were ever what the national image projects and what I seem to remember about the "old" America of my childhood is a thing I wonder about more and more. It is fashionable to regard American history, starting with the Mayflower, as one long ruthless landgrab and ceaseless exploitation of imported labor, slave and "free." Yet I am not convinced that the old America of unswerving rectitude, spareness, homespun plain talk, philanthropy, rough equality, earnest endeavor, was simply a myth. Those traits consorted naturally with a business ethic ("Honesty is the best policy," "First come first served," "One man's money is as good as another's"), and the manifest good will of the American, always stupefying to Europeans and still noticeable in some young people, is both a moral quality and an intangible asset to the national corporation; take the Peace Corps. When Charles Wilson said that what was good for General Motors was good for the country, he was expressing a deeply held belief which in its day had had a certain foundation.

What we forget now is that a commercial ethic was once held to be immensely progressive in comparison with a caste or feudal ethic, because of its built-in egalitarian tendencies and the competition for popularity between firms and products. The enlightened philanthropic bourgeois, an Eighteenth-Century culture hero, was nowhere found in such numbers as in the New World, and specimens of the type, like Ben Franklin, were counted among the country's chief natural resources. A sense of this is still found in Henry James.

The pursuit of gain was felt to be a relatively harmless activity, when it did not lead to miserliness, which seems to have been rare on this continent: we have no leading misers in our literature; making money, not saving it, was the American "way." Your money was supposed to work, like any self-respecting person, and not lie idle. The enormous conviction of superiority to wicked old Europe was linked to the idea of innocence; the American was an open book, neatly ruled and ready for the auditors. The persistence of this idea into our time may be explained by the fact that it was always *comparative*. Succeeding waves of immigrants confirmed the thesis that America was "better" than the Old Country. It is hard to see how this belief survived in big-city slums and New England textile towns, but it did. Even today, when the original virtues have long vanished from public and most of private life, the sense of moral superiority, far from diminishing, has acquired a messianic fervor. Not just the "pigs," but the very groups in revolt against the "pig culture" often seem bent on exporting the American way of life, in their own version, to less enlightened parts of the world—e.g., Susan Sontag, critical of the superficiality or "thinness"of Swedish avant-garde morals, of Cuban and Vietnamese "puritan" attitudes toward grass and free sex, e.g., young draft resistors who arrive in Paris and are shocked if the apartment or room they move into doesn't have an elevator or a telephone. And the militant blacks, I understand, look down on black Africans, who, lacking the American experience, are insufficiently revolutionary.

I suppose you could say that all this is touching, just as elderly U.S. tourists are touching when they complain that Japanese taxi-drivers don't speak English or when they are afraid to drink foreign tap-water or "can't abide that strong coffee" in Rome or Madrid. It proves that the American innocence is real, not hypocritical. (I can think of few outstanding hypocrites in our literature either.) It is an innocence or unconsciousness of the self as capable of wrong-doing. As U.S. foreign policy has grown wickeder, the man at the controls becomes proportionately more naive and insular, as unaware of a pattern in his day-by-day decisions as any Phantom or B-52 pilot was of selecting civilian targets in his bombing runs against North Vietnam. In contradistinction even to Johnson, who doubtless had somewhere a lingering fear of hellfire, Nixon is a pure technician, assessing with his gauges various pressures and adjusting operations to them. As a technician, he probably experiences pride of workman-ship, and his official career, in his eyes, has been a search for formulae—the "Southern strategy," "Vietnamization"—inventions of applied political science which will be associated with his name. Whether one of these formulae can release us from Vietnam is almost immaterial. Vietnam is one of those problems that a U.S. President has to learn to live with, as they say, and to get rid of that problem would pose a lot of new ones. Safer to stay with the kind of trouble you know. And Vietnamization, in its current interpretation, unlike a clear "Win" policy, seems to guarantee an unspecified and

almost indefinite U.S. presence in that trouble spot. Nixon's
conscience, let us say, is now at peace with Vietnam as an issue, and,
no more than Lieutenant Calley, does he feel he could have done
more—or less.

*Would you care to comment on the present political and/or cultural
situation in France? What is the state of the student movement? Are
there any new developments in French literature? Is the "structuralist" trend in literary criticism making any headway, and how is the*
nouveau roman *faring?*

I am rather ignorant about new developments in French literature. I
cannot understand what is printed in magazines like *Tel Quel,* and I
have given up trying. My only motive for making the effort would be
to "keep up," and I feel that is a dubious motive. My Paris literary
friends say they can't understand the latest avant-garde either, which
is reassuring since they are (a) French or French-trained, (b) not
stupid, and (c) sympathetic in principle to innovation and personally
to some of the innovators. The only French book about which I was
enthusiastic last year was *Les Guérrillères* by Monique Wittig, a
strange and beautiful fiction—a sort of epic—that comes out of the
Women's Lib Movement, although to say that is misleading since in
some ways it is more like *The Song of Roland* than like, say, Betty
Friedan. The year before I rather liked *Que l'Amour d'un Grand Dieu,*
by a young woman called Adelaide Blasquez, who works on *La
Quinzaine* and is the daughter of Spanish Republican exiles. This too
had an element of feminism and seemed to be somewhat influenced
by Nathalie Sarraute, the only older French writer (and she is really
Russian) for whom I feel spontaneous sympathy and admiration. All
these women have in common a glint of humor or dry sense of the
absurd that is certainly not typical of the *nouveau romanciers.* I think
the *nouveau roman* has had it. (Nathalie Sarraute never belonged to
that group, also sometimes known as the École du Regard, and got
lumped with them by mistake.) But structuralism in literary criticism is
more than making headway. It has practically taken over the field.
The French are suckers for fashion, and suddenly *le tout Paris* is a
structuralist. To an outsider, this is a comedy. The question is, though,
whether any of the younger structuralists are making discoveries that
could not have been made without the methodological commitment.

To me, the best modern literary criticism has been written by Michel Butor. Another perceptive writer is André Dalmas, a railroad official and editor of *Le Nouveau Commerce*. He is particularly good at calling attention to and analyzing young novelists.

What do you make of the cult of the movies now rampant among American youth? Is the cinema as an art-form really worth the overwhelming attention it is now receiving? Does European youth share the excitement of this cult?

I don't much like movies and seldom go. Above all, I dislike arty movies. My taste goes to *Divorzio all'Italianó*, on the one hand, and *Z*, on the other. And *Dr. Strangelove*. These films, of course, are hated by those who make a cult of the movies. The rage for movies among the young started in France, I think, some time before it took hold in the U.S. If you are looking for students in Paris, the place to find them is in a movie house, though this is perhaps slightly less true than before May, 1968. I don't think the cinema as an art-form deserves the attention it's getting. In fact I don't think it *is* an art-form and least of all when it pretends to be. That doesn't mean that there can't be beautiful moments in movies or that even on rare occasions an entire movie can't seem beautiful. But a chair can be beautiful without chairs as a class being considered an art-form. I feel the same way about photography as I do about films. They can document, amuse, agitate, teach, maybe convert. They are a *useful* art. The ones in both cases that surpass that category were often made as socially instructive documents, like *Potemkin*, or as reportage, like Walker Evans' photographs done with Jim Agee for the Department of Agriculture, or as plain entertainment, like Chaplin and Buster Keaton. If you want, you can say that the ones that survive are "found" art, like Marcel Duchamp's toilet. I don't think I really believe that, but in any case movies are *popular*, made for mass audiences, and there's some horrible contradiction between this fact and the cosy élite notion of art, made for the precious few. Nothing ages more than the "beauty" passages of a movie; take the Teutonic Knights in *Alexander Nevsky*—I once thought that was lovely, and now it seems pure corn. I should hate to see *Marienbad* in a few years.

In defense of movies, I should say that they seem to be able to get on film images of modern life that the novel flinches from. Even a movie like *Easy Rider*, which I disliked, did show a sort of drugged pastoral that you don't get in fiction. The same with some of the depression landscapes in *Bonnie and Clyde*. Maybe this is because landscape has become so inaccessible to the ordinary person. Nobody paints it any more or tries to describe it in words, so that the few parts of it that have not been gutted unroll on film like a lost dream. Yet this is related to the camera's capacity for lying. A fragment is represented as a whole. The U.S. Southwest highways that flow by in *Easy Rider* are not all that lyrical in real life, which doesn't have a cutting-room available. *Lolita* is more truthful. For some reason, words seem to insist on at least a minimal accuracy, unlike moving pictures. For example, if I wanted to make a documentary on Vietnam, I could produce a poetic and highly persuasive account of the pacification process, with backgrounds of paddy fields and bamboo, with smiling children in clean clothes and a venerable wrinkled peasant running to tell the lieutenant where the V.C. is hiding. This would be a lot tougher to do in a report, partly because the reporter's eyes and ears are suspect, whereas the camera is felt to be trustworthy in that it cannot "make up" anything, which renders it easy for the viewer to identify with it. Of course we all know that the camera selects, but we are momentarily taken in by its vivid synecdoche; it's natural to believe our eyes ("Show me") as opposed to somebody's word. The selective powers of the camera are probably why movies and some still photographs are the last refuge of lyricism in a highly unlyrical world.

A further defense of the movies is the fact that they are a universal language. Particularly for the young. Whatever their nationality, they have all seen the same films; and this gives Germans, French, Americans, etc., a common vocabulary as well as something to discuss with each other. The images require no mediation, and whether you see a film in the original version, with subtitles, or dubbed, the translation of what is being said is the least important part. With plays, poems, and novels, the translation may be a real barrier. This discovery about films as a communications channel may account for the high value attached to them, as though they were a sort of currency.

Is a significant distinction to be made between American radicalism of the 1930's and that of the present period? In what ways has the "youth culture" now sweeping the United States influenced political moods as well as movements of protest and confrontation?

I think I rate the radicalism of the Thirties lower than you do. I am fond of it because it was part of my youth, and I value the mental clarity that was associated with it: sharp analysis, the habit of making distinctions, avoidance of rhetoric. These qualities, to which I'm attached like a limpet (or is it a barnacle?), are almost totally absent from today's radical movement, though Europe is better in this respect than the U.S. You can reason with a young French Maoist and each score points off the other. Maybe because drugs haven't yet taken hold there. Also French young people (possibly Italian too) don't despise their Old Left parents and treat them as cop-outs; they may actually respect them. And this in turn is because the older generation is on the whole poor or at best in moderate circumstances. The second or third generation of French radicals has not had to watch its parents living one way and talking another. I would venture to formulate a little law: the more affluent the parents, the less mental clarity you find in the children.

But to speak of my doubts about the radicalism of the Thirties, what did we accomplish? Almost nothing that I can see. When I say "we," I mean the group of Trotskyites and Trotskyite sympathizers or fellow-travelers around *Partisan Review.* We fought the good fight against Stalinism when we were very much outnumbered and outweighed, materially speaking. And most of us did not "sell out" on the ideological plane to the various New Deals and New Frontiers or join the Conservative fringe. But that was a rather negative accomplishment, and as for our battle against Stalinism, we were losing until U.S. foreign policy finally hardened into anti-Communism after its wartime vacillations. Then suddenly most of the old Stalinist fellow-travelers turned in our direction, and the Twentieth Congress clinched it. Some of us (you and me included) were OK on McCarthy, but again history took care of that, and I would not like to claim that our disputes with Hook and others had any influence on events. Meanwhile, like most American writers, professors, and editors, we were getting richer. And less revolutionary. Not just because we had more money, but because we were getting older, and because, according to our analysis, it was not "a revolutionary situation." That was doubtless true, but just here our clear-mindedness perhaps did us a disservice. We were *writers,* not organizers or revolutionary cadres, but, looking back, it seems to me that I personally might have done a little more than write books. For instance, I had never seen the inside of a factory, since I was taken on conducted tours as a schoolchild, until I went to North Vietnam and was taken on another tour. My only contact with workers has been with plumbers, carpenters, and so on. We talked (and still talk) about the reactionary politics, at least on the war issue and often on the race issue too, of the U.S. trade unions; we are right, but it is a strange reason for having no interest in them.

In a revolutionary situation, it may be good to be clear-minded and be radical, too. But in a non-revolutionary situation, this leads to an ironic detachment. And irony, self-irony and all the other kinds, is the present-day American curse. That is, among intelligent people. Perhaps we picked it up from the Jews, so numerous in the intellectual class; but it is now a distinguishing trait of the American, whatever his origin, at roundtables and international conferences.

The young do not lack this irony, though with them it's often uncompanioned by humor. But on the plus side, they are seeking a radical experience. Whether they cut their hair and try to convert workers in factories, like one Maoist faction, or make bombs in basements, or simply live poor among drop-outs, they're making some kind of connection with the latent revolutionary elements in society—where else would they be found except near the bottom? At the very least, they're integrating their politics with a life-style. But there a question pops up. Are these kids just wearing costumes, dressing up, playing revolutionary with bombs and bicycle chains, or are they for real? The humorlessness of so many of them does not prove they are serious but often suggests a catatonic stupor induced by the weight of the symbolism in the drama they're acting out.

Their disgust with their affluent parents has taken them a long way from home, though Mother may gently try to keep them away from the pushers by letting them plant marijuana in the herb garden or take the whole family on an LSD trip. There are times when one thinks that the strategy of the youth style is simply to test the limits of their parents' permissiveness and thus generate more disgust; for if Dad will smoke pot with you, why didn't he do it before, and if he won't, he is only a pretend liberal. In fact he is a fake either way. Yet disgust, with all the boredom and satiation it contains, seems more keyed to rebellion than to revolution. It's itself a by-product of affluence. The means of venting it cost money; when you add up the cost of drugs, travel, doctors' bills, bail, legal fees, damage to parental property, contributions to the Panthers and the Young Lords, it comes to quite a lot, though less perhaps than a coming-out party.

But maybe playing in the cellar, which they call the underground, they will blow the house up, and maybe it is time that happened. The slow work of subversion indicated by "our" radicalism seems inappropriate to the modern situation. Vietnam seems a demonstration of how little "our" methods worked even when we finally became active in debate, demonstrations, boycotts, canvassing. If the young have been radicalized, they owe it more to the police than to us.

I see that I haven't answered the second part of your question. In fact, I don't find much connection between the youth culture and the older political modes. Each seems to be doing its own "thing." The few older radicals I know who have adopted their children's rhetoric do not seem very comfortable about it. During brief periods of university involvement, faculty members have shown a tendency to copy their students. I would ascribe a lot to this to simple ingratiation.

The term "avant-garde" is now bandied about in America as never before in our history—certainly far more frequently than in the days of the classic avant-garde. Are you truly convinced that there is a genuine avant-garde grouping in American art and literature today? Some people insist that our literary production is as good as it ever was, pointing to writers like Mailer, Barth, Pynchon, et. al., as examples of artistic advance. Do you think that the writers who emerged in the 1960's measure up to previous literary generations?

No, I don't think there's a genuine avant-garde grouping in America, though I haven't read some of the writers you mention. I think Mailer's last two non-fiction books are both something new and very good. But I don't find anything avant-garde in them. They sum up, fuse, and refresh some older modes. There's a breeze of freedom blowing through them. What I know of the so-called new avant-garde is just the opposite. It seems constrained and frigid. I can't see this as a period in which an avant-garde could possibly flourish. Everybody is more interested in politics than in "advanced" culture, unless I confuse my own interests with the general mood.

Do you think that the relation between art and politics is surfacing again as a major problem today? What do you make of the emergence of black writers as an important literary force? Is there anything truly meaningful in the demand that literary standards be adjusted to accommodate the "black experience," so called?

Yes, I think the relation between art and politics is surfacing again today or, rather, that a new relation between them is arising. Mailer is an example and *Les Guérrillères,* which I mentioned, by Monique Wittig. The only new books I respond to now suggest some such new relation, even those that don't appear to on the surface. But what's happening has nothing to do with "socialist realism" or "commitment." Partly, thanks to experiment with language, what the Russians used to denounce as "formalism" is finally in a position to shape revolutionary political material. On the other hand, it looks as if there *might* be, at least in France, an interplay between workers and intellectuals—something that hasn't happened since Zola. If this comes about, there will be a new kind of advanced literature aimed at the speaking to masses, another version of what Tolstoy was trying to do late in his life for the peasants but using maybe techniques derived from comic strips, techniques of foreshortening derived from the *nouveau roman.* At the moment, it is only a vision; I can't cite any examples. But as I understand it, there is the hope of making a radical break with bourgeois literature, all of it, including the low kinds of it that are supposed to appeal to a mass mentality. Whether that is possible, I don't know; to break with bourgeois literature, it seems to me, would be to break with the whole inheritance and long accretion of language. But that's too difficult a subject to discuss here.

I'm not familiar with the younger black writers. But Ellison, Baldwin, Cleaver certainly don't require any downward adjustment of standards to accommodate them. Cleaver isn't on the same literary plane as the first two, but *Soul on Ice* is intellectually far more sophisticated than the maiden efforts of many of our white writers, e.g., *This Side of Paradise* or *From Here to Eternity.* As you've pointed out in the distinction you once made between redskins and palefaces, American literature has always had a double standard. We must be unique in this. A good deal of "black experience" writing probably falls into the redskin category, while Baldwin and Ellison are palefaces. I don't know where to put Richard Wright; on the cusp, I guess. But if the "black experience" is going to be expressed in the black idiom rather than in the white man's grammar, it will be a dialect literature—not the first in history. I don't know why people who've accommodated jazz and spirituals should be so uptight about this. And if we ever get black liberation, there won't be any more "black experience" to write about or at least the present gibing vocabulary won't fit it. Meanwhile some terms from that vocabulary will have passed into current usage; I'd expect "honky" and "uptight" to appear soon in the dictionary, but I hope not "rapping."

Miss McCarthy Explains

Jean-François Revel/1971

From *New York Times Book Review* (16 May 1971), 2, 24, 26, 28, 30. Copyright © 1971 by The New York Times Company. Reprinted by permission of New York Times Company.

Jean-François Revel, author of the recent "Neither Marx nor Jesus" (a great success in France, to be published here in the fall) conducted this interview with Miss McCarthy in her apartment near the Gare Montparnasse. "In seven years," M. Revel said, "I had been in Mrs. West's flat [Miss McCarthy is married to James West] only at night, for parties and dinners. It looked strange to me in the daylight—smaller, quiet and provincial." He used a tape recorder, which, he said, gave "a professional, 'technotronic' side to our conversation." M. Revel also pointed out that although he has taken part in many interviews this was the first in which he was the interviewer.

In your new novel Birds of America *what made you choose a young boy, an American student, as the main character of the story?*

It just sprang like that out of my mind. I sat down and started typing out notes to myself about a new novel, and the notes begin: "On Equality. . . ." They ramble on about the question of equality and suddenly (I've got these notes still) there come the words, "The action should begin with a young man." A student, in Rome, and so on. But the boy just sprang there. In reality he's based on several boys but especially on one I knew here who was going in the Sorbonne. He had a plant that he took for walks. The other thing about him that I never got into the book was that he was very anxious to procure a skull. He's been to an exhibition of engravings by Bresdin at the Bibliothèque Nationale, which made him want to learn to draw, and he decided to start by drawing a skull. He wanted us to tell him how to get one, but I don't think we ever succeeded. We could find skeletons but not skulls. So, anyway, the boy was just there in the middle of the subject.

It is also a kind of philosophical novel. At the end, Immanuel Kant himself speaks to the young boy, Peter, and tells him, "Nature is dead." Is that the philosophical meaning of the novel? Do you think yourself that nature is dead?

I believe it. Moreover I agree with Kant, if I understand Kant. You remember that quotation at the end about the beautiful things in nature proving that man fits into the world, etc. If nature—in the beautiful form that we normally think of it: that is, the outdoors, plants, farms, forests—if all this were to disappear, which it's doing, there'd be nothing stable left to stand on, no ground for ethics. Then you'd really be in a Dostoevskian position: why shouldn't I kill an old pawnbroker—because there's no longer a point of reference or a court of appeals. Nature for centuries has been the court of appeals. It will decide one way or another. Not always justly; but nevertheless (especially in our Anglo-Saxon tradition—it's very strong in Shakespeare), the appeal is always to this court, to Nature's court. And if this is gone, we're lost. And I think we're lost, I'm not an optimist.

What do you think about the reaction against the ruination of nature? Today people look more and more for natural products, natural life, don't they?

I really believe that Gresham's Law is operative in these things. I don't think there's a natural selective process in masses of people that causes them to choose the better product. Well, I'll take the example of a turkey. I just bought a turkey at the U.S. Commissary. It was a frozen turkey. I don't like frozen food, anyway; but normally American frozen turkeys are better than French fresh turkeys. But I read all this literature on the outside of the turkey, and it explained that this turkey had been "deep basted" with vegetable oil. The corpse had been injected (the word "basted" of course is hilarious in the context) with vegetable oil. Now I'm sure that next year or two years from now you won't be able to buy a turkey that this hasn't happened to. And the reason is not that it tastes better—I thought it was rather poor actually—but that you don't have to baste it in the oven. So people would rather have an inferior turkey and not have to work.

To take your turkey as a symbol for the biosphere, your conclusion would be that the destruction of nature is inevitable?

I think that's going to happen and I think that in general bad products drive out good.

Nevertheless, your novel is about culture at least as much as about nature. There are not so many birds in it, except at the beginning. Peter seems preoccupied by social, political and literary or artistic matters, isn't he?

Of course, one simple reason is that he's living in the city. There's nature in the beginning; but, after that, once he's living in the city, he isn't much in contact with Mother Nature. What in essence Peter is trying to do is lead a natural life and to try to find some natural life of the mind that would be common to everybody. It would be like an environment that everybody could live in.

But isn't the novel essentially about education? About how to become an adult in our time? Peter belongs to an intellectual family. He studies first in America and then in Paris and Rome. Why?

I think I've forgotten. Well, I tell you, what takes place in the main body of the book is the equality theme. Peter keeps drawing up plans to send to General de Gaulle or Kosygin or whoever. He's bitten by the desire to solve the world's problems. But always, underneath this, is the desire to create balance and equality. That is, the plan for making sewer workers the best paid class in society. Which is very rational—it may not be practical but it's the product of rationality or over-rationality. For instance, Peter is struck by all those headless statues, decapitated during the French Revolution, hence his reflections in his letter to his mother, where he says the French Revolution didn't go far enough—that we should chop off the head of language too. Of course, he's right, you know; and at the same time it's impossible. Unless maybe they do it in China. It's the only place in the world where they seem to be trying to create a biological mutation. By the changing of the Chinese language and the destruction of almost all the Buddhist temples and shrines. They'd like to destroy their artistic heritage in the interest of starting over. The clean slate. Well, anyway, Peter's story takes place before the cultural revolution; but the thought of such a purge crosses his mind. He thinks, "I don't know whether I could stand it, but this is what should be done."

The very existence of culture seems to him an obstacle to equality? Or does it?

Yes. At the same time, being intelligent, he sees all the obstacles to any scheme he puts forward. Like when he gets wound up in the question of tipping, seeing all sides. The categorical imperative, as he says, doesn't seem to work very well in that situation.

Of course, but he still behaves like a born aristocrat. He can't stand ordinary people.

I wouldn't say aristocrat. Rather he's a misanthrope. At home, though, he wouldn't be against ordinary people, the people who work in the Portuguese grocery store or the filling station, or the kids who play baseball. And he won't join the beach club. Ordinary people in their natural setting he doesn't object to. He liked grade-school teachers when he was a kid much better than fancy masters in private schools.

But isn't that super-aristocratic behavior? You know, when one loves peasants and fishermen but cannot stand middle-class people? Since we are living in an age where almost everyone is middle-class, isn't that a kind of snobbishness? Take, for example, the visit Peter pays to the Sistine Chapel: he is almost sick because of the many American tourists there. These tourists are, after all, ordinary people; they are the people.

Yes, but my point is that anybody, a grocery-storekeeper, who had any eyes—that is, who had any real reason to be in the Sistine Chapel—would be just as annoyed as Peter by all that mob. The real problem hits him in the Sistine Chapel. Everything breaks down for him, his principles abandon him there. That is the whole point of the Sistine experience. He finally comes out and says. "There ought to be an entrance exam, it's the only way." At that point, he's become reckless and maddened, he expresses his true feeling, and, being Peter, he reasons about it at the same time. But that has been a most conclusive challenge to his principles. It goes back to what he tells his mother in the letter, where he says that art and equality don't mix, that "the world will have to get rid of the people like you, Mother." In the Sistine Chapel they try to mix. It's the opposite of the previous chapter, where he's happy, having fallen in love with the works of Borromini, the 17th-century architect that nobody else cares about seeing. Borromini of course is nature. I mean that Borromini's world is a kind of fantastic forest. So that Peter has solitude, nature, art, contemplation there—everything he likes.

All through this boy there has to be (I don't know why) this paradox of lover-of-solitude and misanthrope who is passionately concerned about equality. This happens to be a regular human type, of course—the misanthrope-philosopher, but I didn't conceive it that way.

So the philosophical lesson would be that nature is dead and that culture must die, for the sake of equality?
But I didn't write the book to make a conclusion like that. Furthermore, the thing he says in his letter—which perhaps is really what's at the bottom of the book—is this feeling about the idea of equality once having been entertained, nobody can get rid of it. This I have thought for years—that once the egalitarian notion was discovered, say some time in the 18th century, there's been a continual flight from it. Eventually we're going to have migration into space to escape equality. At the same time any person with a child's fairmindedness cannot help thinking that equality's a good idea. If we lose this fairmindedness of children, then we become monsters. In the Middle Ages you weren't a monster if you took inequality for granted but now you are.

Why did you make Peter an epitome of Western civilization? His mother is American and a first-class musician, his father is an Italian Jew and a scholar, his stepfather a German physicist, the third husband of his mother is an internationally known art historian.
I don't know why. I know I made Hans a scientist to make an opposition between Peter and science. Maybe some sort of melting-pot idea—I think it's really that. And America, after all, was supposed to be the land of opportunity and, well, the melting pot.

To my mind one of the most lively parts of the book is Peter's French experience. An obvious failure. Is Peter's a representative case of young Americans abroad, as it is now, according to you?
I'm really trying to be faithful to the experience of these kids over here—98 per cent of them feel that—and they're so lonely. It's not Europe, it's France. I met a young Dane the other day who told me he'd lived here as a student and he said, "Exceptionally, I got something out of it; but the loneliness was so terrible." They all say that. This business of going to the same cafe for six months and even

the waiter won't speak to you. Henry James had exactly the same experience. When he left Paris, he wrote a letter to his brother William James and said, "It would be ignoble to stay in Paris just for the restaurants." But I think it's gotten worse. I remember, right after the war, in the 40's, when I was teaching, I had students who later came abroad on those Fulbrights and, though they were often very poor, they had a much better time and they enjoyed it in those years.

Are there formal problems for you, a problem of the form of the modern novel?

I think about them in connection with other writers, that is if I'm doing a criticism or a review. But when I'm writing a novel I don't look at it as some event in the history of the novel. The only formal problem I think about when I write is the formal problem of a sentence or a paragraph. I can't write any differently from the way I write.

Do you feel any esthetic pressure on you of the new theories of the novel, or of the well established theories of the new novel?

I do believe in a sort of "Tel Quel" doctrine, that you must listen to the language, that language tells you what you want to say. If some word is sticking out of a sentence, say, and it looks ugly, it is telling you what you don't want to say. Language is continually giving you messages, because language is a repository of everything on the verbal level that's been experienced by human beings.

What you magnanimously call the "Tel Quel" doctrine is that language has no content, no meaning, the content of language is language itself. Do you agree?

That I don't believe. Nevertheless it's obviously not a question of just sitting down and copying something that's out there with the best means in your possession. At least half of it is going to be coming from something that is happening in language, including your own.

There is no plot in your novel. But yet there are normal sequences which are close to traditional realistic writing. Isn't that so?

Well, actually I think the form of *Birds of America* is rather strange. Because it isn't a realistic novel. Anybody who thought that was a realistic novel would be crazy. Still the oddity is only conveyed by tone—only by tone and not by the exterior formal devices.

That's true. Birds of America *is no more a realistic novel than is* Lolita, *for instance. But there are in it situations and characters, and you always indicate who is talking to whom.*

I suppose we all do it less than we used to because of the modern novel, even the people who write traditionally. We indicate who is talking much less than we did, simply by osmosis from the avant-garde novel. The reader also has gotten used to having to work a little harder to identify speakers. In Nathalle Sarraute's novels, it's always clear really who is speaking; but you have to work for it and you sometimes have to do a repeat to be sure. I remember when I first started to read *Ulysses.* I got up to, I think it was page 56—I couldn't get any further. And I tried again and it was always page 56. Then suddenly one year I sat down and read the whole thing, and it was no longer difficult, and this was because so much Joyce had gotten in the atmosphere that Joyce himself suddenly became transparent.

Do you think Joyce is really transparent now for the average reader, the public who is not professionally or passionately devoted to literature?

I have a marvelous idea. People do not any longer expect to understand. It's really a very frightening development. They pick up some book and they really think it's all going to be normally unintelligible. This expectation leads to a loss of ability to understand, so when people come to something that is understandable they no longer get it and make the most incredible misreadings. This reading-impairment is a product of *la nouvelle litterature.* Have you given any thought to what it is in people that makes them want a story? Because this is a very deep thing—obviously—and I don't think anybody has ever posed the question, that I know of anyway. I've posed it to myself but not very seriously. It would be a rather interesting subject for speculation and might mean that you could rescue the plot.

You have been here, living in France, for almost 10 years. Has this had any impact on your writing, or what kind of impact could it have in the future?

I think eventually I would lose my subject matter. Of course, this book took a long time to write. I started it way back in '64. Then I had those two Vietnam trips in between. Anyway, aside from that, I don't think the international theme—the confrontation of cultures—-

exists any more. Not because of formal developments. It no longer has any bearing: maybe air travel killed it.

In my case, living in Paris and writing more or less in the realistic tradition, I couldn't do a novel about French people, because they'd have to talk French. I couldn't even write about English people. I'm incapable of writing at length about anybody except an American, so it's not only a question of being out of touch with the native speech but of being out of touch with the native subject matter. Joyce could write about Dublin while he was in exile because he was not interested in the present. Bloomsday, June 16, 1904, was all the more real to him because of the distance in geography as well as time. But if you're not that type of writer, by staying abroad, you eventually lose your subject matter. Certainly in my case the subject is social— is always social.

Do you plan to go back?
I don't think people's movements should be dictated by artistic needs. It would be horrible, evil, for one to make one's artistic needs the motor of one's life. George Orwell was against it too, on sort of puritan grounds. Maybe I'm a puritan too, I don't know. Of course it's true, about the egotism of writers—this monstrous egotism that we seem to have. Bellow is a most ghastly example of it. I don't think that wives and children and dwellings ought to be sacrificed to the needs of the artist, though there are certainly moods when I feel it. But on the whole I believe in a certain amount of submission to fate and also to chance. All that, too, is part of the natural and the vitality of the natural. Some subject has to propose itself to me—not me proposing myself to the subject. In writing, there has to be some element of the Tolstoyan. "I cannot be silent." That's more true, of course, of political polemics; but you don't sit down and decide to write a polemic. You reach the point of saying to yourself: I cannot be silent any longer, about whatever it is.

Somebody wrote rather wittily about a woman poet in America that her only relation to poetry was the desire to write poems. I am rather against the autocratic will. If I moved home to America to pursue my subject matter, the subject would run away from me, I'm sure, as a punishment.

Do you always write your novels slowly? This one was begun in

1964; and The Group, *which was published in 1963, was begun in 1952.*

Not always, just those two. *The Group* became a terrible problem—partly a moral problem—not about sex of course. But I began to feel as though I was persecuting those girls and just hammering away at them and knocking their poor heads together and that I ought to stop that, this just could not go on, and so I put it away for several years. I didn't work on it at all and wrote another novel instead and then I went back and reread it and I thought, this isn't so bad, I had been exaggerating. This happened repeatedly during those 11 years, and I did several books in between. Whereas, with this one, Vietnam got in the way. That is, I felt that I could not go on writing about a boy of that age and not do something myself about Vietnam; that the whole book would have been some sort of *trahison* if I had just sat on my bottom. I wrote those two books, accomplishing nothing, doing absolutely no good. When Johnson fell out of office, we had one joyous moment of feeling that we had all accomplished something. In any case, after those trips, I felt I was free to go on.

Do you really think that the American writers who wrote about Vietnam didn't accomplish anything?
Well, it's true. I'm so discouraged. I really thought when Nixon first came in that he wanted to get us out of the war, for whatever motives. I think maybe he did; but the office doesn't want to get the President out of the war, which means that I think this war was "not an accident," as Trotsky was fond of saying. It must come out of something very deep that we had not noticed in American life, because it took us all by surprise—this slow involvement in Vietnam, and it took us by surprise about America. A European could say we should have known before, but we were sort of like Peter's mother in imagining that there was this ideal American republic, with some shortcomings. I find the situation extremely alarming now and, I don't know, I see no prospect of getting out of there; and, after all, the war is expanding.

Mary McCarthy

Arnold W. Ehrlich/1971

From *Publishers Weekly* 200, No. 4 (26 July 1971), 19-21. Reprinted by permission of R.R. Bowker Co. Copyright © 1971 by Xerox Corporation.

"My breath was taken away by the unfavorable quality of the reviews." The speaker is Mary McCarthy, the setting the art-filled Park Avenue apartment of her brother, Kevin, the noted actor, and the subject the reviews of *Birds of America.* Miss McCarthy, a long-time resident of Paris but in New York for a few days during a sultry late June for radio and TV appearances, relaxes on a sofa, lights up a cigarette, and appears smiling and expectant despite the lack of air conditioning. A veteran of many literary engagements, wearing with honor her own wound stripes, nevertheless she waits "for the pain to be drawn."

"What particularly bothered you about the reviews?" *PW* asked.

"The bitchiness," was the prompt answer. "The reviews of *The Group* were hostile but at least they weren't violent. The quality of reviewing in this country has declined since *'The Group* came out. I'd rather have something like Norman Mailer's perceptive but unfavorable review of The Group, in the *New York Review of Books,* than what I have been getting."

She was particularly annoyed by John Aldridge's criticism of "Birds" in *The Saturday Review.* ("The serenity of the book is so total that one might almost suppose Miss McCarthy has finally developed beyond the point in her career where she felt she had to prove, with all the pounding fists of her being, that she deserves the title of foremost lady intellectual of American letters.")

"But at least that wasn't syndicated," she commented, and proceeded to another gripe—"the sinister case of standardization of opinion in this country, and the abominable practice of boilerplate reviewing." She had been keeping count of her magazine and newspaper reviews, not including syndication, and on the date of the interview her score was "29 favorable, 24 unfavorable, and 9 middling. But the real power," she added with her famous cat grin, "is reflected in the number of times identical reviews appear over the country. I can't believe there isn't someone intelligent enough in every decent-sized town in this country to write an original review." On the other hand, William Hogan, of the *San Francisco Chronicle* had reviewed *Birds of America* three times—"all favorably." Puzzled but obviously pleased grin.

Another "bitchy" review that vexed Miss McCarthy was Helen Vendler's in the *New York Times Book Review*. "Doesn't she have the reputation of trying to destroy famous writers?" she asked. "And that caption" (she meant subhead: "Mary McCarthy again her own heroine—frozen foods a new villain")—"that was pretty bitchy, don't you think?"

What was her reaction to V. S. Pritchett's long piece in the *New York Review of Books,* which *PW* interpreted as a velvet-glove putdown, as only a superb English writer can pull off?

"Oh, I don't agree with you at all. Do you really think so? I read it twice. I thought it was favorable and counted it among the favorable category.

"Normally, in London I get better reviews than in America," she said, when asked to compare the quality of reviewing in the two countries. "You know, there's a young French girl who has been doing her thesis on my work. One day she came to me looking very puzzled and said, Did I realize that reviews of my books have always run 60 percent unfavorable? No, I didn't realize it." Dazzling smile, radiant self-composure, the stance of a literary warrior knowing it was her turn to get shot down, but tough enough to take it.

We switched to literary chat: What writers did she like or dislike? Her opinions were quick and spontaneous. We start with John Updike. "I liked the first two books—*The Poorhouse Fair* and *Rabbit Run.*"

"How about *Couples?*"

Grimace.

"Norman Mailer?"

"I liked *Miami and the Siege of Chicago* and *Armies of the Night.* I'm anxious to read 'The Prisoner of Sex.' Have you read it? Will I like it?"

(Yes and no.)

"Saul Bellow?"

"Up through *Herzog.*"

"Philip Roth?"

"None of it."

"Malamud?"

"Just the short stories. I think he's a better short-story writer than novelist. But then, many other critics think I'm a better essayist than novelist." Cheshire cat grin.

"Walker Percy?"

"I haven't read him."

"John Fowles?"

Blank stare. Ditto John Barth and Thomas Pynchon.

"Anthony Burgess?"

"Now there's a writer I really like, especially 'The Clockwork Orange.' No, I didn't know there's a movie coming from his book. There should be more people like him around."

"Nabokov?"

"Yes, but 'Ada' was a struggle to finish. I skipped pages, which I rarely do with a writer like Nabokov."

What other writers appeal to her? "Oh, I liked Frank Conroy's *Stop Time* and do you know a writer named Paul Bailey? You don't? You should. Read *After Jerusalem* and *Trespasses.* Alison Lurie is another writer I like—she has a nice *écriture.* And in France, Nathalie Sarraute and Monique Wittig."

As to future writing plans, "a few little things are biting at the edge of my mind," Miss McCarthy said, but there is a long-range plan, a book on "the Gothic," similar in structure to *The Stones of Florence* ("a book I did in good conscience"). "I have seen almost everything Gothic in France," she said, "and it might just turn out that there is some connection between the architecture and politics of that time with the spirit of 'relevance'—God, how I hate that word!—today. I've become so political that unless there is some thread of connection with what's happening today, I don't see any point in doing it."

Another writing project she is eager to undertake, this one for the *New Yorker,* is coverage of the Captain Medina trial, due to get underway in August at Fort MacPherson, Georgia. "This one you do because it has larger overtones."

Would she like to go to China? "Oh, I don't think so," she smiled. "It's not the place where a sensibility like mine can wander. Besides, I don't speak Chinese and they don't speak French."

Miss McCarthy gave *PW* a tour of her brother's apartment, and we admired the collection of contemporary art and the beautifully appointed kitchen. At the door she invited us to visit her in Paris and we went out into the polluted city with a feeling of pleasure after an hour in her company.

Is America a Terrible Letdown?

William F. Buckley, Jr./1971

Transcript of the *Firing Line* program taped at Lewron Studios,
New York City on 39 June 1971, and telecast on P.B.S. on 8
August 1971. Reprinted by permission of Southern Educational
Communications Association.

Mr. Buckley: Mary McCarthy has a new novel which she calls, *Birds
of America.* It is the chronicle of a 19-year-old college student who
discovers the ornithology of American life after a summer in Europe.
It has not been received with uniform enthusiasm, suggesting that
American courage is not dead, at least not in the critical community,
courage being what it takes to cross swords with Mary McCarthy,
who long ago established her reputation as a lethal duelist. She
graduated from Vassar after an unhappy childhood, concerning
which she wrote in her autobiography, *Memories of a Catholic
Girlhood.* Indeed, I might interrupt to record that it was not the
Catholicism of her background that she blames for the ugliness and
sadism of her foster parents. She began her career as essayist, critic,
and novelist immediately on graduating. She taught at Bard College,
served as an editor of *Partisan Review* and as its drama critic. Her
novels include: *The Company She Keeps, The Groves of Academe,
Charmed Life,* and *The Group,* and exclude *Little Woman* and
Rebecca of Sunnybrook Farm. Miss McCarthy used to call herself a
Libertarian Socialist, which shows her gift for oxymoron. It isn't clear
what she would call herself now, though it is clear from the two books
she wrote immediately before her latest novel, that she disapproves
everything about our role in the Vietnam War. Her tracts in question
are called Vietnam and Hanoi and were published in 1967 and 1968,
after trips to Indochina. It is a matter for discussion whether her
biases, as recorded in those books, affect her art and her novel and,
if so, whether they help or hurt. We are here to discuss the question,
"Is America a Letdown?" I should like to ask Miss McCarthy wherein
America especially let her down.

    Miss McCarthy: Oh. I didn't know this was the question we were
going to discuss.

Mr. Buckley: Are you prepared?

Miss McCarthy: Well, I dislike self-pity. So that I would never speak in terms of America let me down . . . let itself down.

Mr. Buckley: Well, then . . . let other people down.

Miss McCarthy: Yes, well, I think there's been a—it seems to me that there's been a great change in America, oh, starting sometime after the Second World War. That the quality of people in politics—of the general—what's called the quality of American life, deteriorated; that when you see, nowadays, some leftover of from, let's say, the Roosevelt Administration, it's, you know, it's like seeing some old Cathedral Pine standing there. And if you meet an American diplomat leftover from that time, he's very outspoken, he's very frank, he doesn't care what he says to whom, and you can hardly believe your ears. In the sort of current soft, pasty, American political scene. And, yet, those were the people—I was very proud of America when I was a young person. That doesn't mean I was uncritical of it. And I'm not proud of it anymore.

Mr. Buckley: Um-hmm. Well . . .

Miss McCarthy: I'm proud of a few of those Cathedral Pines, and I'm proud of a few people today on the public scene and maybe there'll be more.

Mr. Buckley: So you think, therefore, that the great qualitative changes took place during the last generation, which interests me because the principal criticisms of America as lodged in the thirties were that America was so committed to the riguors so capitalist doctrine that America didn't care about the people who were left out. And between the time that you admired America and, now, when you think so poorly of it, a whole series of laws were passed of a kind that tended to appease the critics of America during the thirties. Even so, even when we don't have the kind of hunger, unemployment, want, misery of the material kind we had then, you still think that America has gone downhill rather than up?

Miss McCarthy: Well, I know Harlem has gone downhill since the thirties. And, certainly, Upper West Side has gone downhill—it's the only part of New York I've seen much of since I've been here—has gone downhill in the most striking way in ten years.

Mr. Buckley: Well, but what happened in Harlem among other things surely was that people decided to go there.

Miss McCarthy: Yeah.

Mr. Buckley: They decided to go there because they preferred it over against where they were.

Miss McCarthy: Yeah. Also they were driven off. Driven out of the fields, really, by changes in agriculture. It became no longer economical.

Mr. Buckley: Well, as a matter of fact, the rise in productivity in the South exceeds a rise in productivity in the Northeast so, therefore, they came here for other reasons. Not dishonorable reasons but they didn't come out here in the Grapes of Wrath sense.

Miss McCarthy: No, no. I didn't say that.

Mr. Buckley: You said what?

Miss McCarthy: No. That is, if productivity has risen in the South, is that because of machines or because of the labor?

Mr. Buckley: Well, it's a combination . . .

Miss McCarthy: Yeah . . .

Mr. Buckley: . . . always.

Miss McCarthy: All right. So, you need less labor for the same amount of productivity.

Mr. Buckley: Yeah, but the reason for the migration into New York is because it is, of course, the land of opportunity and because of a fleeing discrimination and a lot of other things. But it wasn't, in point of fact, because economically they couldn't make out there. What I'm trying to say is that the America that you have grown to abominate is an America which took your advice.

Miss McCarthy: Don't say abominate.

Mr. Buckley: . . . took your advice.

Miss McCarthy: My advice . . .

Mr. Buckley: In the thirties.

Miss McCarthy: I was not a great activist in the thirties.

Mr. Buckley: Took the advice of people you loved.

Miss McCarthy: Leon Trotsky.

Mr. Buckley: It does sound platonic, doesn't it? As a matter of fact, Leon Trotsky seems almost like a conservative. Here's what I'm really wondering, Miss McCarthy, and a lot of people who read your books wonder whether America has actually become calous in a really important historical sense in the last thirty years or whether it was headed, necessarily, in the direction which you couldn't anticipate in the thirties, or whether, as I say, something suddenly happened that made it unlovable?

Miss McCarthy: Well, I think it's partly—excuse me—but I think capitalism has a lot to do with it. I mean I think that capitalism is the most successful deteriorator of society—of human life that's been known yet. And that—I've never been in Russia but I have been in Poland for a considerable time and a little bit in Hungary and Yugoslavia, and what strikes you about those countries, is, you know, how refreshing they are because they're so backward and reminds me very much—Poland when I first saw it—the streets, the city— reminded me very much of my childhood, of the way things were, then. This means that socialism is unable, though it's able in Russia to achieve pollution, too, but not on the scale that capitalism has been able to do it. I think any logical conservative, like you, Mr. Buckley, would have to be anti-capitalist. If you're not anti-capitalist, I don't believe you're a conservative.

Mr. Buckley: Hm-mmm. Well, anti-capitalist because—you were about to say, because—of pollution and stuff like that?

Miss McCarthy: Pollution, this thing that we're on . . . Television. Of . . .

Mr. Buckley: Well, now, you've got people like C.P. Snow, a socialist who says, in fact, he—you know, he likes to project; this is one of his things, but he says, in fact, that capitalism shows already the resources for defeating pollution in the way that the socialist societies haven't done. Capitalism is a sort of a problem solving technique. I'm not saying it's going to make people happy, even if pollution disappeared.

Miss McCarthy: I would like to believe that was so, but I don't see any signs of it, and it seems to me that there has . . .

Mr. Buckley: Well, for instance, they predicted, in 1976, the kind of pollution that comes in from automobiles, which is, for instance, 60 percent in New York City, would simply be a historical problem. It won't exist any more. Now will this be a triumph for capitalism or a triumph of what?

Miss McCarthy: I should think that could equally well achieved under capitalism or socialism.

Mr. Buckley: Well, it's achieved under socialism by not having any cause to begin with.

Miss McCarthy: Yeah, now they're beginning to get—now

they're beginning to have parking problems. They didn't have that when I was there—when I lived in Poland.

Mr. Buckley: Well, you can have parking problems when you have three cars and space for two of them.

Miss McCarthy: Yeah.

Mr. Buckley: But, it seems to me, if I may say that in your novel, you more or less take it for granted that the people of refined sensibilities sought to be anti-capitalist, and you more or less disdain, in the sense of making the argument as though it were a little bit sort of—

Miss McCarthy: Well, it's not that kind of a novel. I mean, it's a novel . . .

Mr. Buckley: Well, Peter's a very inquisitive guy. He likes to reason—this Peter is the . . .

Miss McCarthy: Hero.

Mr. Buckley: . . . nineteen-year-old hero, yeah. And he sort of likes to reason, and he likes to examine things—as a matter of fact one critic said, of course, the only good joke to be found in Miss McCarthy's book is that the author is so preposterously out of date about the objects of her concern.

Miss McCarthy: He didn't notice the book was laid in '64, '65, and he talks about 1971 to prove how out of date I am.

Mr. Buckley: That's right.

Miss McCarthy: Great observer.

Mr. Buckley: Yeah. But the point is that the kind of moon that is discussed after the summer in Rocky Port, Maine.

Miss McCarthy: It's not Maine, by the way.

Mr. Buckley: They said it was Maine. I thought we were supposed to conspire about where it wasn't. It probably was in New England, though.

Miss McCarthy: Well, the place names that are given are Providence, Brown University, Westerly, so it has to be somewhere around there.

Mr. Buckley: Around there, yeah.

Miss McCarthy: It can't be in Maine.

Mr. Buckley: But the point is that there you were lamenting, for instance, the in-roads of the supermarket—what it, in fact, did to the availability of . . .

Miss McCarthy: . . . slow movers.

Mr. Buckley: Yeah, sure. And the kind of jars where you did jelly and all that kind of stuff. And all of a sudden, four or five years later, you can't go around the street without running into antiquey shops that give you that kind of thing. Doesn't that suggest, really, that history anticipates your criticisms of it, in some cases.

Miss McCarthy: Well, I haven't been back to the scene of Rocky Port recently, but even in those days, in '64, there were plenty of those antiquey gourmet shops that—I believe this is Hilton Cramer you're quoting—and his whole point is that there's all this gourmet cooking—Julia Child french cooking, etc.—that existed back then. That is, it was mostly in the form of frozen croissants, just like in France, to take home and heat up. But the point is, that the natural food of America, which is what Peter and his mother happened to be concerned with wasn't being made anymore, and I don't think is being made anymore. That the whole French cooking business is part of the whole process I'm describing. You see what I mean?

Mr. Buckley: Yeah, yeah. I do see what you mean. Murray Kempton once said to me that American technology has almost succeeded in removing all of the taste out of bread.

Miss McCarthy: Yeah.

Mr. Buckley: And we get a peacetime use of nuclear energy, we will remove that last bit, and I understand that completely. But, I think, this probably ends us up understanding the difficulties that you have in reconciling yourself with capitalism which really is the difficulties that you have in reconciling yourself with people who express their preferences differently from your own. Ward Just—I think, one of his reviews says one hardly knows how one . . . he said that—which I thought was most interesting—that it was Lionel Van Deerlin of the *New York Times*—it is almost a parable—Mary McCarthy, preaching pure forms to committed political beings of whom she feels she is one, and there's the rub, whether anyone so adamant of pure forms as one who writes Miss McCarthy's fastidious and conclusive prose can, at the same time, be anything but contemptuous of the vulgarities implied in an egalitarian political vision. Some people go out and pay .25 cents for the kind of bread that you disdain. Now, does that mean that we oughtn't to have the kind of society in which they are free to buy the kind of bread they want to buy?

Miss McCarthy: The question is whether people are free to manufacture that kind of bread, and not whether the consumer is going to buy it. It's, of course, true; there is some sort of Gresham's Law. It seems to be in these departments, on the borders of aesthetics, though not in the center of aesthetics, that it does seem to be true that bad bread drives out good. And it seems—apparently, it's more profitable—it's easier, cheaper to make bad bread—I imagine that it's cheaper to make bad bread—certainly, to mass produce it—to mass produce bread than to make bread on a smaller scale at the local baker. It's even coming in in France, now. Since I've lived there, first came sliced bread. And as soon as I saw sliced bread, I knew. And now they have bread wrapped—either sliced or not sliced—wrapped up in some sort of plastic, or whatever, to keep. And once you get the very idea of bread keeping, your bread's going to be bad, and it's going to be cheaper to make, cheaper to process. There will be more profit, I think. In the end—the bad bread will cost as much or more.

Mr. Buckley: Why more profit—if it's competitive.

Miss McCarthy: Yeah, but this competition business doesn't seem to work very well.

Mr. Buckley: Well, it's very easy to examine the reports of these national bakeries. They make about 1/3 of 1 percent on a dollar. And the very fact that they advertise is because they are trying to get you to patronize their bread rather than the other man's.

Miss McCarthy: Which is exactly the same. That is, that all those breads are indistinguishable from each other.

Mr. Buckley: This may be what Mr. Just is talking about when he calls you a bad reporter because, probably, within about three blocks of where we're sitting, you can get 95 different kinds of bread. Now this isn't necessarily true if, you're stuck in Rocky Port, or wherever.

Miss McCarthy: It wasn't Ward Just who said that.

Mr. Buckley: It was somebody else?

Miss McCarthy: Yeah.

Mr. Buckley: Lionel Van Deerlin.

Miss McCarthy: Yeah.

Mr. Buckley: (Laughing) That's all right. Competition among critics. In other words, so many people really like to believe about America certain things which you are strangely acquiescent, given your critical nature, in encouraging them to believe, such as that you've got to get that ghastly bread in order to eat bread in America. You don't.

Miss McCarthy: No, you can make it at home.

Mr. Buckley: You can buy it. Do you want me to introduce you to where you can buy it? Non-bad bread?

Miss McCarthy: In New York, I think, you can buy it. There are a few places . . . In Stamford, Connecticut?

Mr. Buckley: You can buy it there; you can buy it in Stamford Connecticut. Pepperidge Farm . . .

Miss McCarthy: Oh, Pepperidge Farm bread is not bad. It's not bad, but I wouldn't call it good, either. It has gotten steadily worse over the years—at least so it seems to me. And the great problem in Maine is to get a loaf of unsliced Pepperidge bread. Every now and then you can. Unsliced means it does keep somewhat better, and it's the same dough, of course, but it isn't drying out in the wrapper.

Mr. Buckley: Yeah, but let's pay this tribute to American technology since we're using bread as a sort of synecdoche and that is that the existence of deep freeze makes it possible to get fresh frozen—or rather fresh made—bread, I mean, the kind that you make yourself and stick it in there and it will last for a couple of weeks.

Miss McCarthy: It is not the same.

Mr. Buckley: Nothing's the same. But the point is that it's very good. Now, you can make a case for ancient society in which you made your bread everyday and spent two or three hours of your day doing that. Americans have opted otherwise, and the question is— are we against the system that made it possible for them not to have to bake bread everyday?

Miss McCarthy: I think it's possible for a town baker to make bread, you know, on a daily basis. And there are plenty of countries where this is still going on, and if you say that so called fresh frozen bread—a very funny idea in itself—that fresh frozen bread is better than Tip Top, I'll agree with you . . .

Mr. Buckley: Yeah. Anything is.

Miss McCarthy: (Laughing) But, I refuse to be so damned relative about it. That fresh bread is better than fresh frozen bread.

Mr. Buckley: Yeah, of course. But the bread that was made at three o'clock in the afternoon is better than the bread that was made at four o'clock in the afternoon, which doesn't mean that we should organize our life so as to have made our bread just before we eat it.

Miss McCarthy: It's a bit undigestible if you eat it that quickly.

Mr. Buckley: But I'm interested to know, was it inevitable in capitalism that it should become so ugly in the estimate of people like yourself and, if so, why were we so late in discovering it?

Miss McCarthy: I don't know. I don't know whether it was inevitable in capitalism—I rather think so.

Mr. Buckley: Why?

Miss McCarthy: The whole notion of production for profit seems to me to beg any question of the value of the thing produced, which seems itself to be at least a dangerous situation—sort of a flashing red light situation. Maybe it didn't have to go that way, but it has gone that way with a sort of galloping rapidity. Don't you agree with some of these . . .?

Mr. Buckley: No, I don't.

Miss McCarthy: I'm not talking about capitalism. Don't you agree with my estimate of the results?

Mr. Buckley: No. I think that there's a great deal that is culturally an affront—and asthetically an affront. But I have always ascribed that to freedom, not capitalism. And I don't see how you can give up one without giving up the other. For instance, it seems to me that the moment you're committed to free speech, you have signed on to listen to an awful lot of crap, and to read an awful lot of very poor books, and listen to a lot of poor music. I know somebody who wrote me a couple of weeks ago and he said, quite frankly, that the only thing to do is to pass a law and this law ought to say that bad music can't be played over the air waves.

Miss McCarthy: And then you have to define what's bad music.

Mr. Buckley: Well, I wouldn't undertake to do so. And, then, he said, in two or three months, you find a sudden change in the national taste. Gresham's Law will, for the first time, have been—it's very attractive—extremely attractive. People are going to live 'til they're 70 years old and die without hearing the art the Fugue. Now, I think this is too bad. Now, does this, however, mean that my commitment to culturally high standards ought to require me to take the logical conclusion of being anti-freedom the way they are in the Soviet Union?

Miss McCarthy: You mean in terms of broadcasting?

Mr. Buckley: Well, no, in terms of anything. In terms of giving people, making people eat, listen to and read what you think is better than that which they would, otherwise, choose to do.

Miss McCarthy: But anybody who has a program makes that decision all along the line everyday. I mean, you decide—you exercise a form of censorship in whom you don't invite to be on this program with you. It goes on all the time.

Mr. Buckley: Yes, sure. No, I'm not denying I have sovereignity over how I spend my time and the time over which I dispose.

Miss McCarthy: No, but sovereignity over your listeners.

Mr. Buckley: I'm asking whether somebody should have sovereignty over the whole operation, which is the socialist alternative.

Miss McCarthy: That's why I'm called libertarian. That is, for something very decentralized as possible. For the decisions to be spread out, otherwise, it's completely utopian, and it's much more utopian now than when I said it, I think. But I still think this would be the ideal and it would be hard to work out and practice, especially with problems of how to distribute heavy industry in such circumstances, and the question of maintaining freedom. None of these questions are, you know, are breezes—I don't think so.

Mr. Buckley: No, I don't either. But it seems to me that at any particular point in history, one is on that side or the other side because to disdain association with either side, I think, is, probably, dishonorable. And you never have; so, I'm sure that this goes for you, too.

Miss McCarthy: I think it's all right for some people to do that. I think it is all right for a philosopher to do it.

Mr. Buckley: Yeah, but you're not . . .

Miss McCarthy: I'm not a philosopher.

Mr. Buckley: No, that's right. Now, you say that you wrote a couple of years ago that your hope is that there will be an evolution in communist life such as to grant extra freedom and more pluralism.

Miss McCarthy: And look what happened in Czechoslovakia after that.

Mr. Buckley: Sure. Now, in this morning's paper, Georgie Markov, who is the relevant commissar for what writers should write, or whatever . . .

Miss McCarthy: I saw that.

Mr. Buckley: He denounced all Soviet writers who are in official disfavor and said, quote: "no matter how great a talent any writer may possess it can be expressed with full clarity only in the atmosphere struggle for implementing the great social transformation that is waived by the Soviet people." This was a direct assault on Solzhenitsyn and a few other people who are in jail. And, yet, this, strangely, is the society concerning whose romantic aspirations you continue to identify with.

Miss McCarthy: No, I never identified with the Soviet Union, so let's not get into you know, an unreal argument. I agree with you. However, I will just add one thing about that quite dislikeable country—that, at least, Solzhenitsyn has not been liquidated, which would have been true in the Stalinist period. So, you could say there is minimal progress.

Mr. Buckley: Neither was Denisovich liquidated.

Miss McCarthy: No, but writers were. There's a long list of . . .

Mr. Buckley: What do you call what happened to Daniel and Sinyavsky?

Miss McCarthy: They're living. There's a whole lot of difference between being living and dead.

Mr. Buckley: A lot of people in Auschwitz lived quite for a long while until they were killed.

Miss McCarthy: Yes, but then they . . .

Mr. Buckley: We don't know whether Daniel will live tomorrow. If he does, its a heroic . . .

Miss McCarthy: But we don't know whether we're going to live til tomorrow. Now, I am not approving of the imprisonment of these people . . .

Mr. Buckley: There's no government organization that is going to sequester me or you in America and do to us what they did to Daniel and Sinyavsky. You don't want to profane their own experience by suggesting that the pressures on you are similar, do you?

Miss McCarthy: I said nothing of the kind. I mean—don't ascribe positions to me and then attack them.

Mr. Buckley: You say you never . . .

Miss McCarthy: I said there'd been a marginal improvement in that these people were still alive, that Krushchev is still alive; but the improvement is very, very marginal.

Mr. Buckley: I think it's moot. I think it's very possible that it would have been more humane to execute them than to subject them to whatever it is they have been subjected to.

Miss McCarthy: Well, they wouldn't agree with you.

Mr. Buckley: Well, nobody does, because that's how instinct asserts itself.

Miss McCarthy: Yes.

Mr. Buckley: But there are people who have committed suicide rather than face that, and even though millions of people went to Buchenwald and went to Auschwitz having some idea of what was in store for them they did it, in fact, commit suicide. It doesn't mean that it wouldn't have been more humane if they had been executed before being exposed to the rigors of Auschwitz, does it?

Miss McCarthy: Auschwitz, yes. Buchenwald, I think, had a great many survivors. It wasn't an extermination camp.

Mr. Buckley: Well, we liberated it. But, now, you say that you have never identified yourself with the Soviet Union, and I remember very clearly in 1952, for instance, your attacks on Simone de Beauvoir when she came over to this country and—in order to say the kind of things which, unhappily, you went to Hanoi twenty years later to say about. But you said a year or so ago, "Nor, frankly, do I think it admirable to try to stop communism even by peaceful subversion. The alternatives to communism offered by the Western countries are ugly in their own ways and getting uglier. What I would hope for, politically, where we went through that—they, the communists, have a better base, in my opinion, then we have to start from in dealing with such modern problems as automation.

Miss McCarthy: I think the smaller countries still do. That is, the satellite countries and such countries as North Vietnam. I still think that it's a possibility that they have a better base.

Mr. Buckley: Would East Germany be in the category of a satellite country?

Miss McCarthy: That wretched country—I don't know. And, yet, I don't feel the way about it that I feel about, say, Poland, Hungary, or Yugoslavia. I don't know anything about Rumania.

Mr. Buckley: I do. (Laughs) No, what I'm trying to say is that it's easy enough and it's right, in a sense, to be optimistic. But it seems to me that in the categorical commitment—the kind that you made, say, rather than us—that, then, is pretty categorical. You're saying, "I would rather be on the side of the communists, than on the side of the West."

Miss McCarthy: No I didn't say that I said what I said . . .

Mr. Buckley: You said—I do not think it is admirable to try to stop communism even by peaceful means, the alternatives as to communism—offered by the Western Countries are ugly in their own ways and getting uglier now you're suggesting are you not or are you?

Miss McCarthy: Yes. I think, still, I think—I don't know about East Germany and I don't know East Germany, either. I still think and, perhaps, I'm being too optimistic that such a prospect exists in Poland and that it exists in Yugoslavia. When I was in Poland, I knew a lot of people, the former—what they call former people—they don't call them that in Poland. But the former gentry and aristocracy who were, mostly, working as museum curators, or they were working as agrenomes, running farms. Some of them have collected farms—there are very few. Or they were working in the movies, and so on. And I saw quite a few such people. In Russia, they wouldn't exist; they would have been, I suppose, liquidated. And their view at a given point in the conversation—they were anti-regime, very anti-Russian, very anti-East German, also—at a given point in the conversation they would always say, "But we could never go back to the way it was before. This is better."

Mr. Buckley: They could hardly remember how it was before.

Miss McCarthy: No, these were people of a certain age. After all, communism is not that old—it's post-war, in Poland.

Mr. Buckley: It's been a long time since Poland had much control over it's own destiny.

Miss McCarthy: Well, Pilsudaki was functioning up to the war.

Mr. Buckley: Sort of. Sort of.

Miss McCarthy: Not that he was an admirable figure. But these people were as well equipped to remember what Poland was like before as we would be to remember what life was like under Truman.

Mr. Buckley: Well, the answer is that this is, of course, extrememly interesting, and it doesn't tell us very much about what would happen in Poland if there were a plebiscite because there hasn't been a plebiscite. And we know that such an evolutionary movement as you encourage took place once in Hungary; ten years later in Czechoslovakia—the juggernaut came and put an end to it.

Miss McCarthy: Yes.

Mr. Buckley: Now, even so, your public identification at this moment of American history is with that tanks rather than with the freedom fighters, and this seems to me, extraordinary.

Miss McCarthy: No, I am not identifying with the tanks. I am against American penetration into those countries.

Mr. Buckley: You don't think, even by peaceful subversion, we should try to stop communism.

Miss McCarthy: Yes. By U. S. peaceful subversion, by air drops of American wrist watches or alarm clocks or whatever. I am against that, and I think the people in those countries, on the whole, would not really welcome this on our part. I feel about the United States that the United States, at the present time, is like a sick person who should be in isolation until he recovers, I'm not worried about isolationism. I think it would be the best thing that could happen to this country.

Mr. Buckley: Well, are you in a position to cite, for instance, people who have fled from those countries who agree with you.

Miss McCarthy: Yeah.

Mr. Buckley: Who?

Miss McCarthy: Well, it's sort of difficult to cite by name.

Mr. Buckley: What about all the ones who'd know?

Miss McCarthy: Uh-who? I'm sorry. I'm mixed up.

Mr. Buckley: (Laughing) You mean whom most recently? I don't know of any defector from Poland or Czechoslovakia or Russia or China or any of the people who crossed into Hong Kong or who have died trying to cross the Berlin Wall, who said to the United States, for heaven sakes, let up. Don't try to stop . . .

Miss McCarthy: Oh, well, that's the attitude of a lot of Poles in Paris—not all of them, but a great many of the Polish refugees in Paris, is an attitude of somebody like it was—I haven't seen him recently—of somebody like Czeslaw Milosz whom you probably know.

Mr. Buckley: Oh sure, I read his book. But, his book is one in which he says there is nothing, in fact, we can do about it in a nuclear age. They've got the noose around our neck and there's nothing we can do about it. But there isn't anything at all in Milosz, that I saw that would suggest that there are any points that he has in common with you.

Miss McCarthy: Well, I'm talking about his conversation—not about the captive mind, which was a long time ago.

Mr. Buckley: Yes, but nothing much has changed since then, has it. They just finished quelling one attempted self-assertion in Poland a few months ago.

Miss McCarthy: I can't tell about what's-his-name—what's Gromyko's successor's name—I'm blanking out on his name— Gierek—there's some thought that there is a slight improvement. But whether this is something real for the people, one doesn't know yet. Milosz was absolutely miserable in the early years of his defection in France, and I remember having coffee with him and his trying to make me explain to him—he said, "You people, what do you live for? What do you live for?" And if you say, "Well, I live to do my work and see my friends and so on," this seemed to him a completely unsatisfactory goal in life. And this is true of many people who have left those countries. Others become absolutely fanatical, some of those young Polish defectors were way to the right, not only of you but of Agnew or whoever. And, in fact, I told some Polish official who came to see me one criticism I have of your regime is it's ability to produce reactionaries. And it's true that they can produce the most rabid reactionaries. Especially among some of the young people who have defected.

Mr. Buckley: Well, undoubtedly any regime that clamps down on human freedom produces people who, however mistakenly, feel that human freedom can be augmented by going in wholly the other direction. This happened in Germany, and this happened in Italy, and, I think, it's—it's probably natural. But, in fact, haven't we had a sufficient experience with what it is that we're up against to render, at least, irresponsible, at most, quite literally shocking, the notion that America and the West ought to cease to represent some kind of an alternative to the kind of misery that, for instance, Soviet writers are subjected to?

Miss McCarthy: We should offer an alternative. That is, we should exemplify an alternative.

Mr. Buckley: Well, for instance, on the matter of writing. You're not suggesting, are you, that you have any difficulty in publishing your books?

Miss McCarthy: No, but I do have difficulty in getting them reviewed, not *Birds of America*. But, I think, and maybe I'm . . .

Mr. Buckley: Because of what?

Miss McCarthy: Well, this is very mysterious. My book on Vietnam got, perhaps, ten reviews in the entire United States, and my publisher was absolutely thunderstruck. It was easier to say where it wasn't reviewed than where it was. Never reviewed in the *New York Times* Book Review, etc. My publisher said he had never seen a case of a book on a controversial subject by a well-known author—this was after the success of *The Group*—that received, virtually, no notice. So, he said, they're going to make it up to us on *Hanoi*. I even wrote to the Editor of the *New York Times* Book Review, saying, "What's happening? Why don't you review this book?" His answer was, "Patience." I'm still waiting. That was in 1967. So, anyway, my publisher said . . .

Mr. Buckley: And you think this is because . . .

Miss McCarthy: I cannot explain it. My publisher said, "All right, they're going to make it up to us on *Hanoi*, I think *Hanoi* got three reviews in the entire United States. Maybe I'm slightly underestimating—there might have been four or something like that—it's was a fantastic thing. Now, it can't be that Washington did it, because the *New York Times* opposed our Vietnam policies. So, it couldn't be that Washington did it. Among the places that these books didn't get reviewed were the *New Republic, Nation,* and the only people—

Mr. Buckley: How would you account for that?

Miss McCarthy: I can't. It is a mystery. And, to the point that people writing in for biographical information for these compilations of writers and this and that, would always stop my books with *The Group* and I'd write back and say these titles exist. They are quite unaware of it. The very fact these books existed was not known. It is a mystery. And, of course, it's nice to be able to get your books published, anyway, but it's a strange business.

Mr. Buckley: I think, though, you have said four or five times, that you don't know. You, nevertheless, obviously intended to leave the impression . . .

Miss McCarthy: No, I didn't.

Mr. Buckley: . . . that it's because your book was so much opposed to American policy.

Miss McCarthy: No. I didn't.

Mr. Buckley: Well, then, how is it relevant in any way to a conversation that began by asking whether or not you were satisfied with the freedom to publish in America?

Miss McCarthy: Well, I think that freedom to publish is not just a thing by itself; there ought to be some possibility of the fact publications becoming known.

Mr. Buckley: Um-hmm.

Miss McCarthy: Wouldn't you think so?

Mr. Buckley: Well, I certainly do. I certainly do. But I think that— well, Ward Just, in *The Washington Post*, reviewing one of these books, said "One hardly knows how to deal with this book, so transparent are the biases, so evident the intention to color Hanoi white and Washington black."

Miss McCarthy: Hm-mmm. He's sort of a square.

Mr. Buckley: Yeah. I thought you'd have something appropriate to say about it. But could it be that some editors, reviewing this book, thought it so blind and so undiscriminately . . .

Miss McCarthy: Why didn't they attack me?

Mr. Buckley: Well, why didn't they review Robert Welch's book on Eisenhower?

Miss McCarthy: Didn't they?

Mr. Buckley: No.

Miss McCarthy: Not at all?

Mr. Buckley: Not at all.

Miss McCarthy: Well, there's another mystery. Can you explain that?

Mr. Buckley: (Laughing) Yes.

Miss McCarthy: (Laughing) All right, explain it.

Mr. Buckley: Well, they thought it was preposterous. They thought it was preposterous.

Miss McCarthy: No, the few reviews I got were from people like *The New Leader*—that is, old, cold, warriors—who still thought it worthwhile, you know, attacking me and saying all that type of thing—not that Ward Just is an old, cold warrior—he's not. But those people still thought it was worthwhile. I don't know. And I don't think those books are bad.

Mr. Buckley: Well, I think all of your books should be reviewed, ex-officio, myself, simply because it's interesting enough if you write a bad book.

Miss McCarthy: You mean that's news?

Mr. Buckley: But the point we were trying to make is that here, in your general condemnation of America, by contrast with your general romanticism about the other side, we're trying to enumerate what are the existing differences. We have agreed that you can publish. Now, can you speak freely here?

Miss McCarthy: Right. Yes. I have never had any inhibition on my ability to speak freely. And I'm not one of those who thinks it's because nobody will pay any attention to you. It's the same as living in the Soviet Union and not being able to speak. It's not so. On the other hand, there is some way in which our country has turned into sort of a bad circus, of which this little program is part, and that everything turns into entertainment. It's been true of . . .

Mr. Buckley: You never disdained entertainment, did you?

Miss McCarthy: No, but—so that the bite goes out of everything. I can remember thinking this back as early as the Army-McCarthy hearings—that they were taken by the public as a—as a show.

Mr. Buckley: Well, they were.

Miss McCarthy: Well, they were.

Mr. Buckley: True. True.

Miss McCarthy: But they were more than that, too.

Mr. Buckley: They took it as that, also.

Miss McCarthy: Yeah.

Mr. Buckley: You said in what, I hope, were words that you would like to take the occasion to withdraw—you said, a year or so ago, "If, as a result of my ill-considered actions, world communism comes to power, never mind. Some sort of life will continue as Pasternak, Solzhenitsyn, Sinyavsky and Daniel have discovered. And I would rather be on their letterhead than that of the American Committee for Cultural Freedom."

Miss McCarthy: Well, I certainly would be much more honored to be on a letterhead with Solzhenitsyn than with Sidney Hook—my God. . . .

Mr. Buckley: It isn't clear what it is to be on their letterhead since, of course, they don't have a letterhead—they're not allowed to have a letterhead.

Miss McCarthy: Well, there is a human rights group you know . . .

Mr. Buckley: . . . there are only letterheads to try to save them, and you're welcome on all those letterheads, I'm sure. But then, what really astonishes me is the same sentence in which you mention Solzhenitsyn, Sinyavsky and Daniel as living in an almost ideal state.

Miss McCarthy: I didn't say that. I don't think they were living—I was—there is no thought in my mind that those people are living in an ideal state, either then or now. And my remark about if my efforts to lead to the triumph of world communism is a joke at my own expense. As is the idea that anything I would do would lead to any cataclysmic . . .

Mr. Buckley: You mean you were just entertaining?

Miss McCarthy: That was a joke, but you can put jokes in with serious . . .

Mr. Buckley: Yeah, sure, but here when you're discussing the American Committee for Cultural Freedom, you chose to break its back over the fact they once engaged in the question of Joe McCarthy—whether he should be routinely denounced or non-routinely denounced.

Miss McCarthy: No, it wasn't that. It was whether he should be denounced at all. I remember that very well.

Mr. Buckley: Yeah.

Miss McCarthy: I remember that very well. And I remember at that very Waldorf Conference, Sidney Hook, of the American Committee for Cultural Freedom saying, "Well, let's wait to make up our minds about McCarthy when all the facts are in." They were in.

Mr. Buckley: Are you opposed to that?

Miss McCarthy: They were in.

Mr. Buckley: Oh, were they?

Miss McCarthy: Yes.

Mr. Buckley: But, now you say . . .

Miss McCarthy: Nothing new was added after that.

Mr. Buckley: Okay. Well, that's interesting. A lot of people disagree with you, including historians. But it is odd that at the same time that you were, in effect, saying Joe McCarthy has done worse to America than the people have done to Russia, who have persecuted Solzhenitsyn . . .

Miss McCarthy: I didn't say that.

Mr. Buckley: Well, you said you'd rather be on that committee than on the Cultural Freedom Committee.

Miss McCarthy: I would. I consider it a more distinguished group. This is a silly argument.

Mr. Buckley: Yeah. Because the Committee for Cultural Freedom, after all, had everybody on it.

Miss McCarthy: Not me.

Mr. Buckley: If you don't like Sidney Hook you can say it didn't have Sidney Hook. But it had everybody else. It had Dwight Macdonald—all your friends—Danny Bell—everybody—you dislike all those people?

Miss McCarthy: I don't dislike Dwight Macdonald. I love Dwight Macdonald.

Mr. Buckley: Okay. He's on it. Now, at precisely the moment when you chose Joe McCarthy as sort of the metaphor of everything that's gone wrong with America—something that Toynbee once said . . .

Miss McCarthy: No. What has gone wrong with the American Committee for Cultural Freedom.

Mr. Buckley: Yeah. Yeah. You're writing a book—a novel *The Groves of Academe*—in which the protagonist discovers that the only way he can protect himself in this college is by pretending that he's been a communist, because by being anti-McCarthy, in effect, he absolutely guarantees that he can survive the whole thing.

Miss McCarthy: Yes.

Mr. Buckley: So, simultaneously, you are acknowledging that culture never paid any attention to McCarthy except to disdain him, and to pooh-pooh him, and yet you use him as a symbol of persecution in America.

Miss McCarthy: No. No. My point in *The Groves of Academe* is that there were certain colleges—certain small progressive colleges—of the type of Sarah Lawrence—of Bennington, perhaps; I'm not sure. In any case, where the one way of guaranteeing your job was to say you were being fired for being a communist. But that would not have been true, let's say, at the University of Missouri—to pick it out of a hat—I have nothing against the University of Missouri. But this was a special circumstance, creating irony.

Mr. Buckley: Hm-mmm.

Miss McCarthy: Any political climate generates ironies around its opposite.

Mr. Buckley: Yeah, but the point is, that in America, precisely, to have been an anti-McCarthyite made it much, much safer for you in academic circles and even in government circles.

Miss McCarthy: It depended. Not—I think—I know it didn't— there were lots of cases up before the AAUP, Association of University Professors, of people who were fired for being—or being suspected, in any case, of being communist. I, personally, at that time, Bill, thought that there was a lot of hypocritical breast-beating going on among people who talked about the loss of their cultural freedom. They had not lost it. It's fine to fight for somebody's who's lost it but pretend you've lost it when you are vociferating is disgusting I think.

Mr. Buckley: Hm-mmm. So you acknowledge our democracy?

Miss McCarthy: Not mine. I never did that. And I always took— in fact, I gave a broadcast on the BBC in which I made this point.

Mr. Buckley: Yeah. And Richard Rovere did the same thing. He said, "I find attacking McCarthy as dangerous as drinking my early morning cup of coffee."

Miss McCarthy: In certain circles—yes. In our circles.

Mr. Buckley: Yeah. So, therefore, you never considered Mc-Carthy was that kind of a menace?

Miss McCarthy: Not to me. I think he was a tremendous menace to our State Department. I think our State Department will never recover from the Senator McCarthy period. But people of fairly high ability, independence, stayed out of the State Department because they were expected to get more of this kind of scrutiny. I think you can date the deterioration of the State Department to that time.

Mr. Buckley: Yeah. It tends to be more popular in the telling— this particular myth—than in history. I remember Evelyn Waugh was anti-McCarthy, begging some American scholar please to reveal the names of the people who had been driven out of the State Department by McCarthy—a challenge that was never, for some reason, accepted. Maybe for the obvious reason.

Miss McCarthy: I don't think, Mr. Buckley, there were some
driven out that were public cases and so on. But I'm not talking
about that and for some obviously good reason—I don't know—I
forget. But what I'm talking about is people not wanting to qualify for
the State Department. Gifted people are not wanting to go into that
work. And there, I think was where the damage was—not the firing
of people, but the lack of applicants.

Mr. Buckley: Of course, you have to admit that the responsible
people can hold that communists ought not to apply to the State
Department.

Miss McCarthy: I think it's idiotic for—yes, of course, I agree.
But I've always held that communists should have the right to teach.

Mr. Buckley: Yeah. And that's an interesting point of view.

Miss McCarthy: It seems to me it's a libertarian point of view.

Mr. Buckley: Yeah. It's a very difficult point of view which,
probably, we don't have time to get into, but it's a point of view that
the President of Harvard, the President of Princeton, the President of
Columbia and Yale disagreed on, in 1951.

PANEL PARTICIPATION

Mr. Buckley: Mr. Leiberman.

Mr. Leiberman: My question refers back to the discussion on
capitalism, and—when cars are manufactured in this country . . .

Mr. Buckley: When who?

Mr. Leiberman: When cars are manufactured—this was probably
before the advent of the assembly line—people made the cars by
hand; and if they didn't get much money, what they got was
satisfaction out of the job. And, now, people are making cars by
screwing in that little bolt and getting money returned for satisfaction.
And, so, aren't these people who are really the majority, the workers
of this country—aren't these people the victims of capitalism rather
than the people who are benefiting by it.

Mr. Buckley: Well, the event you referred to took place in the
early part of the nineteenth century, when Eli Whitney discovered the
replaceable parts. People haven't made cars individually except as an
application. You can still make a boat. I know somebody who made
a boat; he worked on it eight years. Now, he's a very lovable eccentric, but if you had to pay for that boat, as a result, he's not availing

himself of other things. —you'd have to be a millionaire in order to buy it. Now, I don't deny—I'd be the first to concede that any time you have mass production you have a sacrifice in the sort of artistic input involved. What you get at the other end is leisure, which you can use to cultivate whatever it is that you want to cultivate.

Miss McCarthy: That's the problem. You know, what is given to people to cultivate, in the way of leisure?

Mr. Buckley: Your books for one thing.

Miss McCarthy: Oh—

Mr. Buckley: My magazines.

(They both laugh and audience laughs)

Miss McCarthy: That doesn't take up their full time.

Mr. Buckley: Well, it's a good start. If what you say, then, is okay—having made it possible because the guy doing the screw, therefore, makes cars available at $2100 instead of $21,000, which is what they would cost if you hand made them—then, having, all of a sudden, finding himself with 55 leisure hours per week—he doesn't know how to spend them. You are making another criticism than one of capitalism. You're talking about a whole other set of dislocations, right?

Miss McCarthy: I think so. It would be the same under Socialism.

Miss Ippolito: I would like to direct my question to you, Miss McCarthy.

Miss McCarthy: Yes.

Miss Ippolito: You were condemning capitalism before. My question is you really cannot—well, actually, it's a statement— capitalism must be before socialism. I do not see how a country that is to be socialized can exist without first being put into a capitalistic form.

Miss McCarthy: Well, that Marx's thesis.

Miss Ippolito: Hm-mmm.

Miss McCarthy: And Lenin tried to jump that stage. That is— thought that you could proceed directly from a more or less pre-industrial society—there was some mercantile capitalism, even in the beginnings of industrialism in Russia, but, basically, that you could make this jump. And the Chinese, also, are following a Leninist line and making this jump. There's a great deal of thinking, or theorizing, anyway, going on—people trying to go back to Marx. And putting that Marx was right in his analysis that this stage has to be gone through first. I don't know. I'm not an economist. It may be so. But the theory is in any case, that in non-industrialized countries like China, that the only way the working class can be mobilized for modernization is through an authoritarian state. That is even Walt Rostow's argument, if I recall right. And it's true that in those countries they don't have any strikes; the working class can be mobilized for rapid modernization since there are no strikes. And living in a country like France where there is a strike every two minutes, you never know—it often runs the calendar strikes for the weeks. You brace yourself by what you can do and what you can not do that week. Living in a country like that, there are moments you think, "Oh, you know—I'm joking—(She laughs with audience) live in one of those countries where the worker's can't strike because it's their state, supposedly.

Miss Ippolito: However, though, these countries have had a great deal of difficulty in keeping their workers interested, because their workers are lacking in a great deal of goods. They are not getting the benefits of this mass mobilization.

Miss McCarthy: North Vietnam is a very special case, and the only communist country, I idealized, was North Vietnam. And it's true that they were getting the labor out of the working class and that there was tremendous release of national energy, but they were under attack by a much stronger power with a long history of patriotism—of national patriotism. And I still wonder what North Vietnam would be like now if we hadn't attacked them. That is, it might of fallen into some miserable stagnation. We don't know. And whether they will be able to use this energy that we dowered them with, in a sense—or partly dowered them with—I would not give us all the credit. How they will be able to use this in peacetime is a very interesting question. But whatever they achieve, assuming that they will be able to extend freedom, they did have to decentralize on account of the bombing, which, in itself, was a relative form of freedom of . . .

Mr. Buckley: Well, so did Russia, under Stalin, in the last part of the Second World War.

Miss McCarthy: Not, I think, to the same extent, but I'm not sure. But, in any case, even if something very good on a peacetime basis continues and develops there, it still can't be a model for us, this small country in southeast Asia alas can't be a model for us and I think that the idealism of China—the idealization, rather, of China—on the part of youth is based on the fact that (a) we don't know much about it, so that nobody can idealize the Soviet Union anymore. We know too much about it. Partly that, and partly that there is absolutely no sense of judgment. Young Maoists haven't the faintest conception of how these principles would work in an advanced country like the United States.

Mr. Buckley: Mr. Kiviat.

Mr. Kiviat: Miss McCarthy, you were recently quoted as saying, "The worst thing that could happen in America would be to win the war in Vietnam."

Miss McCarthy: Yes.

Mr. Kiviat: In your book, Vietnam, you repeatedly pointed out the horrors of war such as the napalm, the American beer cans thrown in the temples. Don't you think it's intellectually dishonest to base an opinion on foreign policy on the asthetic values alone or even primarily on them, without going into the politics of the situation?

Miss McCarthy: Is napalm a question of asthetics.

Mr. Kiviat: I think it is, because I think you're denying—you're taking the superficial question, which is the horror of all war, and you're attacking—you're supporting one side and attacking the other on the principle that the war itself is bad without going into the politics of it.

Miss McCarthy: That war itself or *the* war?

Mr. Kiviat: Well, you're bringing out the reactions of war—the actions of it, such as napalm and what's happening to the country-side. It still can be terrible and it still can be bad but one side can still be right and the other wrong, and such, the war itself might be right. And I'm not defending the war, but don't think, perhaps, you were intellectually dishonest when you . . .

Miss McCarthy: (Laughing) No, I don't. No, thanks, I don't.

Mr. Buckley: (Laughing) You want to elaborate on that, Miss McCarthy?

(Laughter from audience)

Miss McCarthy: The point that you are trying to make is really not clear to me. I mean, the idea that you think a napalmed child is so repellent on an aesthetic basis but okay, otherwise.

Mr. Kiviat: It's repellent on any basis, but it still doesn't touch the question of which side is right.

Miss McCarthy: South Vietnam, of course, is so much more wrecked by our bombers than North Vietnam. I don't know how long it will take them to recover. Also, simply from our presence, aside from our bombing, in the South. This wreckage, I think, the aesthetics there is ethics, too. And it's not my personal aesthetics; it's what those people there have to live with in comparison to how it was before and there were a few isolated places like Hue—this was before TET—where you could see what it had been before, and where American troops were not allowed as a punishment to the natives. And, there, you have some sense of what it was before, and you have some sense in North Vietnam of what it was like before. I think that the aesthetic here is the ethical, and as far as my remark about the worse thing that could happen to our country would be to win this war, that doesn't really enter into this thing. My point is that it would be bad for us to win, and that this victory would only encourage us in further adventures of this sort—that there would be no break on it. I think this country—I do think this country—maybe it's sentimental to hope that it could go through some examination of conscience.

Mr. Buckley: Thank you, Miss McCarthy. Thank you, ladies and gentlemen and members of the panel.

Mary McCarthy Returns
Bob Lundegaard/1973

From *Minneapolis Tribune* 29 April 1973, Section B, 1, 2. Reprinted by permission.

"Whenever we children came to stay at my grandmother's house, we were put to sleep in the sewing room, a bleak, shabby, utilitarian rectangle, more office than bedroom, more attic than office, that played to the hierarchy of chambers the role of a poor relation . . .

"Those weeks in my grandmother's house come back to me very obscurely, surrounded by blackness, like a mourning card: The dark well of the staircase, where I seem to have been endlessly loitering, waiting to see Mama when she would come home from the hospital, and then simply loitering with no purpose whatever . . ."

[From *Memories of a Catholic Girlhood*]

Novelist and critic Mary McCarthy returned last week to the scenes of her childhood in Minneapolis for the first time in almost 40 years.

The yellow house at 2427 Blaisdell Av. S., where she and her three orphaned brothers lived from 1918 to 1923, has been torn down for an apartment building. And Blaisdell Av. itself, a lazy thoroughfare in World War I days, is a busy one-way street. But "the best house on the block" is still standing. That belonged to Mr. Harrison, "who had a housekeeper with a daughter my age named Antoinette. He taught me to swim, and he had a bathing suit that came up to his chin and a long white beard."

Across the street was "the man who had the Hupmobile agency" and in the next block was the home of her grandparents, which is also standing. But the clapboard is covered by masonite shingles, and the huge garage where her grandfather kept his Pierce-Arrow and Locomobile is now a private home. She remembers that the garage had a turntable, pushed by hand, that rotated the cars so that they didn't have to be backed out. But the house of her grandfather, grain merchant J. H. McCarthy, surprised her. "It looks so shabby!" she

153

exclaimed. "I remember it as being grander. That's what memory does to one."

Memory also fooled her about the hill she went sliding down in Fair Oaks Park ("I thought it was much steeper") and the construction of St. Stephen's Catholic School at 2123 Clinton S., which she attended. She was sure it was made of wood; it is a brick building. "I'm disturbed by that," she said, frowning slightly as she entered St. Stephen's Church across the street. The church was empty. "The confessionals are gone," she whispered. "Where do people go to confess?" Then she walked farther and saw it. She was looking for the confessional in which she hid when she ran away from home. "And in the morning," she pointed upward, "I took refuge in the balcony." Another time, she recalled, "I ran away to the art museum and hid behind the statue of Laocoon. That's probably not there any more."

There wasn't time to verify her suspicion about the statue. The neighborhood tour was a brief stop on her way out of town to catch a plane for Seattle. She was in Minneapolis for a day to deliver the Joseph Warren Beach memorial lecture at the University of Minnesota. It was her first visit here since 1934, the year after she graduated from Vassar. She later recreated the Vassar and post-Vassar times in her most famous novel, *The Group.*

Miss McCarthy, 60, said she hadn't returned before this because no one had asked her to. Besides, although she didn't say so, the city must hold painful memories for her, judging by her account of the Minneapolis years in a 1957 book, *Memories of a Catholic Girlhood."*

At 6 she was oldest of the four children arriving with their parents from Seattle in 1919. A flu epidemic struck down both parents within days of their arrival, and the children were farmed out to relatives who—at least through Miss McCarthy's prism—seemed straight out of a novel by Dickens. The children were fed a steady diet of parsnips, rutabagas and kale, were locked outside for hours without toys in below-zero weather. Their mouths were taped shut at night. They were also forbidden to have friends, read books outside of school and eat candy. Miss McCarthy was even beaten for winning a statewide essay contest to keep her from getting "stuck up." Small wonder she ran away.

When they were eventually rescued by their West Coast grandfather, Miss McCarthy returned to Seattle, attended a convent school
and Vassar, and headed for New York with her first husband, an
actor. She described some of those New York days Thursday to a
seminar of English majors at the university. "I was terrified" looking
for a job, she recalled. "One man wanted me to ghostwrite a book
about sunspots."

She tried to review books, "Edmund Wilson (later her second
husband) was an absolute pushover for young, pretty book
reviewers. Katherine Ann Porter walked away with a stack two feet
high, which she never reviewed and never returned. "But Malcolm
Cowley looked at me through his bushy brows and growled, 'Young
lady, I only give books to people who are geniuses or starving.' I said,
'Well, I'm not starving.' "

She was, however, a genius. In no time she was reviewing for *The
Nation* and *New Republic,* then the prestigious (but poor-paying)
Partisan Review, taking on the literary establishment from Brooks
Atkinson, drama critic of the *New York Times,* to Orson Welles and
Clifford Odets.

She established a quick reputation as a literary scold, with impossible standards and a scathing wit.

But in conversations at the university Thursday and in an interview
Friday, she was invariably congenial, flashing a crinkly smile and
showing an interest in the other person's viewpoint. In fact, she
complained to her lecture audience, "My problem is that I fail to
communicate because I write clearly. What I intend as a compliment
is taken as an insult."

She agrees with the economic aims of Women's Liberation, but not
that "Women can be equated with an oppressed minority like blacks,
or that the release of this oppressed minority will save the world."
She gnashes her teeth at being praised, as a biographer did, for
having "a mind like a man," but she doesn't seem bothered by
interviewers who describe her hair or figure, although they wouldn't
do the same for Hemingway or Faulkner. "But it's true," she says. "I
am more interested in my hair than most men are."

She caused a stir at the seminar by insisting that women's writing is
different from men's, and that a "blindfold test" of authors would
disclose the difference: "Women's writing is more polarized. Women

are either from the Sense or the Sensibility school of writing, if you take Jane Austen as Sense and say, Charlotte Bronte, Virginia Woolf, Katherine Mansfield—all those—as Sensibility. "You don't have that much polarization in male authors."

But, someone wondered, what about "Pride and Prejudice"? Couldn't that as easily have been written by a man? "I don't think so," she said. "I don't think the whole excitement about the marriage could have been written by a man. Her preoccupations were feminine preoccupations."

Miss McCarthy apologized for staying out of a discussion about brutality in the modern film. "I'm lost," she said. "I see movies so seldom. I did see *Last Tango in Paris,* but I didn't like it. I couldn't stand Marlon Brando."

Asked what writers had influenced her, she said, "I've never been able to find anybody. When I first started writing, I'd been reading a lot of Henry James, and his prose style is very catching. But it lasted for just one story."

What about influences she had rebelled against? "That's more like it, but the only one I can think of offhand is that I loathed 'Of Human Bondage.'"

What audience is she writing for? "A very tough question. I'm writing for somebody. Not myself. Not a friend. Not a wide audience. One writer called his audience 'my 21 readers,' and he had about the right number."

Besides Minneapolis, her stops on this trip include Seattle (to visit an ailing relative); Carmel, Calif. (to visit friends), Berkeley (for another lecture); Syracuse (for an honorary degree); and New York (to see her dentist). Plus side trips at beginning and end to Aberdeen, Scotland, to lend moral support to an old friend, Hannah Arendt, who is lecturing there. Then back to Paris, where she has lived since 1961 with her fourth husband, James West, a government official.

Although she is vehemently anti-Nixon, and has written three books opposing the war in Vietnam, she is not all that enamoured of Paris and its government either. For one thing, her neighborhood in Montparnasse is being threatened by a "hideous skyscraper"—a building with 13,000 office workers and a 3,000-car garage. "I find the Pompidou government very, very depressing. I don't think it's as bad as the Nixon administration, but I have a French friend who isn't so sure. He says that at least Nixon doesn't pretend to be cultured."

Mary McCarthy: Portrait of a Lady

Joan Dupont/1978

From *The Paris Metro,* (February 1978), 15, 16, 78. Copyright ©
1978 by *Paris Metro.*

In the movie *Julia,* Jane Fonda as Lillian Hellman plays on the
typewriter as though it were a honky-tonk piano, a cigarette clenched
in her pretty teeth. At one point, in a fit of pique against the
machine—*The Children's Hour* is lagging—she throws it out the
window into the snow. Now, that's the kind of spirit the public likes to
see women writers display: mannish, manic. But I saw Mary
McCarthy standing on the Place de la Concorde at high noon, a
Sulka shopping bag clutched to her side, her face powdered pale,
dressed in pearl-grey like a widow, hair and handsome chin set. She
stepped cautiously, feet splayed in sober pumps, as if she might fall
unless she took it very easy. And this is the caustic beauty who wrote
The Company She Keeps, a collection of savage vignettes, the Vassar
graduate, author of that catty best-seller *The Group.* Has age
chastened her?

Mary McCarthy is not that old—65—but she is that honest. While
furious at descriptions of herself as "the grand old lady of American
letters," she knows she is no longer the radical rebelling against her
Catholic girlhood, the Greenwich Village bohemian married to
Edmund Wilson, in and out of Trotskyism, on to fresh passions, other
marriages, and many men.

Today she is married to James West, a U.S. diplomat, and she lives
in Paris because "Jim's job is here." She is clearly content in this
latest incarnation and dresses for the part. Invited to Versailles to
meet Jimmy Carter, she introduces herself and receives a big kiss. "I
wanted to congratulate him on his stand on human rights," she says,
sounding like some lady from the garden club.

The French know her mostly as the author of *The Group* and *Birds
of America,* from which she recently gave a reading at Beaubourg. In
the American community, she is a legend, but unknown, unseen
except within her small circle of friends. Or perhaps merely

unrecognized? "I wouldn't know her if I passed her on the street,"
says one young writer. And I didn't either, until she was pointed out
to me.

Close up, in her rue de Rennes apartment, she looks much better.
She still—or again—wears her hair bobbed as in Vassar days, with a
side part. The forehead wave falls soft, caught back by a discreet
barrette. She almost overdoes dressing down, and black seems to be
a mode with her, not a mourning. It appears that she often wears
these somber tones: black, grey, or navy. Today she is done up in
demi-deuil, as the famous recipe has it, like a white-breasted truffled
chicken. The blouse is cream, buttoned to the throat; sweater, skirt,
stockings and low-heeled shoes are black. Her smile is gracious and
she talks in a deep, educated drawl. It is, as a matter of fact, a
seductive voice, reminding me of Miss Barber, Chairman of the Fine
Arts department and house mother at Vassar. She too combined a
decorous appearance with a sultry voice and we all wondered about
Miss Barber.

Once McCarthy left Vassar, she embraced every leftist cause, then
satirized everything she belonged to: Communists and Liberals in
The Company She Keeps (1942), utopians in *The Oasis* (1949),
marital musical chairs in *A Charmed Life* (1955), and Vassarites in
The Group (1963).

Like a volcano, she erupted in the Sixties over Vietnam, and again,
in the mid-Seventies over Watergate. But it is hard to believe that it's
been only ten years since Mary McCarthy travelled to Saigon and
Hanoi and wrote a series of brilliant sketches for the *New York
Review of Books* describing the Americanization of Vietnam.
"Nobody has a nose for American stupidity like Mary," says a friend.
And it is true: "Flying to Hue in a big C-130, I heard the pilot and the
co-pilot discussing their personal war aim, which was to make a
killing, as soon as the war was over, in Vietnamese real estate. From
the air, while keeping an eye out for VC below, they had surveyed
the possibilities and had decided on Nha Trang—'beautiful sand
beaches'—better than Cam Ranh Bay—a 'desert.'"

Lately, she has not been heard from much. She has not given an
interview for years; she is leery. What do you plan to do with the
tape? she wants to know, and there is no satisfactory answer because
I have no idea nor any ulterior motive beyond having her words

right. So deft herself at getting revealing words out of people, she is well aware that another can get mileage from the tapes. Several years ago, she gave a taped interview to furnish background for her biography and found, to her horror, that she had been betrayed, that much of what she had to say about Edmund Wilson—who was still living then—was going to be printed. The case was settled, but she has been burnt and has it in for the biographer. She plans to write her own memoirs: "My publisher says I should write my intellectual autobiography and I like the idea.'

She talks some more about Jimmy Carter; how she wrote to his mother on behalf of a Soviet dissident and how his mother had answered—*a nice letter*—and the garden club matron rematerializes. I can't quite believe in her. The aging seems premature, something that has happened in her head. It's all very well, being dressed from top to toe by Lanvin, living easy, dining with the Ile St. Louis set, but the suspicion that she has gone soft is distressing. Mary McCarthy means something to my generation: honesty and audacity. But somehow, her previous lives—the stubborn militant, the randy, adventurous woman, the hard-hitting critic, have not left traces on the complacent surface. Whatever this new image is, and it will take a while to get it in focus, it is one she has chosen to accept and present to an audience.

She has told me to sit down wherever I like. There is not much choice: two small couches against opposite walls, diagonally across from each other in the muted room. We each have a table in front of us, too small to hold much, already crowded with bric-a-brac. My table has an enamel and silver display—might just one *objet d'art* be an ashtray?—arranged with a doctor's attentiveness to his waiting room, an ophthalmologist say, whose intention it is to *discourage* smoking. So I am surprised when she coughs—the end of a heavy cold—and lights up. "Everything is an ashtray," she explains, perched stiffly on the edge of her couch. She is capable of holding quite still, the arched brows do not flex, even her hands are quiet.

Having heard about the feasts she cooks, sparkling dinner parties she lovingly prepares and hosts, radiant in white silk, all this sobriety is baffling. We are in a dark room, sipping coffee and viewing negatives.

The very first question makes her balk: what does she think of

France and how do her impressions, living here, stack up with the
ideas she may have had before?

"I don't think I can answer that."

But she has been involved with France for so many years, starting
with the Sacred Heart Convent School, where she was taught by
French-speaking nuns.

"That was all so long ago."

Indeed, when she speaks French her accent is educated, Amer-
ican-tinted, as though it were a language aired only on rare
occasions.

Then what does she think about France now, after having lived
here for 16 years?

"I don't think I want to talk about it much." Silence. A clock
chimes the hour. Then she finds the anecdote, the thread that leads
her out gracefully. She used to talk about France a lot. In 1963, she
did a program for the BBC in which she described how lugubrious
her quartier was then, with funeral processions and chrysanthe-
mums, crepe bonnets at the Bon Marché. The French read about it
and were outraged. A smile has slipped into her voice now.

"I talked about the thing every foreigner notices, the lack of
hospitality and how you never see the inside of a French house, or if
you do, they're not French, but Italian or Jewish or something." By
the same token, she finds France "a perfect place to work because
nobody is bothering you with invitations, at least, no French person
is, not like New York, London, or Rome." She thinks much of her
best work has been done here, over these last years, but her real love
is Italy.

It doesn't sound as if Paris is much fun for her, even though she
can work well here. As a literary executor to the estate of her friend
Hannah Arendt, she has been editing a two-volume work, *The Life
of the Mind,* from papers the German-born philosopher left upon her
death in 1975. The book is scheduled for publication in New York
this March. Now she is writing a novel "about the present, but with
many things accumulated from the past." The characters are not
French, however, because "I don' think I can have a French character
in a book." She writes slowly, with many revisions and freshly
sharpened pencils standing in waiting beside the typewriter. She
works all day; some afternoons are set aside for German lessons and

a secretary who comes in to help with correspondence. So she leaves the house rarely during the day—those shopping forays.

Yet, she is fun-loving. That becomes evident as she warms up to the stories about the good years: the summer of '45 on Cape Cod, making bonfires on the beach, getting sand in her typewriter as she translated Simone Weil, swimming nude at night and talking Tolstoy with critic Dwight Macdonald, writer Niccolò Tucci, and critic-philosopher Chiaromonte.

Her feeling about that summer "had nothing to do with a love affair. I *was* having a love affair . . . or several. But, what I'm talking about was an intellectual kind of emotion." Intellectual emotions are all right; she is not about to discuss the other kind. The affairs, even evoked remotely, sound as though they had bounce.

Her childhood had been particularly chilling. Orphaned at the age of five, she and her brothers were sent to live with an Uncle Myers who, as it turned out, was not an uncle, but paid to do the job. He applied himself with incredible, even mysterious, brutality, laying it on heavy with the lash. "When I got out of that it took me a long time to realize I wasn't going to be punished for something I had or had not done." Her brother, actor Kevin McCarthy, was the only one with whom she had some sense of solidarity. Then, from the age of 11, she lived with kind but uncommunicative grandparents whose great distraction was playing double solitaire. This was the sinister and solitary life vividly described in *Memories of a Catholic Girlhood,* a book that has more imagination and compassion than most of her fiction.

The convent was a release from those silent mornings shared with her quixotic Jewish grandmother. It is well-known that the convent is a fertile ground for passion—that's where Emma Bovary got her start. Mary McCarthy's passions were more cerebral, but touched with romance: admiration for a French Sister, love for Lord Byron. Years of being hemmed in made her fierce about injustice and she pictured herself as Shakespeare's Portia, an exceptional woman.

The certainty of being exceptional started early—after all, she had had an exceptional childhood, between the Protestant grandfather, the Jewish grandmother, the Catholic paternal grandparents, fanatically harsh Uncle Myers and Aunt Margaret, a woman who had constipation constantly on her mind. What was hard to take was the uncertainty: at the convent she was laughed at by her schoolmates, and so in her striving to be outstanding, to dominate intellectually, to comprehend and repair injustice she was encouraged by her elders but ridiculed by her peers. In her novels we get sudden glimpses of the precocious child, lavishly praised for her large vocabulary and gift for languages, dogged about being taken seriously.

Life has been better to her since; she has also worked hard. "In one's life, there are developmental plateaux, going upward, one hopes," she says. Vassar was the first real high: "There were some quite exceptional women teachers at Vassar then."

After college she married an actor; 1936 saw the end of that marriage and the beginning of real political engagement: phase II. "When I came back from Reno, the Spanish Civil War had broken out. It was the period of the Moscow trials. Had I still been married to that particular man, I wouldn't have gotten involved with those things." When the Stalinists rejected Trotsky, she became Trotskyist.

She was living in Greenwich Village, revelling in being young, poor, and alone. This is the period barely fictionalized in *The Company She Keeps*, her biting collection of short stories published in 1942 in which everybody's intellectual and moral shortcomings— including the heroine's—are laid bare by a wicked pen. It is among her most successful fiction, but she rejects it now. "I don't like the way it is written; it's so juvenile. The prose is too *rhythmic*," she complains. "It's not my idea of prose." What is her idea of prose? "It should be *prose*." It might be the young Mary McCarthy she rejects, the woman who wore flamboyant ill-matched clothes, flirted with Communism and criticism and went quickly to bed. She was far from a lady in those days and not yet an author.

Then came her second marriage, to author and critic Edmund Wilson. But she dates her third phase, not with the beginning of this marriage, but with the end, in 1945—that beautiful summer spent on Cape Cod.

"Reuel and I left Edmund the summer of the Atom Bomb," she says. This sounds strange: Reuel is their son, a small boy then. Somehow she makes the move—a woman leaving her husband— sound like a delegation walk-out. Admittedly, the marriage was tumultuous, but she denies that competition may have been a factor. She does not call Wilson "Bunny," his nick-name, nor does she give him much credit: "I got very little out of that marriage. Intellectually, I mean." It amuses her that everybody assumes Wilson was her mentor, although she allows that he did encourage her to write fiction. If there were stories along the line of Willy and Colette—or worse—we are not going to hear them today. Her tone never takes off to the querulous; the marriage is summed up the same way she treats psychoanalysis, about which she also says, "It didn't do anything for me. Analysts believe that you should stay in your situation. I changed my situation and found that life was different."

Why did she get married again, and again?

"I like being married," she says simply. "I like to serve."

She and Reuel were living in New York. "And it really was not possible for me to have a live-in-lover. My son was fine about it, but I was afraid he would start talking to his friends and they would talk to their Mamas . . . it would be uncomfortable for him." She made him fanciful recipes and read to him every night.

Although she has a cook, and a maid, she still enjoys cooking, starting from scratch, making elaborate meals for friends. "I started when I was married. My first husband cooked—you know, the things men cook—spaghetti." Whereas she can make lasagna from the dough on through. "I think I inherited that from my grandmother, not that she actually cooked, but she set a very good table. I feel pangs for her. She was a very reserved woman." The woman across from me is reserved too, but she has her joys.

"I'm not as happy as I was when I was younger, but nobody is. I have a lot of energy, but age is not a happy business. Your friends die, then you feel more and more cut off. You're not as close to people . . . except maybe your husband." The voice has gone bleak.

And what about her beauty?

"Well, I mind that." *Die Zeit* has just published a piece she wrote about Hannah Arendt's death. "They've got a most ghastly picture of me—I look like the craters of the moon—and they must have had quite a search to find that picture because it was taken 10 years ago!" She rises to get the paper and show me the picture. It is grim. "They have some lines here that I don't have." The patrician face is alight with rueful amusement.

I raise the question of rivalry among women intellectuals.

"Oh yes, there is competition," she says, "but not with Hannah because she is—was—an infinitely superior person. Also because you can't feel competition with someone you admire. I like to see something beyond, I like to look up."

And Lillian Hellman?

"I can't stand her. I think every word she writes is false, including 'and' and 'but.'" Her steady smile has grown into a full grin. "I met her in very unfortunate circumstances for *her*." This was in 1948 at Sarah Lawrence where she taught, after Bard. Hellman was up visiting President Harold Taylor and sounding off to some students, "about how John Dos Passos had betrayed the Spanish Loyalists because he didn't like the food in Madrid! I didn't introduce myself and I think she thought I was another student. Anyway, she paid no attention to me. She was just brain-washing those girls—it was really vicious. So finally I spoke up and said, I'll tell you why he broke with the Loyalists, you'll find it in his novel, *The Adventures of a Young Man,* and it wasn't such a clean break. She started to tremble. She had rather aging wrinkled arms, bare, and on them were a lot of gold and silver bracelets—and all the bracelets started to jangle. It was a very dramatic moment of somebody being caught absolutely red-handed. And so, somebody like that writes a book like *Scoundrel Time,* and I think that it's still scoundrel time, as far as she's concerned."

This has been, not her longest speech, for she has been mono-loguing, but the most impassioned. The past is very present suddenly. She is still angry. Anything about the Stalinists gets her going.

And McCarthyism?

"I didn't have any problem making up my mind about Joe McCarthy. I wrote and spoke—well, that was it: I wrote and I spoke." She also tried, with friends, to start a magazine. "I was very anti-Communist of course—anti-Stalinist—with a Trotskyist background."

Her anti-Communism had been established for years and so she was in no danger of harassment herself. "I never would have joined the Communist Party, and you didn't really join the Trotskyist party—very few did. Most of my friends didn't."

McCarthyism upset her enough so that she contemplated going to Harvard Law School to arm herself with constitutional law, but she was dissuaded by an old friend, a judge. "I acceped his advice and I was rather sad because I loved the Portia image."

In 1952, she published *The Groves of Academe*, her novel about a progressive college that resembles Bard, and a liberal President who sounds a lot like Harold Taylor. The professor hero—or anti-hero (heroes are scarce in her books)—is fired and mobilizes the faculty on his side by pretending to be a victim of the witch hunt.

"People talk a lot about the climate of fear in those days and how nobody dared speak out against McCarthysm: that was a lot of balls."

I cast an anxious glance across the room, disbelieving that the pale lips have uttered such words. She continues, blandly, "At least in my experience. Maybe in some backward colleges in the West or Middle-West you could lose your job for speaking out against McCarthy. I am not convinced. Of course, the places I taught were just the opposite. 'The climate of fear' was all greatly exaggerated, I think," she laughs comfortably. "Well again, as in all my experiences—like Women's Lib—*I* was never persecuted."

Again she emphasizes that she likes men—she has been married four times—never suffered oppression, except from the notorious Uncle Myers, enjoys "Feminine things, like cooking and gardening." Describing herself as "somebody who likes to admire," she does not admire the major writers held in esteem by the women's movement. The run-down becomes a staccato exchange:

Virginia Woolf: "She's not my taste."

Doris Lessing: "I don't care for all that heavy self-examination—narcissistic."

Simone de Beauvoir: "I've said enough about Simone de Beauvoir. And written enough."

Susan Brownmiller: "Haven't read it . . . I've never been raped . . . of course rape is monstrous."

Kate Millet: "I find it very hard to get through that stuff. Although I liked that part, in her first book, on Henry Miller. I thought she brought out something that was there. No, I didn't read *Flying* or *Fear of Flying*—well, I did."

What did she think of it?

"*Nothing.*"

To her credit, she still harbors malicious enmity for Hemingway: "I hated Hemingway. He can go right in there with Lillian Hellman. In fact, I think they'd make a wonderful pair; I think Hemingway is untruthful too."

As for other women writers, she likes Frances Fitzgerald and her *Fire in the Lake,* but has not read Gloria Emerson's *Winners and Losers:* "I can't bear Gloria Emerson. She has attacked me in print." Nor does she thrill to the name of Diana Trilling: "Diana disapproves of me. She's a kind of Mrs. Grundy."

To boot, two writer friends have become involved with the women's movement: Barbara Deming and Monique Wittig.

Of course, to the woman who has found that "being a woman is an advantage, like being the exception-Jew-or-nigger," the movement seems to be a tempest in a teapot brewed by misguided harpies. Is it because, living abroad, she missed out on what was happening in the Sixties? No, she was exposed to it in the Seventies when she attended an arts panel in North Dakota. "It was the most hysterical thing I've ever been present at—frightening. The main group was graduate school level—if anybody can achieve that out there. One of these dervishes got up and told how she had to wash her husband's shirts every night—he was a factory worker. His shirts smelled of sweat and it made her sick. Well, I was sitting next to Gwendolyn Brooks, the black poet, who feels even more strongly about Women's Lib than I do and she said, why didn't the woman get a washing machine! But this poor sweating male! I was frightened, not so much for myself, but for my country.

"It's worse out there because they live in a prairie and have nothing else to put their minds to but feeling injured, and they don't make any contribution. Everything is mechanical, produced like a TV dinner. If they had had children, there was no evidence of it. Their husbands worked; they contributed nothing. And I thought that technology had a good deal to do with the origins of some of the passions around women's lib. That is, technology had deprived women of a sense of usefulness. Of making a contribution.

"I don't mean that I disagree with the goals of equal pay, and so on, it's the domestic side that I find so repellent. I can't see the point of devoting yourself to the constant emotions of competitiveness and envy. And I don't see why people should dislike serving. I quite enjoy serving."

Of course, when you are McCarthy, you have a choice. And if you get fed up with that choice, you have a wide range of options. If you are less exceptional—and most women are—your field is limited. I would like to wedge this point in, but she has the floor and is not about to give up.

"And the idea of trying to apportion with absolute equality the domestic tasks—I find this so ugly. You cannot have equality in this kind of sphere anyway. It doesn't have to be between men and women. It can be between women, a lesbian couple. It can be between mother and daughter, but you can't have it: some people are more gifted, some can work harder. You can't have it and I wouldn't want it. I think that most women who have careers or artistic occupations *do* work harder than their men often, but I wouldn't like it if my husband were out there in the kitchen cooking."

She probably wouldn't like what he cooked, either, unless he happens to have gotten beyond the spaghetti stage. He does, she allows tolerantly, run a better vacuum cleaner than she does.

"About those phases in my life," she adds, "the last one was in 1960, when I went to Poland and met Jim. That was really when I left America too."

Might she return someday?

That is going to be open to question upon his retirement in a couple of years, and it sounds as though there might be some worry or regret, though not about leaving France necessarily. They spend summers in the U.S. in a house they love in Maine, acquired in 1967 during the Vietnam war when "It seemed the right time, somehow, to have a home in America."

But having a beautiful summer home is not the same thing as living there full-time, after all these years away. She is aware, for example, that she has lost touch with the language. From her serene rendition of aristocratic values it sounds as though she managed to steer clear of '70s jargon, the "I-see-where-you're coming from," or "You're-really-into-your-head."

Is she more conservative politically today?

"Yes, I'm more conservative. Maybe I've come . . . I started out conservative: although I'm a rebellious person I was a great royalist, even through college. And then, there is no Left anymore. Either they're not Leftist or they vanished. Former young French Leftists have moved to the Right or they have bombs and I cannot sympathize with terrorism. My French friends will probably vote for Mitterrand or the ecologists."

She knows enough about the evils of capitalism, "Money that creates money is the original sin, as the church felt in the Middle Ages," and still has hopes in moderate Socialism, "But I don't see anything around to encourage Socialism. Ten years ago, we hoped for Poland or Hungary. Now even the Swedes and the Danes have rejected the Welfare State—people can't take it. Young workers resent paying heavy taxes to an old age program, paying for people who don't contribute."

And how would she feel about her privileges being taken away? Would she suffer?

"I don't know if I would suffer, but I wouldn't like it," she smiles.

Then hasn't she—wasn't she about to say it herself—come full circle?

"I said it, but I took it back."

It is time to end. And we have not said a word about sex.

"Oh, but I wouldn't talk about sex; it's in my writing, but I don't talk about it."

She rises saying, "I enjoyed that very much," as though we had just spent a long, pleasurable afternoon working on some tricky Latin lesson. She knows the text far better than I do, and I didn't really get my questions in, but she supplied more answers than I'll ever know what to do with. Diligent tutor, she dispatched the homework, working quietly and well, infinitely scrupulous. Also, true to her record is real life, she ran some risks and took her responsibilities.

Three hours of even very mellow Mary McCarthy are heady. So much articulateness stuns. But I will have to go back to the books to find the head-strong rebel, and how had I ever missed the royalist? All those well-chosen words need weeding. Is it that one can identify with the intellectual, but not the aristocrat? Yet, throughout her books, even in *The Company She Keeps,* a lady loiters.

"I cannot remember the moment when I ceased to air my old royalist convictions and stuffed them away in an inner closet as you do a dress or an ornament that you perceive strikes the wrong note," she wrote in 1953 ("My Confession," from *On the Contrary*). Mary McCarthy has still not emerged from that particular closet, and, despite her lucidity and great control, some contradictions are hanging out. However, apparent lofty detachment could be protective cover for a shy and sensitive inner self.

Living out of touch with America and remote from France may
have a scary side, like weightlessness. It's not all Olympian calm up
there. If she has turned, coming almost full circle, domestic con-
tentment may play a part. There is a temptation to say that the
exceptional woman likes having room for herself, and only the best
company, at the top.

There is still an artist in the house. Yet it does look as though,
knowing something about charmed lives, having led several, she has
chosen shelter.

A World Out of Joint

Miriam Gross/1979

From *The Observer*, (14 October 1979) 35. Reprinted by permission of *The Observer*. Copyright © 1979 *The Observer*.

Most of my books have been in some way political, but I suppose this is the first one which deals directly with what you might call headline material: terrorism, hijacking and so forth.

I've only met one person who has actually been hijacked, but of course once political hijacking started—as opposed to people blowing up a plane to collect the insurance on their mother-in-law—everybody, the minute they got on to a plane or even waiting in the departure lounge, began to ask themselves what they would do if this happened to them. I know I certainly did, in so far as I'm anybody or everybody.

You also couldn't help surveying rather suspiciously the other people travelling with you—and I must say a certain colour consciousness came in: you tried not to, but you couldn't help looking more carefully at black people or Arabs than you did at the white passengers. And you found yourself trying to guess who were the security guards.

People, in my view anyway, inevitably began to project themselves into such a dilemma and ask themselves how they would behave—just as during the war and right after the war people asked themselves how they would have behaved under Nazi torture; that still goes on as a matter of fact. And it was partly this which drew me to the subject. I was also interested in reading in the papers about passengers who'd been hijacked finally disembarking and saying things like: "The hijackers were perfect gentlemen." Middle-aged housewives making these statements.

But once I started the book it came to me that I had to show at least one of the terrorists from the inside. I realised that it would be refusing the jumps not to describe such an event from a terrorist's point of view as well. It was as if they were speaking out of the dark: 'Hey, teacher, we're here too.'

I don't think this means I've romanticised them—terrorism is terrifying. But we've seen, after all, that in many of these cases the terrorists find it impossible to commit murder or use extreme violence on someone they've gotten to know. That happened to Moro, I believe: the people who'd been holding him apparently had to send for other Red Brigadists to execute him. They couldn't do it them-selves.

It's true, I suppose that I have a certain sympathy for the main terrorist character in my novel; it would be hard not to respond to his kind of total dedication and self-sacrifice, though not of course to extorting sacrifice from others. But I also show how terrorists paint themselves into a corner because their aims are impossible—that's the whole point.

Actually it wasn't really hijackings which got me started on the book. People aren't the only hostages in the story: there are works of art. The book really grew out of the Kenwood House Vermeer case. I started noticing that people, including myself, were much more concerned about the Vermeer—Oh dear when they started cutting strips off the canvas!—than they were about any human hostage. And the whole question of the value people put on works of art is very interesting, especially for someone who cares about art and beauty in every way, as I do.

I think really my criterion is aesthetic or I think the aesthetic and the ethical are the same—to me, a beautiful action is a good action and a good action cannot be ugly. Nevertheless, one can't help questioning one's own way of life and one's principles, the fact that one cares so much about art and about the appearance of things.

I'm ashamed to say, for instance, how many suitcases containing clothes I took to North Vietnam—like going away to college. The North Vietnamese pretended not to notice, perhaps they didn't notice, perhaps they don't think in such terms. Though some of the ones I met were interested in works of art, food, books and nature: on our travels the one I got along with best was the one who could identify all the trees and plants and who also taught me the Vietnamese literary man's recipe for making tea—you watch while the water comes to a boil and when the bubbles are the size of a crab's eye it's not soon enough, but when they are the size of a fish's eye it's time to make the tea.

But the main thing that came home to me while I was in daily contact, amid the air-alerts, with the North Vietnamese was religious—their current religion was Marxism-Leninism though with a wayback Buddhist background; and this made me realise how much I was a Christian. It was not even a matter of confronting it, but, let's say, of noticing it. I don't believe in God—that's just a fact, it's not an act of will; I can't even conceive of God, so there it is. But ethics came to me in the frame of Christian teaching, and even though I don't believe in an after-life I'm still concerned with the salvation of my soul. I'm quite incapable of switching to an atheist's ethics, if there is such a thing.

It really takes a hero to live any kind of spiritual life without religious belief. Not that I've any sympathy with all the born-again Christian movements in America right now. I think they are false and shallow—most of them don't believe in God any more than I do— the whole thing is ridiculous, and typical of a hideous society with all its PR. Even though it clearly corresponds to some nutritional or vitamin lack in people's lives.

Aside from Christian doctrine, the thing that has most formed my cast of mind has probably been Shakespeare. Whether the two are connected in some way I'm not sure, but it seems to me that throughout Shakespeare there is a deep rejection of the will. The will naturally allies itself with abstractions, and abstractions in Shake-speare are always wrong. In comedy they simply lead to comic conclusions, beginning with *Love's Labour's Lost* where the young men make their absurd vow and try to stick to it. And anyone who thinks that he embodies what Ibsen called 'the claim of the ideal' is shown to be wrong in Shakespeare, like Angelo in *Measure for Measure* or Lear or Coriolanus or Shylock with his insistent idea of a pound of flesh—a bloodless abstraction, evidently.

Shakespeare's view of the will and its capacity for abstractions, as opposed to the things of nature, to the instinctive and the concrete, spoke to me very young and still speaks to me. I believe in humility, in a certain modesty towards what is outside, towards what is not I. Or not me. The assertion of any absolute idea is really a claim on the part of the mind to control the world, to control reality. It's a proclamation of sovereignty, and I don't want that, I don't believe in it; I think one must respect the created world which has its own laws,

including unjust laws, and its own harmony. We must listen to
messages from that world, and this comes over very strongly in
Shakespeare where the rustics are always right, they have the last
word. The rustics and the clowns and even the fools. That corresponds to my sense of the way things ought to be.

The trouble is that we are destroying, have practically succeeded in
destroying, this guiding sensory world. It is disappearing before our
eyes. When I was travelling through the French countryside last
week-end, for instance, I thought Oh God, the next generation and
the generation after that will never know what the natural world was
like; they will look at a landscape of Fra Angelico as you might look at
a bit of Byzantine ivory, as something strange. What the French have
done to the countryside is even worse than what the Americans have
done to theirs. The factories and the housing developments and the
pylons (though these have a certain Paul Klee charm) have
devastated it.

The energy crisis might save us if we know how to use it. People
did have that hope at the time of the original oil embargo in 1973;
they believed that we might go back to simpler ways like the bicycle
and give up the whole business of the growth rate which capitalists go
in for and which the socialist countries have to compete with too. But
this hope very rapidly faded.

There is probably going to be a third party in our presidential
elections, an ecology party headed by a man called Barry
Commoner who has written some interesting and rather inspiring
articles about energy, and I may well vote for him. Certainly I think
the idea that there is any such thing as a Conservative today is
absurd. The people who call themselves Conservatives are in favour
of capitalism, which is one of the main forces involved in the annihila-
tion of nature—and it's accelerating all the time. No Conservative
wants to restrict this in any way. Any true conservative ought to be
against nuclear energy, for instance, and they aren't.

I feel that America now is horribly sad and discouraging and I
don't think there's much to choose between Carter and Kennedy. I
have a certain sympathy for Carter, but it is probably sympathy for
the underdog—he's become the great public underdog. And I don't
feel the attraction of the Kennedys at all. On the contrary. The
convent-girl in me doesn't respond to them. I don't think they are

Christians; they may be Catholics but they are not Christians, in my belief anyway.

I've become much more sceptical and pessimistic in the last few years about politics in general. I was a believer in socialism with a human face, and all that; I don't know whether it would work or not, but I do know that nobody will ever give it a chance to. Wherever it has cropped up in the last few years it has immediately been stamped on, whether it was Allende in Chile or Dubcek in Czechoslovakia. Nobody wants to see it triumph; at least that's what it looks like.

The only political causes that I still have any active connection with are in Poland and Czechoslovakia. I belong to a couple of committees so I get news, and I do have a romantic attachment to Poland: I've lived there, and it seems to me the one place where socialism might just conceivably been given a try. Partly because of the play between the Church and the State there is a dialogue between the dissidents and the authorities of a kind which is non-existent in the Soviet Union. And I admire the dissidents for managing to maintain some intellectual balance. In Russia they all seem to go in the Solzhenitsyn direction—the Soviets have a superb recipe for producing reactionaries. I admire Solzhenitsyn, incidentally, as a writer and as a person, but it breaks my heart to see what has happened to his thinking. I keep hoping that this is a passing thing with him; for a long time I was writing him imaginary letters gently correcting his bull-headed views.

As for my current views on Vietnam, it's all rather daunting. I've several times contemplated writing a real letter to Pham Van Dong (I get a Christmas Card from him every year) asking him can't you stop this, how is it possible for men like you to permit what's going on? One can allow for a certain amount of ignorance at the top for what is executed at a lower level; that's true in any society. But this has gone past that point. I've never written that letter, though; it is still in my pending folder, so to speak. Of course it shouldn't have stayed there, but it did. I might have signed the Joan Baez protest about the boat people, but I was never asked.

Well, socialism with a human face is still my ideal. Living under such a system would require quite an adjustment, but it would be so exciting that I hope one would be willing to sacrifice the comforts of life that one has become extremely used to. I think that the excitement would make all the difference—I hope it would. But anyway, it all seems so remote now. Take what we were saying about beauty, the aesthetic. It has become a class thing, a class privilege.

That wasn't always so: it wasn't so in the Middle Ages for instance. Until recent times people—even very poor people—lived in beautiful and harmonious surroundings. It's true that more people nowadays are interested in looking at works of art—they are fighting for a place in front of the Mona Lisa. But I think that all this is tied up with an interest in money. Money itself has lost its value; art somehow is regarded as treasure, and the public is interested in seeing treasure. Look how they lined up to see the Scythian gold exhibition.

The only hope, the only clue, that people in future will have to what to me are absolutely lifegiving things, is through education. But so much education now is a kind of non-education; perhaps universal literacy is creating a world of illiterates. Alberto Moravia once said a very good thing in conversation about *analfabetismo* and the statistics on it. He said that the ratio of literacy to illiteracy is constant, but that nowadays the illiterates can read and write.

But it also seems to me that lots of the people who could formerly read and write no longer can. Every time I write a book I face the problem that people—and that includes book-reviewers—can't read any more. In my last novel, for example, the hero is attacked by a black swan. One reviewer described it as a white swan, another as a goose. And in the very first review I read of my new novel, I found one of the characters described as 'a narrow, venal woman.' This is the poor dumpy collector who tries to lay down her life for her painting. This is terribly discouraging.

When I showed the review to one of our neighbours in Maine he said that if you were a teacher you would accept this as normal—the fact that your students cannot read what is in front of them, cannot read the text. And I do think that people have lost touch with language, which is, after all, a kind of silting in of human knowledge and of the human capacity for definition and identification.

Some things have improved, I suppose. Maybe in the sexual field, where fear and ignorance still prevailed—not so much when I was young, but in the generation which preceded mine. Of course it's better that people shouldn't be taught, for instance, that masturbation is a terrible evil or that it can lead to insanity. On the other hand I don't think that masturbation is very good for a person as a steady practice, partly because it is so in-turned—it's like jogging. (Look at the face of a jogger. It's not like the face of a pedestrian, who is in contact with the ground, or a cyclist, who is in contact with his machine. The jogger is in contact with some idea, some abstraction.)

As for Women's Lib, it bores me. Of course I believe in equal pay and equality before the law and so on, but this whole myth about how different the world would have been if it had been female-dominated, about how there would have been no wars—and Women's Lib extremists actually believe these things—seems a complete fantasy to me. I've never noticed that women were less warlike than men. And in marriage, or for that matter between a woman and her lover or between two lesbians or any other couple, an equal division of tasks is impossible—it's a judgment of Solomon. You really would have to slice the baby down the middle.

I myself don't object to the idea of serving, though I would if I had to do it all the time. I rather like a certain amount of structure and hierarchy, and I don't object to the idea that someone is better than I am. I enjoy the sensation of looking up. I think most people do, but they are not supposed to now. My greatest friends have been people that I looked up to. Unfortunately they are mostly dead. I don't think I would much enjoy a friendship based on equality—that is, that the person was absolutely on my level, no better and no worse. It would be like having a friendship with your self.

I also like marriage and domesticity—I'm the marrying type. Hannah Arendt who was my confidante, among other things, was always saying to me: 'Why do you have to think of marriage? Live with the man; you don't have to live with him even, you can see him. There's no need for all these divorces and re-marriages.'

Hannah was in favour of deception, she thought frankness was madness. And she was right in a way: frankness can be cruel. But I can't bear deception. I really hate it. Of course divorce is a terrible thing: it's a kind of murder, as I've said in one of my stories. And yet I've done it over and over. There's this obstinate thing in me that nothing will do but marriage.

I've been married to my fourth husband, Jim West, for nearly 20 years now. I like that companionship of marriage, and perhaps the security. I like the rites and rituals of domesticity. I like bringing Jim breakfast in bed. He does mine, but not as often; and I prefer it that way. Every object in this room is part of our common biography. That Greek bull, for instance, and that little falcon next to him are part of being together in Sicily, with an old lame Yugoslav woman, an art dealer. So that your house or your flat becomes a kind of shrine. Your love for each other may be going through rather shaky periods, but these solid objects are still there, like witnesses.

All this is somehow connected with the idea of immortality or perpetuity. One has to believe that love is eternal, even if one knows it is not. And also one can't bear that anyone should die and these objects don't only embody our past together but also other people. That plant behind you was given to me by a young Brazilian photographer, and so I feel that he is growing there in his jungle plant from Brazil, here in this room.

More and more as I get older—or as I get old—I have the feeling in my head all those people, my grandmother, my schoolmates, my friends, can survive. I'm carrying all these people's lives around in my skull, and they're not dead as long as I can remember them. Of course many of my friends have died: the two people whose views I care most about are no longer living, and in a sense there's almost no one to talk to any more. And these deaths, more than I realised, have taken their toll, as they say.

I absolutely hate being old. I reached a very happy plateau seven or eight years ago (oh God, I've now got to 67 isn't that awful?). I was very happy, I felt well physically, I felt wise, serene. I felt I had learned something. I did not regret my youth because then I hadn't had this sense of wisdom.

That's utterly gone. The wisdom has gone, tranquility has gone. I don't really know why this has happened. It may come back, though I think it's partly a matter of the physical decay of the organism. More and more I realise what a large part physiology plays in moral attitudes and emotions and so on. I've always been conscious of having quite an equable disposition, of being rather cheerful—I know I can lose my temper, but in general I think I'm not irritable; I have a lot of self-control and I think I've treated myself and everybody else with care. All this seems to be dependent on one's physical well being.

I've now become very irritable in the mornings. I used to wake up, you know, delighted. I love the morning, especially the early morning and the sun rising, and in December we can see the morning star before sunrise from the kitchen. Well, now some days I wake up very, very irritable and I realise that what I thought was me was just my constitution.

I think this is a particularly bad moment for me because of the business of my novel just coming out—it's just like being in the stocks, you're standing there with your head pushed through. I still foolishly always hope that I'll get entirely good—no, that's not the main thing—that I'll get interesting reviews, but I know that it isn't going to be any different from before.

I'm not talking about fame. I hated it when *The Group* got the best-seller treatment. There was a time when I thought it had ruined my life. I didn't like the exposure, it made me into a different kind of person. I had to change my hairdo: I couldn't stand the sight of that bun in the photographs. And I hated the whole business of interviews and TV. I felt I'd been corrupted. Not that I was a corrupt person, but that the world which I despised had somehow eaten its way into me and I had been corroded perhaps more than corrupted.

I've said to myself that *Cannibals and Missionaries* is my last novel. Something I've observed is that one loses one's social perceptions, they get blunted and dimmer as one gets older—it's partly a matter of eyesight. You can continue writing poetry and essays and so on, but to be a novelist you have to have this alert social thing.

I've started working on a new book, but it's not a novel. It's what my publisher calls an intellectual autobiography. But again, you're working from memory, which doesn't improve with the years. I've always had a very good memory—though I wish I hadn't lost the letters from a crucial period of my life, in the 1930s: I didn't pay my storage bill, they were in a trunk. But anyway, that's what I'm doing. You know, one only has this much time on earth.

A New Kind of McCarthyism:
Actor Kevin Interviews Sister Mary
on Her Books, Loves, and Life

Kevin McCarthy/1979

From *People Weekly* 12 (12 November 1979), 92,95,96,99.
Reprinted by permission of Kevin McCarthy. All rights reserved
to Kevin McCarthy.

*You're widely celebrated for your so-called caustic wit. Does it come
naturally? Are you proud of it?*

Of course it comes naturally and I don't know if I'm proud of it. I
enjoy it, I enjoy laughing

*You seem to get a great deal of open pleasure in your own natural
gaiety, in your own irony and humor.*

You mean laugh at my own jokes? Yes.

*In print you have the reputation of being cold and ruthless, you
know, a bitter quill dipped in venom. When critics say you are
seeking revenge on someone or something, what is your response?*

Balls!

Do you like writing?

It's a terrible job. I can produce 19 variants of one page—often! Of
course I rewrite. That's why it's a terrible job.

Who is your audience?

I think quite a few simple people, not illiterate, but very ordinary.
I'm not an author that's greatly loved by an elite.

*Do the figures of our parents, whom we lost in the 1918 influenza
epidemic, come back to you?*

No, not unless something evokes them. As far as I'm concerned,
they've really turned into their photographs.

Were you ever jealous of me?

I don't know, Kevin, maybe as a young child. But I was *envious* when you ran away in such a dramatic way.

I remember saying when I got back to that dismal foster home, "I ran away to an orphan asylum." I was looking for an orphan asylum to go to. But you ran away twice!
I think we four kids were difficult children, already a handful.

Did you ever go to a psychoanalyst?
After I was married to Edmund Wilson I was sent to three, don't you remember? But I don't recommend psychoanalysis. I think the whole thing is an absurd series of myths. It's never in any way been empirically verified.

Why did your marriages break up?
I don't know. But it's never been incompatibility, except, let's say, with Edmund Wilson. And in that case, there was no other man in the picture when I left him. It was [laughing] desperation!

I and my wife, Kate, are, you know, 35 years apart, and we're about to have a child. I have three children by my first marriage and a grandchild, Jessica, almost 6. Is it an okay thing?
I think in this case, yes. Kate is going to be 29, has been married before and has a child. And you, Kevin, seem tremendously young for your age. But usually it's grotesque—these ancient men with 18-year-old girls. You never see it the other way around.

When you look back on childhood, do you feel you are compensating in your career for some of those wounds?
That sort of psychiatric stuff doesn't compel my belief. Its tendency is to take any mystery out of our experience, and to imply one has a kind of knowledge one doesn't have.

Then what is your secret?
Well, as far as you and I go, I think it's natural that we as orphan children—rather looked down on, different from other children—would try to distinguish ourselves favorably. I know that as a child I had this attention-getting business very strongly, and [laughing] alas, I still have.

Would you say that my becoming an actor was to get attention?

Yes, it could be. And I suspect our Irish father was drawn to the theater and drama, which might have been an early influence.

I vividly recall realizing in my first Shakespearean play at the University of Minnesota that I could speak—I could speak out! But you, too, wanted to be on the stage, didn't you?

Yes, but at Vassar, when I played in Chaucer's *Knight's Tale*, I shook so hard that this paper mâché tower I was in nearly fell over and the audience was laughing. I still have stage fright, a fear of appearing in public.

You seem to me fiercely indomitable, always ready to take up arms. Why?

For the fun of it, perhaps! Or a mixture of fun and principle. If nobody will speak out on a subject, well, *I* will.

I admired your courage in going to the battlefields of South and North Vietnam.

Well, I wasn't the first woman journalist. Barbara Deming [from a Greenwich Village journal, *Liberation*] got to North Vietnam first. And during those bombardments, I was scared. Once we had to flatten ourselves in a ditch when the American bombers came over. I never went on patrol. I felt I was rather weak, but I wouldn't have learned anything about the rightness or wrongness of our actions by going on patrol. It was the most dangerous thing you could do. I felt it would be a kind of betrayal of Jim, my husband, if I were killed.

Let's talk about Chappaquiddick.

I don't give a damn about what Senator Kennedy was doing with Mary Jo Kopechne. I don't find that reprehensible. It's what happened afterwards. It's the cover-up—all those distinguished Democrats getting together to figure out how to play it. The original thing could have happened to anybody, but what happened afterwards could happen chiefly to a politician, and a politician who put his career first.

What about Pope John Paul II?

I'm not really very sent by this Pope. To me, he looks too much like a football player. I don't see him as a spiritual man, like Pope John, whom I really did love. This new Pope has been taken in by the discovery of PR techniques. There are superman touches. He'll say anything depending on the audience.

You say you're against jogging. In fact you compared it to masturbation, a word we would never have used as kids.

I don't like the way people look when they jog. There's something very abstract about the idea. It's some terrible turning back on the self, I feel. It's like going for a walk wearing a pedometer, like our Uncle Meyers. The jogger isn't even really running; he's on some sort of a treadmill.

I can't imagine being as directly and openly critical of another actor as writers seem to be of each other. Why do writers have the long knives out?

I would call it plain speaking. As a writer, you don't have to function as part of a group. With actors, there's getting the show on that night, and that requires a bit more closing ranks.

In talking about Truman Capote's In Cold Blood, *you objected to it because, you said, violence is the ultimate pornography. Is that a phrase you would go with?*

Yes. Now that sex isn't forbidden, violence is the only thing that gives people a thrill anymore. It's the only thing, generally, that's forbidden.

You were quoted as saying, "I don't like John Updike anymore." True?

I did say that, but before I had read his marvelous African book, *The Coup.* He's so gifted, but I think he should give his private life a long rest.

Have you ever read James Michener?

No, no. But as Jim Agee once said, reviewing *Oklahoma!* without having seen it, you don't have to have seen it played to know it's bad.

What do you have against Lillian Hellman?

Well, I've never liked what she writes. And there was a little episode back in 1948 when I was teaching at Sarah Lawrence. She was in a sun parlor telling the students that the novelist John Dos Passos had betrayed the Spanish Loyalists. She was defaming Dos! I couldn't stand this woman brain-feeding these utterly empty, innocent minds, and thinking she could get away with it.

A young novelist, John Casey, said all Mary McCarthy's characters have feet of clef. Isn't the senator in your new book a thinly disguised Eugene McCarthy?

There's no attempt at disguise; it's supposed to be an improvisation on the theme "Gene McCarthy." It was great fun to do! To be inside his mind, to be his voice. Reading it aloud the other night, it was right on target—right into the old catcher's mitt. You know the real Gene McCarthy is extremely funny, but extremely perverse. When anything is expected of him is when he will not deliver.

You and the poet Elizabeth Bishop were at Vassar together, weren't you?

Yes, she was a class ahead, but she doesn't figure in *The Group.* They were mostly high-C-average people. She was too bright and original. I think she was, along with Robert Lowell, our best poet. And now they are both gone!

Can you ever get to the point where you let the activities of your mind rest and sort of drift and dream?

Never!

Thank you, Mary.

Thank you, Kevin, my dear.

Writing Dominates Mary McCarthy's Life

Maggie Maurice/1980

From *The Burlington Free Press*, 8 May 1980. Reprinted by permission of *The Burlington Free Press* (May 1980), Copyright © 1980 by *The Burlington Free Press*.

The story goes that critic Edmund Wilson locked Mary McCarthy in a room and forced her to write.

Mary McCarthy smiles when asked whether it is true.

"No—and yes," she said.

"When we were first married, I was 25. I had done reviews. 'Oh, you draw up a crushing brief against a play,' Edmund said. I had tried a detective story and could never get beyond the corpse. I gave up trying to write.

"Edmund said, 'I think you have a talent for fiction.' It was a new notion for me. My teacher at Vassar had said I had a critical bent but little creative ability, so I was interested. We had a small guest room and he told me to go in there and take the typewriter.

"He shut the door. He did not lock it," she said, smiling again as she remembered back to 1937.

That first story was accepted by Robert Penn Warren in *The Southern Review*. She later included it in her book, *The Company She Keeps* (Simon and Schuster 1942).

Writing in one form or another has dominated her entire life. Writing is what brought her to St. Michael's College this week. She gave a public reading Wednesday night, sponsored in part by the Vermont Council on the Humanities in conjunction with the college's 75th anniversary celebration.

She arrived in Burlington with her husband in an 18-year-old white Mercedes. For the next 24 hours the air exploded with new possibilities and vast horizons already explored in literature. She had lunch with the top writers in the community. She conducted an open class and she read. The only thing that almost gave out was her voice. The ideas kept coming.

Wearing a blue tweed suit with pearls and a victorian pin, she has

184

a natural exuberance. For years she wore her straight hair pulled back in a bun. She cut her hair after *The Group* came out, which was the same year she bought the 1962 model five-passenger sports car. "They don't make them anymore," she said. The first night she was in town someone offered to buy it.

She really laughed about that.

Sitting in her hotel room with a view of Lake Champlain, she talked about what she'd been doing, about her books, especially her favorite, *Memories of a Catholic Girlhood.*

She has lived in the Montparnasse section of Paris since 1961 with her fourth husband, James West. Last Friday she changed her address from 141 rue de Rennes, Paris, to Castine, Maine 04421.

"Jim retired from the State Department at the end of December. We used to spend summers in Maine, but now we'll be there five months. It's awfully uprooting. There are compensations, but if you've lived 18 years in one place, it feels like home. To me, of course. His work was in an office and it's gone. We've rented our apartment and I'm not acclimatized yet."

Her latest novel is *Cannibals and Missionaries,* which was published in October. It's about a committee of liberals flying to Iran to investigate tortures and illegality under the Shah. It takes place in 1975.

"I have a sense of deja vu about the Iranian situation," she said. "The book was based on an Iranian I met in Paris. And there was such a shaky little committee but it never got off the ground. The Iranians are strangely indefinite, maybe yes, maybe no. If you deal with the Arabs, it is more clear cut.

"The Iranians specialize in cloudiness. I don't watch the news— we have a tiny Sony television that rarely works. But if I did, I would probably recognize Bani Sadr. He was in Paris in the early '70s."

Mary Therese McCarthy was born June 21, 1912, in Seattle, the oldest of four children. Her parents died when she was 6 during the influenza epidemic of 1918.

She and her brothers spent five years in Minneapolis in the custody of a great-aunt and uncle who "had a positive gift for turning everything sour and ugly."

Their clothes were worn thin, the food was terrible (the uncle ate well, however), the children were never allowed to go out to play.

They were beaten with a strap. Twice she tried to run away; both times, they found her and sent her back.

When she was 10, she won a prize in an essay contest. Her great-uncle beat her to keep her from becoming stuck up. Something congealed within her right there.

In 1955, she wrote, "I cannot feel grateful nor do I believe artistic talent flowers necessarily from the wounding of the stem on which it grows."

But five years of misery were apparently crucial in shaping the writer. She wrote it all in *Memories of a Catholic Girlhood*. Louis Auchincloss in his book on women writers, *Pioneers and Caretakers,* thought it was unsurpassed by any of her fiction.

Today, her brother Kevin is an actor. Preston, a former bank officer, has just remarried. The youngest brother, Sheridan, is dead.

"It's interesting how four children developed," she said. "As the oldest, I was furthest from what we might have been. I suffered more but I was less affected because I had another standard, I remembered my parents. My uncle couldn't get to me mentally; I feared him physically."

She is closest to Kevin. "We do a lot of laughing when we think about our uncle, that candy he had in the cellar. We never had a piece."

In the book, she wrote:

"Looking back, I see that it was religion that saved me. Our ugly church and parochial school provided me with my only aesthetic outlet, in the words of the Mass and the litanies and the old Latin hymns, in the Easter lilies around the altar, rosaries, ornamented prayer books, votive lamps, holy cards . . . A desire to excel governed all my thoughts, and this was quickened, if possible, by the parochial school methods of education, which were based on the competitive principle."

It is hard to buy copies of her early books now, although they can be ordered. Second-hand bookshops don't have any by McCarthy. "People don't part with good books like that," said Sallie Soule of Bygone Books.

Mary McCarthy is working on a new book based on lectures she's given on the novel. She likes Tolstoy, Stendhal, Shakespeare, much of Nabokov. Her latest discovery is Victor Hugo. She has just finished "Les Miserables" in French.

She mentions her husband who has gone for a walk. "He's very handsome, isn't he." The two view the world without as something to learn from, whether it's spending Easter in Auvergne ("the most Romanized province in France") or having lunch in the Chicken Coop in Mexico, Maine ("I would trust those people on jury duty").

She remembers being in Burlington in 1949 for a writers conference. "I went to a party and we got into a fight over Alger Hiss," she said.

To would-be writers, her advice is specific. "Read a great deal. Do some reporting, reviewing. Write criticism. You have to be close to 30 before you have enough social experience to write novels."

At the end of the interview, she stood on the steps enjoying the fresh air. She wanted to save her voice for the reading. St. Michael's, founded by the Society of St. Edmund, is a Catholic college. Miss McCarthy, who has lost her faith but feels indebted to her Catholic training for her attraction to Latin, has come full circle.

"I looked at the list of other writers (Margaret Drabble, Margaret Atwood) and decided to come," she said.

The Novelist Mary McCarthy

Joan Kufrin/1981

From a book of interviews by Joan Kufrin, *Uncommon Women*, New York: New Century Publishers, 1981, 73-91. All rights reserved to and reprinted by permission of Joan Kufrin.

She wrote recently, "For both writer and reader, the novel is a lonely, physically inactive affair. Only the imagination races."

Yes, and there's the *fun*! In what other medium is the spectator invited to enter the mind of another human being? Novelists *want* to tell us their secrets, *want* to tell us what they know of life, what they imagine it can be. All of their pasts go into their novels—their educations, their states of mind, their heart and soul. Even what is left out is an indication of what they think is important.

The best novelists are like close friends: They alone can tell you what's wrong with you (or the world), and you don't mind somehow—at least for long. No wonder we feel an intimacy with novelists we trust. How many of our friends always tell us the truth? How many of them don't try to con us a little?

For me, Mary McCarthy has been one of those novelist friends. Though I might not like what she says, she tells the truth. These days, that's important to me. It was important in the early 1960s, when I read her novel *The Group*. I, who had grown up in the cloistered 1950s, gasped. There, in delicious, juicy detail were what lay ahead of me—career, love, marriage, sex, children, and not, I blushed to learn, in that chaste order.

She touched with precision so many of my experiences I did not doubt that she *knew*. All other ramifications of that novel—the shaky premise of "progress," the author's disdain for certain tides of thought that swept over America from the Roosevelt to the Eisenhower years, her satirical treatment of the characters—all this went over my head. All I knew was that I recognized myself in *The Group*.

By 1971, when her novel *Birds of America* was published, I had married and had children. My concerns, which once lay in the dubious realm of self-fulfillment, had switched to the war in Vietnam, the environment, and the loss of individual equality, ironically, in a world where individuals supposedly were seeking it. Splendidly, so had hers, and she told me about them in such a way that I could understand what I thought.

In the intervening years, I met her five other novels, and came across her nine volumes of nonfiction—everything from criticism to reportage on Vietnam and Watergate, travel, and essays. I found that Mary McCarthy not only had opinions on everything—more important, she had ideas, and she wrote about both in a lucid, graceful prose, the likes of which is fast becoming extinct in the English language.

It is to her novels, though, that I find myself often returning. That, and because she thinks of herself primarily as a novelist, is why we visit her in Maine—to talk about the novel, her conception of it, the writing of it, its joys and limitations.

A word about plot, before we begin. Critics have always pointed out that plots are thin in McCarthy novels, as though plot were all. Well, says Mary McCarthy in her latest book, "Ideas are utilitarian. They have a purpose. They are formed in consciousness with a regulatory aim which is to gain control of the swarming minutiae of experience, give them order and direction."

One must, I think, accept *that* idea of ideas if one is to read Mary McCarthy—that we live by ideas, whether we know it or not, and if we understand what we live by, we understand, perhaps imperfectly, what we are doing on earth and what is possible and not.

She is sixty-nine now. The once black hair is mostly white. Her face, nearly unlined, is to me quite beautiful; smiles frequently flash across it while she speaks. When she laughs, her hazel eyes crinkle up and almost close.

She had been ill for several months, and though she is now recovering, she walks slowly and carefully. She is gracious, insists on tea before talk. We sip, thus acknowledging the basic civility of human discourse.

Throughout our conversations, she calls out from time to time, to check on activities of her household. She notices states of comfort, inquires about plane departures and arrivals, and listens closely to the answers.

Her home, which she and her husband, James West, bought

thirteen years ago, is a stunning example of Federalist architecture, built in 1805. It is in a quiet Maine town, on the main street. Vases of brilliant marigolds and zinnias from the garden brighten the rooms. Half the year, the Wests live here in Maine; the other half, now that James West has retired from the Organization for Economic Cooperation and Development, in Paris, his previous station.

Before we begin the interview, a neighbor, who is a poet, drops by to discuss the meaning of a phrase that the Wests' houseguest had been seeking. It seems appropriate. Where most neighbors lend cups of sugar, lawnmowers, rakes, Mary McCarthy lends and borrows words and definitions. After all, words are her tools. Incidentally, she uses only the best for her meanings. Let the reader beware!

When I knew her better, I asked if she enjoyed making her readers run to the dictionary.

"Ha, ha," she had chuckled. "No. I don't do that on purpose. I'm unaware of it. I hear about it from readers who make jokes like 'Do you want to give a copy of the *Oxford Dictionary* with each volume?' But I'm unaware of it."

You really are? You really think we know all those words? I had persisted. I had in mind *hagiolatrous,* which had infuriated me as I bumped into it in one of her books.

"Yes, I do," she had insisted. "One of my problems as a college teacher was always that I couldn't realize that anybody knew any less than I did!" We had laughed merrily, but all that was when I knew her better.

Today I ask, when you, Mary McCarthy, are excited about a novel, can't put it down, breathe to yourself "This is a *good* one," what about it excites you?

The answer is instantaneous. "The way it's written. I don't like the word style very much. But the *way* it's written, when the whole nature of it is right there. Just as what an artist does is right there in the line he draws.

"There are all these other remarkable things that you may get excited about in a novel too—some perception, understanding of the character, even some remarkably intelligently managed plot. But those, I think, are secondary rewards.

"I've got this new book on the novel out [*Ideas and the Novel*]. For it, I reread Stendhal, particularly *The Red and The Black,* and with a quickened appreciation simply for the way it is said, the way it's *written.*

"Such marvelous compression from the very beginning, and how much is got into the crucial chapter—I think it's the third. Everything you need to know and is essential, and at the same time quite amusing, is all got into something like two and a half, three pages. And there it is. The whole history of *Julien!*" She beams.

You wrote once, "The writer, if he has any ability, is looking for the revealing detail that will sum up the picture for the reader, in a flash of recognition." With you, is that intuitive, or must you really search for those details?

"Intuitive. Yet there is a principle of search behind it. It wouldn't come if you weren't looking for it. But it isn't as if you take eighteen possibilities and finally choose the nineteenth. I think just one finally appears, wearing its feathers."

Do you have a sense of wonder at where these telling details come from?

"Yes—but that's part of the *interest* of the whole thing!"

Are there techniques of journalism that the novel should use? Objectivity without judgmental input?

"There isn't any such thing, of course. Even journalists are not objective, and the good ones know they're not. You have to want to be as objective as you're capable of being to do regular journalistic work; but you also must *know* that you are not capable of total objectivity.

"The journalist can't put all details in. He chooses. I think one fault in certain novelists is that they are *too* journalistic, too current. That is, they are too much bent on representing what is the style at a certain moment. I think that's one of my own faults at times, and I can see it sometimes in other people. There's a very hazy borderline with detail, between too much detail, where it becomes journalistic, and too little, where it becomes vague. Gossamery."

I don't want this to be one of those pseudoprofound questions, but I can't think of another way to ask it. What is the reason for a novel? Why do *you* write novels?

Again, there is no hesitation in the answer.

"It's to make something that wasn't there before. To make an object as I might be moved to make some kind of object out of twigs and grass," Her eyes dance.

A novel is more than twigs and grass. I protest.

"The reason for writing a novel, rather than writing an essay or reportage or any of these critical pieces, is purely to make something that wasn't there before. Something that will then be there, as part of the world of objects, created by nature or God or man, that is semipermanent. I think it's some impulse like that."

You never, then, in low times, ever say to yourself, 'What good is a novel?'

"No, because if you don't look at it in terms of utility, then you don't ask what good is it."

I ask her about bad novels, and she tells me she doesn't read any she doesn't expect to like. It makes a lot of sense and saves time.

What about the motive writers once seem to have had for writing novels—that of expressing a philosophy of life. Isn't that one of yours?

"In some of my fiction it certainly was a motive. *Birds of America* and *The Group*. But I don't think it was the primary motive for my choosing to put it in the form of a novel. Or to write a novel. There are other ways of expressing that [philosophy]. But it was certainly part of the motive."

How do your novels start with you? (In her life she has written seven, plus one that is often called a novel by critics but which she calls a "philosophical tale"—(*The Oasis.*)

She smiles at the question, probably because her novels do not come easily or quickly. There was a span of eleven years between the start and completion of *The Group. Birds of America* kept stopping because of the war in Vietnam: in the end it took nearly seven years. And her first novel, (*The Company She Keeps*) was not going to be a novel at all but began as a short story.

"I called it a novel. It was sort of a novel." She laughs. "And the publishers wanted to call it that, and so I was perfectly happy to do so. The stories *were* all connected, but they started out as separate stories. Then I saw the possibility of making a connective narrative out of them, with a certain play between "she" and "you" and "I" as the chief character. (In each story the heroine was written from a different point of view.)

A lot of the critics didn't call it a novel either, and they either hailed the writing as brilliant or damned it as "high grade, back fence gossip," but they didn't ignore the first published fiction of Mary McCarthy.

The writing of that book, interestingly, was not the culmination of any long-time desire to write fiction. Mary McCarthy, up to the age of twenty-six, believed she had no "gift" for creative writing. Her teachers at Vassar had told her that.

"Oh, when I was about sixteen, I tried to write a novel in school. I don't think I called it a novel; it was probably a long story. A romance. Later on, the first things I wrote smelled quite strongly of Henry James. I wasn't aware of any imitation, but reading them later on I could see. I'd been reading a lot of James. It wasn't even with great admiration, but he's very catching.

"Anyway, at Vassar, I was discouraged by my teachers, who told me that I had no creative gift. That I had a very strong critical gift. And I accepted that."

You didn't say to yourself, "They may say that, but *I* know differently?"

"No. I accepted that. For a number of years."

Until she married Edmund Wilson, the noted author and critic, in 1938.

"It was Edmund, who, one week after our marriage, said to me 'I think you've got some creative talent. Talent for fiction.' And so he put me in a little room and shut the door. He didn't lock it," she laughs, "and he said, 'Now why don't you sit down and write something?' So I did, and that's all, and it was immediately published."

Lest there be a writer out there, reading this, who is ready to slit her throat, a little clarification is in order. Mary McCarthy had been writing since her graduation from Vassar (Phi Beta Kappa). Not fiction, but book reviews and theatre criticism for magazines such as *The Nation, The Partisan Review,* and the *New Republic.* For a while she worked as an editor for Covici, Friede, Inc., where she learned to edit manuscripts and to use all the printer's signs, which were "invaluable." She was not paid; at the beginning, for her theatre reviews. "Oh, something like $3, but it was a very, very small amount of money."

Could you support yourself as a writer when you were beginning?

"You mean before I was writing novels? No. I had a little inherited income, not very much, and of course I was married. In other words, I wasn't totally responsible for my support. No, I couldn't have. Before I married Edmund I had the job at Covici, so that between those things I could support myself."

After *The Company She Keeps,* were there any rejection slips?

"I don't think I had anything that got *total* rejection. I would eventually sell it somewhere.

"The thing is that I learned to write, first in school, then in college, and then doing reviews and theatre criticism, so that I knew how to express myself.

"Actually, you do learn quite a bit about building suspense in a short book review, even, so that my experience finally caught up with my technique."

I ask her to tell me about how the series of five articles, known as the "bloodbath of 1935," came about in *The Nation.* She had written the articles to criticize the leading critics of her day and talks about them with great glee, as though they had been done only last week.

"Maybe I was twenty-two, or still twenty-one. I was very young, and I had done a few rather sharp reviews. Actually, it was Charles Angoff, later editor of *The American Mercury,* who had the idea of turning me loose on those critics, who were really ripe for it. Oh, and they *deserved* whatever anybody gave them." She grins with remembered pleasure.

"Everything was being praised. The most awful trash was being praised and others exalted. You couldn't tell what was a truly great book from a truly mediocre book.

"Anyway, Angoff and I had lunch, and he suggested my doing this. I said, 'That sounds like fun. I'd like to.' Naturally, it was a chance to *star!*

"Though *The Nation* wanted me to do the articles, with the usual mistrust of young people, they wanted a "mature" person on the articles, too. They felt they needed an older head. So they put the assistant book editor on the articles with me.

"Her name is on all of them. We divided the research. But when it came to the writing, she developed a writer's block. In the end, she did half of one of the articles, the one on the *New York Times.* And she asked me not to have her signature taken off those articles. It was very important to her status on the magazine. Naturally, I said yes."

Did that hurt? Wouldn't you have rather done them all alone?

"I would rather have done them all. And I would rather have done all the research, too, because if you don't do your own research, you don't know what you might have found. They paid me extra, but that's how it came out."

Do you believe there are born writers?

"Yes!" Emphatically.

You don't believe, then, that novelists are born in the classroom?

"No. Certainly not. A lot of them have never gotten through college. It seems to be rather normal *not* to have gone to college.

"I think one reason you can't teach writing—and certainly not novel writing—is that young people haven't had enough experience. They might have enough to write a short story, but they haven't had enough *worldly* experience. You have to have, for a real novel, quite a bit of worldly experience; know how people behave, how different kinds of people behave; develop a certain amount of judgment.

"You don't need that for lyric poetry or even for some other poetry. Nor for tales, or romances, or some kinds of short stories.

"I took all those damn things in college myself. I wasted months in things called narrative writing and playwriting. I would have been better off taking something where you actually *learned* something, even economics, than taking narrative writing.

"We all wrote these extremely boring little stories in that course. Then, to be democratic, you have to sit around reading and criticizing the other ones' writings, which are even more boring to you than your own. It's an absolute time waster! And could convince anybody that he didn't have *any* talent for writing fiction.

"There are certain techniques that you can learn with poetry— how, for example to write iambic pentameter in verse. But with novel writing, it's a question of experience. You don't have enough experience to write about, you don't have enough distance from your childhood. For there always is a certain well of experience there that's to be drawn on later. But I think you don't have quite enough distance from that when you are eighteen."

Mary McCarthy did not have enough distance from her own childhood to write about it until she was thirty-three (*Memories of a Catholic Girlhood*)—no doubt because the memories of it were so bitter and traumatic.

At six, she and three younger brothers were suddenly orphaned when their parents died in a flu epidemic. The children were sent, abruptly, to live with strangers, a distant aunt and uncle who beat the children both physically and spiritually. Mary, at eight, was beaten by the uncle when she won a state essay contest—to ensure that she would not become "stuck up." Conditions were so terrible that Mary's youngest brother, Kevin McCarthy (the actor), tried repeatedly to run away *to* an orphanage in hopes of escaping that miserable pair.

Finally, when Mary was eleven, she was taken into the care of her maternal grandparents, who had not been aware of the situation. The boys were taken by the other side of the family. In Seattle and Tacoma, she received an excellent education, first at Forest Ridge Convent and then at Annie Wright Seminary, where she was class valedictorian. She graduated from Vassar in 1933.

Memories of a Catholic Girlhood is a chilling, compelling book, because though it throbs with truth and a great deal of pain, it is written coldly, dispassionately. After each chapter, an italicized portion criticizes what has gone before and examines it for accuracy. It is as though the author has stepped outside her writing to criticize what she has written. Why did she use that technique?

"The italic stuff was written much later, when I came to put the stories together, to make a volume. First I had just done them, one by one, and sold them mostly to *The New Yorker*. One or two went somewhere else. Then I decided to put them together in a volume, and doing that I became aware of how far they were from the truth, really.

"I don't mean that they were lies, but they were obeying certain conventions that were more like the conventions of fiction. And that's true of all *New Yorker* memoirs: The writer purports to be able to remember, verbatim, conversations which, of course, he couldn't remember.

"And then also, I began thinking about a number of these episodes, and I talked with Kevin, the oldest of my brothers, and also one of my other brothers, about these events in that household. And we were really trying to reconstruct, just get at the truth, as close as we could, with combining our memories. And I hadn't had any help of that kind when I was just writing them for *The New Yorker*. The idea was to have a kind of critique and the thing itself, at the same time."

I tell her that I think she is constitutionally unable to lie.

"Oh, that's not *true,*" she cries, her voice rising for the first time that day. In your writing, I say, to clarify.

"Not in my writing," she agrees. "I don't *think* so. I try. I try. I've written somewhere that I was such a problem liar when I was a child, that when I finally escaped from this environment, this horrible household that made me a problem liar, something about the joy of getting out of that and knowing that there was nothing making me lie all the time, anymore, that I've rejoiced in the freedom from it ever since."

Once, in an article, you wrote that "a story that you didn't learn something from while you were writing it, did not illuminate something for you is dead, finished before it's started."

"Oh, that I know."

And: "In any work that is truly creative, I believe the writer cannot be omniscient in advance about the effects that he proposes to produce. The suspense in a novel is not only in the reader, but in the novelist himself, who is intensely curious about what will happen to the hero." It seems to me that you are writing as much for Mary McCarthy as for the reader.

"I think every writer must be. There may be some didactic writers who don't have this view. But if you're writing something, even nonfiction (though to a lesser extent), simply to copy out some idea that's already in your head, what's the point?

"The *discovery*. That's the whole pleasure. Both in small things, just the amusement of putting certain things together and the illumination there, and also the slightly larger illuminations that you get along the way.

"I always ask myself questions, in pencil, pen, or on the typewriter, at a certain point, early, after the first chapter and usually again after the second and maybe the third.

" 'What is this all about? What are you talking about?' And I'm usually not sure. I put forward various hypotheses. 'Maybe it's *this*.' It usually comes to me—at least the key, the little germ idea, the seed—in one piece. It isn't a general idea, it's a single image, usually, or a cluster of images.

"*Birds of America* began with something that appears much later in the written book. It was a young man in an Italian hotel room, sort of like a runner. And he's at his door, listening at the corridor to hear when the toilet door will open, to make a run for it while it's unoccupied.

"I wrote paragraphs about that young man. Why it was in a Roman hotel room, I don't know. It all just appeared to me, like that. He was young, he was nineteen, which was Peter's [the main character] age. All that was there. It had something to do with equality, which is basically what's behind *Birds of America*.

"You start with something like that, because it's alive. And you don't question what that means. It's like a little germ culture you put on glass, and then it starts developing. It's only after you've written a chapter that's sort of sprung out of it that you begin to know what it means. You *have* to know before you can get much further. As it turned out, those paragraphs didn't enter the book until Chapter 4. But I always knew they were there and were coming.

"As for general ideas in one's work, I'm sure I don't know about some ideas in my work that other people must be able to see and that I'm not able to. About twenty years after I'd started writing, somebody told me that all my novels were about the idea of justice. I think that's true. But *I* had not thought of it. Nobody is going to sit down and say a thing like that to himself, when he's starting to write something."

Of all her books, *Birds of America* is my favorite. It is about a young man growing up, trying desperately to reconcile the world as it *is* with the world he idealizes. It is a familiar tale of loss of innocence, but with the McCarthy wit, perceptions, and perspective, it becomes fresh and alive.

How long did you carry that "seed" of *Birds of America* inside you before you began writing?

"Maybe I could actually answer that. There was a boy we knew in Paris. He was the son of people of my generation, academics, whom we knew very slightly. He used to come around and see us. He had this terrible apartment. I never was in it, but I heard his descriptions of it, and I can well imagine what that room was like, how dark it was. And he bought a plant. And he used to take"—she laughs with delight—"this plant for WALKS, and that was really the germ of the book.

"That was about 1962, two years before I began writing it. But the idea of equality had been kicking around for a long, long time."

She said that of her novels, *Birds of America* was her favorite also. (She also likes *Catholic Girlhood, Cannibals and Missionaries, The Oasis,* and *The Company She Keeps.*)

Is it your best novel?

She seems surprised by the question and takes awhile to answer.

"I don't know. I really don't think the author is the best judge. I can judge them negatively, but not positively. I just know the ones I *like* best.

"*Birds of America* amuses me, and more than that. I like the hero. I like the idea, the ideas. Well, it's close to my heart."

Could you have written that book if you had not had a son? (She and Edmund Wilson had one son, Reuel, who was twenty-six at the time she began writing *Birds.*)

"No. And I couldn't have done it for a girl. I absolutely don't know why, but I couldn't have imagined a heroine of that age, of that generation."

Mary McCarthy abruptly stopped writing *Birds of America* during the Vietnam war, to which she and her husband, James West, were deeply opposed. It would be nearly five years before she would resume steady work on it.

Those five years were difficult for her and her husband. Their young marriage (they had been married in 1961, she for the fourth time) would undergo one of those rare tests of fire that few of us ever experience in marriage, much less in ourselves. As an intellectual, as a writer, as a "name" long associated with liberal ideas, Mary McCarthy was urgently examining possible avenues of protest to the war. Jim West, though he too opposed the war, was a foreign service officer on loan from the U.S. government to an international organization situated in Paris, where they lived. He had been in government service most of his adult life. For him to publicly oppose the war would be tremendously difficult.

Early in 1966, Robert Silvers of the *New York Review of Books* asked Mary to go to Vietnam to do a series of articles against the war, for the magazine. She and Jim sat down to discuss it. Jim felt that if she went, he would have to hand in his resignation to the State Department. And it was not just his career. He had three children and alimony responsibilities to consider. Mary wrote in the preface to *The Seventeenth Degree,* "There it was. I could not invest his life in my desire to go to Vietnam." She told Silvers no.

Three quarters of a year passed. Absolutely nothing changed regarding U.S. policy. Bombings continued in the North. The war loomed larger than ever. Silvers again asked Mary to do the articles.

One morning in January of 1967, Jim called Mary and asked her to meet him for coffee at the Deux Magots in Paris. She wrote: "I knew he had come across town to say yes."

She asked if he were going to resign. "Hell, no." Jim West had replied. "They'll have to fire me." (They did not.)

Mary wept.

Soon after, she visited Vietnam and Hanoi and wrote two pamphlets harshly critical of the U.S. role in Vietnam. To her dismay— and her publisher's—the *Vietnam* and *Hanoi* pamphlets were virtually ignored by reviewers. Though John Steinbeck, who was pro-war, and Martha Gellhorn had gone to Vietnam before her, hers was an important, eloquent voice of protest in this country, and it should have been heard.

Perhaps the pamphlet format was to blame. The books were purposely meant to be neither hardcover (too expensive for wide distribution) or paperback (too little chance of being reviewed). The long, narrow shape of the pamphlets might have been a mistake, too; they didn't fit in normal paperback racks, and clerks didn't know what to do with them.

To this day, Mary McCarthy has no idea for sure what happened to the reviews.

"It *was* a terrible blow, and I will never understand it. My publishers have never understood it.

"*Vietnam,* the first one, was in a way more controversial, and there was more argument in it addressed to our government than *Hanoi.* It's a fact that the format was unusual, and in this country—I hate to talk against America this way—I gather that if something doesn't fit into the slot, they don't know what to do with it, so they don't do anything.

"It wasn't that they didn't sell at all. They were read to some extent. I know they were. They finally reduced the price and had a student edition. They reached a certain section of the public, but not through normal channels."

I asked her, later, in a letter if she had felt that the novel was not powerful enough as a vehicle of protest. She answered,

> The reason I broke off writing *Birds of America* to go to Vietnam was, of course, an itch to act. But that didn't mean that the novel was not powerful enough for me. It was just that it couldn't do what the Vietnam pamphlets did: argue directly against the war. There was also a more complicated reason for breaking off the novel and getting on a plane, which was simply that it seemed wrong to be writing through the person of a nineteen year old American boy when so many of his age group were being killed there, or fleeing to Canada or elsewhere. Unless I had done something concrete myself, I didn't feel I had the right to go on writing about him and his generation.

Does it bother you, still, about the reviews?

"It's sort of stopped. If I think about it, it does."

We change the subject.

You've written eight novels. Has anything lasted, proven true over the years in the writing of them?

"This business of having trouble after chapter one, after chapter two. [In one article, she called it a "crisis of faith."] You mustn't go on at that point. Ask yourself questions, preferably in written form. Try to understand: What are you writing this about? Don't go on until you've done that. Otherwise, it goes right into the sand."

And: "The novel shouldn't, in my belief, proceed from an abstract idea, but from some scene, or moment, that flashes up before your eyes."

A "crisis of faith" occurred with *The Group*, after the third chapter, she says. So she put the manuscript away and didn't finish it until eleven years later. It was published in 1963. It is her only best seller (190,000 copies in hardcover). A movie was made of it; it's a bestseller in Germany to this day; and she doesn't much like it. I ask her why.

"I'm awfully mean to those girls. I stopped writing it about three or four times over those eleven years. I felt that I was just whacking those girls over the head and making them parrot this terrible nonsense. Not that they didn't, in reality, parrot a lot of nonsense, but it seemed to me that they were rather two-dimensional characters and there was a little more to them than I got in. My method prevented it; something like that."

You were hard on Libby, I thought.

"Well, she *is* awful. And she's actually based on more of a combination than any of the other ones. One part of that combination didn't even *go* to Vassar! But she's the kind of girl or woman that I absolutely *detest.*

"The only good thing about *The Group* is that I think it is quite funny." And she laughs, thinking about it.

After that book was such a massive best seller, was it upsetting to you?

"Well, for one thing, it makes people in your field extremely hostile toward you. It does. It promotes a lot of bitchiness and cattiness. I think it's true everywhere, but certainly true in New York. And it makes you look at yourself in a new way. You were quite adjusted to what you were before. My books, I don't think, ever sold more than 16,000 copies, and that was O.K. I mean I could live on the results, then.

"I don't know. I don't greatly admire this society that we live in. So there is a suspicion that there must be something wrong with either you or what you've created if you're a success in it. And it may be an accident or a fluke, that's what you hope. But you wonder." She stares at me for awhile.

Another day we talk about the writing.

Earlier, you mentioned coming across details, rejecting some but seeing the right one, finally, standing there in its feathers. When your writing is going well, is that the fun of it then? Finding the right detail?

A noncommital uh-*hum*. These uh-hums would surface when it was obvious she didn't agree with what I had said but didn't think it important enough to argue about. For her, *fun,* obviously, is not the best word to describe the act of writing.

She considers this awhile. "Really working out *problems.* I don't mean problems outside, problems on the page. Your own language itself gives you a great many clues as to what you're trying to say. The language you use is, after all, an inherited thing. It's thousands of years old. These words can hold accretion of meanings—some of them not so evident, but slightly hidden and they are why you reject one noun or adjective and take another. In that choice there is some meaning and you may find out something about this meaning in trying to make out why you reject the word 'insistent' and use 'steady', for example."

And when the writing is not going well, what do you do? Do you leave it and come back later, or do you work it out?

"I've always worked it through. *I* can't go on unless I feel tranquil about what's behind me. And it's good to have something steady to walk on, to stand on. So that I go over and over and over, sometimes nineteen versions, variants of one page."

Nineteen, I cry. Give me an example.

"They're *all* alike!" She laughs. "No, not every page. Every novel, yes. But not every page. But it happens quite often, and sometimes it just takes three or four variants. And I can't go on until it's settled.

"And then, I either throw the used ones in the wastebasket, or I keep them as back sheets. Then it's a terrible thing"—more laughter—"to start typing on the wrong side of the page [it looks blank but isn't] and you run into your own rejects! Or, maybe looking for some scratch paper, I get out some of the rejected variants and say, 'Now why did I throw that away? It's *better* than what I've got here!' By this time, I've got so far that I can't get back to the stage where that variant fitted, and so you always have to think that your last impulse was the wisest one. Which is not invariably true, in my opinion. But in writing, you have to think your last opinion is the right one."

If you're sure it's the last one.

"Well, then the next one is the last one."

Do you have to let your writing age—overnight, over a few days, a week—to know if it's really right?

"I usually don't. I usually keep doing these things over and over. Sometimes I think it's finished, and then the next day I look and say, 'Oh, God, no. This is not it.' Or I may look back the next day and think I was on the wrong track and the third try back was better, let's start that over again. But not more than a day, usually.

"When I finally put a novel together at the end, I do each chapter, piece by piece, one at a time. I don't jump ahead as some people do, go backwards and back and forth. And some begin at the end! Anyway, I begin at the beginning and go to the end. Nevertheless, when I read the whole thing through, I may make some very slight changes, cuts, or additions. Or see that this or that isn't clear enough. But not much, just slight changes."

Is there a lot of nontypewriter thinking about your novels as you work on them?

"Sometimes in bed. Especially as a book gets toward the end, there's a certain amount of night thinking, in terms of the characters. It depends on the book. Some of them can get quite hallucinating.

"I felt that awful chief character in *The Groves of Academe* was speaking during the night. Speaking to me or in me, almost audibly. I think I know why that was so because I was trying to make myself into *him*. That is, use some part of myself that was like him in order to make him real. And so I was making these ghastly faces. I do that, when I'm composing, make all these faces to imitate the facial expressions of one or another character."

In 1962, in an interview in the *Paris Review,* Mary McCarthy mentioned a problem that bothered her then—the author's voice disappearing in and being completely limited to the voice of her characters. The author cannot say anything that the characters would not say, and a lot of the novelist's energy is consumed in maintaining the characters *in* character. I asked her about the problem in a letter, later on.

The problem I speak of in the *Paris Review* interview is not that of restoring my own voice to that of the characters but of restoring it directly to the novel. That is, not to speak through the characters but directly through one's own voice, as the old authors did, e.g., Fielding, George Eliot, Dickens.

In *Birds of America* my voice probably does come through in Peter but it's not meant to. The case of his mother is a little different. She is somewhat like me and has quite a few of my opinions so such an effect is natural. I think you're mistaken though, about *Cannibals and Missionaries.* What is coming through Henk is definitely not me; there may, however, be something of a Dutch friend of mine in him. As for Sophie, again, no, although it's true that in her journal she expresses ideas I have had on those subjects. In other words, no, I haven't got the author's voice back into my fiction yet except in a couple of short

stories that will be reissued by Avon with *Cast a Cold Eye* in paperback.

What about droughts and plateaus in your work? Do you run into
them, and what do you do about them?

"Just keep on going. You have to ignore them, even though you're
aware of them. If you listen to that kind of music, then you keep
postponing and wait for a better period which may never come.

"That's what Trollope did in his principle of writing every day. I
don't write *every* day, but the idea is that, good or bad, you *write.*
And if this is your life, and it represents what ability you have, it will
come out, more or less on a level with the rest of your work,
whatever the absolute standard is. I've never had writer's block or
any of that nonsense, no."

When I said I thought too many writers made a fetish out of
writing blocks, she added, "They must be real because too many
writers talk about writers' blocks. It doesn't mean they're imaginary. It
must be some phenomenon that is associated with almost clinical
depression and that's it."

Do you expect that reviewers, when they review your books, these
days, have standards of criticism against which they judge you?

She grins. "I don't know why I expect that, since the practice
seems not to bear it out, but yes, I do."

Does the criticism bother you?

"Oh, I *hate* it. Because, stupidly, I still look forward to reading
those reviews. It's not only that you're looking forward to praise,
that's certainly good also, but *learning* something which you didn't
know before, having some kind of *contact* with some other mind.

"With these reviews, especially the stupid ones, a stupid positive is
almost worse. I mean, it *is* because if it's stupid and negative, you can
write off the negative because this person is just a *fool.*" She laughs.
"Whereas, if it's positive and stupid, it gives you pause!"

Is it harmful to be misunderstood?

"Yes!"

You would rather be not read than misunderstood?

"Oh, who can say? I suppose you wouldn't because that would
mean there was no possibility of understanding. Whereas with

misunderstanding of something that's read, there's always a possibility of correction there. And a new look."

The purpose of criticism is the elucidation of art—

"T.S. Eliot," she interjects.

Yes, and the correction of taste.

"I think that is a *most* snobby little definition."

What is, then, a definition of criticism?

"I hate this sort of Brahmin way of saying it, but elucidation of
works of art is a legitimate function—the main function of criticism.
But I should think if you elucidate a work of art you don't need to
bother about correcting the taste."

Do you think criticism today (as in reviews) fulfills this definition,
that is, elucidation of works of art?

"I think this is a very bad period for criticism. The practitioners of it
are mostly so illiterate today. As far as reviews go, I always feel that
certain reputations *need* deflating. And that should be done by
young people. Nowadays, it doesn't seem to be done by young
people. But the best criticism—in terms of reviewing—is and should
be done by them. It's much *peppier!* But in general, as far as criticism
goes, we're in a new low period.

"Why? I don't know. Some sort of failure of education. You can't
call it overeducation, but it's superficial education. It produces
glibness and false authority. At the same time, people are completely
losing sight of the ability, the power, the faculty of being able to write!

"I've written and spoken so much about this it sort of *bores* me,
but all the *prepositions* are wrong. Prepositions are the joints of
language. They're what hold everything together and what express
logical relations. And nobody has a clue as to what is the appropriate
preposition.

"I corrected something on the phone today for a publisher for a
book cover, a reissue of *Groves of Academe:* 'a witty, wicked
bestseller *on* intellectual life.' I said that book was not a bestseller. I
mean it's just *wrong.* And furthermore, *on* is not actually dead
wrong, but it's *vulgar.* And so we finally changed it to 'the famous
wicked satire on academic life.' Well, at least it's correct. And it
doesn't contain a lie."

Did you *ever* have any doubts that what you had to say was of any
importance? That it was publishable?

"I did earlier. I had started a couple of things. One thing I did when I was married to my first husband was to start a detective story. That was to make money. We were very poor, and I thought maybe I could; I read a lot of detective stories in those days. I got to about Chapter 5, and I hadn't succeeded in killing the victim and so I stopped.

"I threw it away, but I think I used bits of it in *The Company She Keeps.*

"I know if I feel I'm writing something that's not of any interest or nobody would want to print it, I stop, rather than go on and send it off."

After her marriage to Wilson, and the birth of their infant son, did she continue writing?

"Edmund was very good about help. He always insisted that we get a nurse for Reuel, even if we couldn't get a housekeeper or cook. And it was a very wise decision. Because I could do those other things; they are not emotionally tiring, you know, cooking and washing dishes or polishing furniture. Since we couldn't get two persons, the nurse was the important one. He was absolutely right because I could really go in my study and shut the door and work a good part of the day, while sort of seeing to running the house and doing the shopping and preparing slightly skeletonlike meals."

Wilson criticized her work, but more as a husband than a critic.

She laughs. "I always show my work to whatever husband it is.

"Edmund was not overly critical. He was always somebody who greatly encouraged younger people's talents. That was one very good side of him. And he often overrated rather than underrated—not when he was reviewing some book that was already out, but when he was interested in some younger person's writing, a relative beginner."

What do you tell young writers who want to know what you think of their work?

"I don't believe in encouraging somebody who I think has no hope, really. But the mixed cases are rather worrisome, whether to encourage them or not. It's quite hard to judge promise in a writer, and I don't think I'm good at it. Somebody like publishers, editors are much better judges of promise.

"I'm a perfectionist, and so I value that in work that's shown me.

It's hard for me to rate highly work that is grossly imperfect. I can miss the real talent that's lurking there. Also I tend to overrate something that has marvelous turned phrases, even though the central conception may be weak. And I like wit. I probably tend to overrate witty writers, I mean the young ones now."

The second morning we talked, Iraq had invaded Iran, and we discussed the latest news we had heard.

Here we are, talking about the novel and art, and war is beginning in the world again. Does it ever discourage you that the words of men sometimes mean nothing in the face of all that's going on in the world? Do you ever think about that?

She folded her arms and thought about that. Finally, she said serenely,

"That does not trouble me greatly. I have always been sort of skeptical about people who say, 'Oh there's a war on, this is no time for art.' They are usually those awful Philistines who have no regard for art, anyway.

"It seems to me, historically, art has often been a great consolation in times of troubles. But there can also be times when it seems utterly inappropriate. And then, all right. So it can wait."

I asked her if there is something she wished someone had told her before she became a writer, and she said no. That writing was an ideal career. One was free to move about, to practice it anywhere. And then she added softly,

"You deal with things that are interesting. And often with things that are beautiful."

I told her that up to now, every artist in the book had answered the following question in the same way.

Are you ever completely satisfied with your work?

"I'll answer something different then. YES!"

When you finish your work, you say to yourself, 'This is good. This is *it.*'

"I really do. That doesn't mean I'm right. Afterwards I may look on things rather differently, but no, I think it has to be a bit like God and creation. He looked upon it and it was *good!*"

The grin was pure McCarthy.

Mary McCarthy: An American Classic

Cathleen Medwick/1981

From *Vogue*, 171 (November 1981), 283, 291, 292, 295, 297.
Reprinted by permission of *Vogue* (November 1981). Copyright
© 1981 by *Vogue*.

Main Street in Castine, Maine, rolls resolutely down to the bay: a
broad lap of blue water, belted by islands. On top of the hill (uptown,
they call it here) the white houses with black shutters line up to face
the street. Their lawns border neatly on the public province—a
neighborly gesture. Yet every house keeps its formal distance, its
private point of view. It is only as you near the docks that buildings
start to coalesce; a proportionate scaling-down of facades seems to
broaden the thoroughfare, and verticals are leveled by the sea.

In the harbor sits a battleship: the State of Maine, in summer
residence—training ship of the Maine Maritime Academy, quartered
uptown. On a midsummer afternoon, crewing boats circle the iron
hulk, and dip their oars into the bay. Crewmen sit rocking in their
orange lifejackets. One day, they will board their vessel and put out
to sea. Meanwhile, their very presence braces the town. In the early
hours of the day, Castine is roused by the chant of male voices—a
phalanx of young midshipmen marching past the green lawns of the
Academy, marking time.

Uptown, in her kitchen, Mrs. James West ties a brightly striped
apron around her waist and sets about making blackberry ice.

The world knows Mrs. West, by reputation, as Mary McCarthy.
Castine knows her, by custom, as one of the gentry who summer
here. She has been coming to Castine now for fifteen years. The
town seems almost indifferent to Mary McCarthy's reputation—her
power and influence as a literary critic, and her notoriety. The controversial opinions of the author of *The Group*, widely considered the
most "malicious" and "delicious" wit of her day, are not in question
here. More important that she is on a first-name basis with her
neighbors; that she looks and acts the owner of a fine old Maine
house; and that she respects the subtle hierarchies that, in a quiet
New England town, form the backbone of social life.

The Mrs. West of today bears a hazy but decided resemblance to the younger Mary McCarthy. That woman was striking, if not beautiful, with her oval face, green eyes remarkable for their long, sensuous lashes (a McCarthy family trademark), dark hair pulled back from her face into a taut, immaculate bun. Her face, jutting out from its severe hairdo, was almost too distinct; she had a character which, she has said, is germane to "all truly intellectual women," that of a "romantic desperado"—but in the classic vein.

The woman who is now crossing her kitchen with a bowl of blackberries is a rather stout New England matron of sixty-nine, with iron grey hair, sturdy legs, and an alert expression that has not changed, substantially, in thirty years. It is a face that makes judgments. The tomatoes on the windowsill, the flowers on the counter, the hair that curls just so far, and no farther, along her cheek (a recent hairstyle—she got tired, she says, of that bun) seem carefully placed; she appears to be a woman who respects order and civility, especially in small things.

Her husband, James West, is a native Mainer, with prim-and-proper lips and teasing eyes. He is a storyteller, and can charm a room full of people when he wants to; more often, he prefers to be watching her. A diplomat, Mr. West moves discreetly within the aura of his wife's reputation. If she has visitors, he will absent himself graciously, returning later with a bouquet of wildflowers ("I am always well in the wildwood," he says). With a clean cloth, he wipes the dew off the porch chairs.

The Wests' house, built in 1805, is a sturdy survivor of the Federal era. This is a house that bespeaks pride of function; its form is perfectly correct. Trim, spare, shingled, its one ornament is a webbed fan window just above the front door; giving the house the air of a dowager who, by way of dressing for a ball, puts on a single antique brooch.

Inside is a cluster of neat rooms, tucked in at the corners. Privacy before space, manners before majesty; the essential New England style. At the house's center, "morning and evening" staircases meet, suggesting public and private destinations. The back staircase, straight and narrow, is a path to the kitchen and pantry. The front staircase sweeps geometrically upward from the foyer and, at the landing, offers infinite perspectives. It is a proper staircase, taking the measure of its guests.

Mrs. West moves around her house quietly, with an air of determination. Houses such as this, in which each room has a name and a purpose—library, parlor, pantry—enforce decisions; where the tea should be served, where to sit and talk. Social behavior is defined by the modest formality of the downstairs rooms, and their furniture. The tightly upholstered loveseat, tough as a bench, invites a certain breed of conversation; the George II lectern, with its open copy of a large volume called *The Monastic World,* suggests Sundays spent in silent, even-handed pursuits, such as reading, or gardening; the long low bookcase, painted white, proffers (with a becoming modesty) its china dish of potpourri.

Mary McCarthy writes that, as a little girl, she lived in a house where there were always "treats" such as "a glorious May basket my father hung on my doorknob . . . the little electric stove on which my mother made us chocolate and cambric tea in the afternoons"—a pretty world for a child to live in. It was replaced, after her parents' death when Mary was six, by the dark, musty house of her guardians; and, as she points out, the great shock to her was esthetic: "I had been rudely set down in a place where beauty was not a value at all."

Here, in Maine, the beauties are inherited, and not nearly so ephemeral. Things last, and time gives them value. Or the value comes from their homeliness. Incidental objects—milk cans painted blue to match the blue wood floor and made into lamps, or a needlepoint sailing ship stitched by a sailor—have a legitimacy here that they could never have in, say, a New York City apartment; they are, in effect, local color, a sign that the Wests, however Continental their tastes in other things, are also Mainers, or mean to be. Still, there are Louis XVI Directoire chairs in the dining room and, in the hallway, a Venini chandelier.

Most of the smaller objects here, Mrs. West explains, were gifts, and remind her of people she loves. Robert Lowell gave her the chandelier. Hannah Arendt, a close friend, gave her the ancient Persian chalice; her brother Kevin McCarthy, the actor, gave her the Chinese ivory hand. . . . "Oh, Mary," interjects James with his

teasing smile, "I gave you a present too—and I live with you." She
smiles back, and shows it proudly: a sturdy Sheffield inkstand, dated
1895.

The Wests have been married now for twenty years. It was Mary
McCarthy's fourth marriage, his second. His work as a diplomat
(recently retired) based them in Paris, where they still spend most of
the year. In Paris, Mary McCarthy writes all day, until about 7:00
P.M., goes out often. Here in Maine, she says, they lead a quieter life:
croquet on the lawn, breakfast on the terrace. Though the Wests
bring a French cook here with them in the summers, Mary especially
likes to cook—jams and jellies, and that wonderful blackberry ice
with its rose geranium leaves for flavor. "I love recipes that involve
pushing things through sieves," she admits, and that idea makes her
laugh.

It is strangely unsettling to see Mary McCarthy, the sharp-tongued
social critic, puttering serenely about her kitchen. It is like seeing a
lioness who is behaving like a house cat: one wonders where her
claws are, and when she is going to use them. As, with a chummy
nod to James West, she passes confidently out the back door with
her wicker basket to go pick flowers in her garden, it seems
inconceivable that this could be the same woman who once, in
another seaside town, countered an unkinder husband's refusal to
help her out with the garbage by giving him a sharp slap across the
face. It could never happen here.

She had, and still has, a reputation for being a mercilessly accurate
critic. In 1937 she antagonized nearly all of her colleagues by
publishing, in *The Nation*, a series of articles reflecting their lack of
judgment and taste. Retaliation was swift; she became known as
"Bloody Mary," "Contrary Mary." Katherine Anne Porter called her
"in some ways the worst tempered woman in American letters." A
reviewer from *The Wall Street Journal* wrote: "Miss McCarthy doesn't
merely criticize authors and actors—she dices them, shreds them,
cooks them at a fast boil and then leaves them to simmer." Not,
surely, in a country kitchen, with tomatoes ripening on the windowsill
and a pot of blackberries on the stove.

Mrs. West is polite to everyone. She respects the conventions. She
will not woo people, but she will not cut them, either. "We're not
social here like in Blue Hill"—the neighboring town—and yet

relations with the townspeople are good, natural. She is not the first or only famous literary figure to appear in Castine. Elizabeth Hardwick has a summer place close by, near the bay, in that part of town called "the neck." And Elizabeth Bishop lived here before removing to her island solitude, some miles off. When Robert Lowell lived in town, there used to be a French circle that gathered to read Molière, Villon, Chateaubriand. So Mary McCarthy is no stranger here; she is, on the contrary, a proper element of Castine life.

A big-boned, elderly woman in a sleepy bayside town. She writes in this house sometimes, at a prim white desk in her study. A stuffed arctic owl (James West's gift to her after she published *Birds of America*) looks down at her from the bookcase. Sitting here in her nurse-white skirt and navy-blue sweater (the exact blue of her wicker chairs) she is an American classic, an arrangement by Whistler in navy blue and white.

Mary McCarthy at sixty-nine, the author of novels, stories, essays (most recently, *Ideas and The Novel*) and non-fiction works (ranging from *The Stones of Florence* to *The Mask of State: Watergate Portraits*), with a career that spans nearly five decades, may well make a claim to be one of America's most accomplished and respected authors. She can still be startling, as evidenced by the lawsuit waged against her by her old enemy Lillian Hellman. McCarthy's statement, in a rare TV appearance on the Dick Cavett Show, that Hellman is "a bad writer and a dishonest writer" and that "every word she writes is a lie, including 'and' and 'the'" was a classic flourish. It brought Mary McCarthy into the headlines, for the first time in years, and woke up the literary establishment with an honest-to-God issue: whether, in fact, critics have a right to lambaste authors in public. So seriously was this issue taken (every luminary from Norman Mailer to Diana Trilling had something to say), and so outraged were Hellman's advocates, that McCarthy came out of it all looking at worst like a formidable critical presence, at best like an oracle speaking eternal truths.

Yet for a number of years Mary McCarthy has kept a certain distance from American literary life. In the past she relished controversy; now she seems wearied by it. She does not appear to the public often: an occasional interview to promote one of her books, an infrequent article, and that is all. As the Hellman incident proves, McCarthy still has power; but, except for that one lapse (even the New England matron has her wicked ways), she has been reluctant to use it. Shuttling from Castine to Paris, from Paris to Castine, she seems to be a woman who is skirting her reputation, a writer in retreat.

What could she be retreating from—her reputation, created mainly by *The Group,* as a popular writer, and the lingering suspicion, despite the propriety of other works (*Memoirs of a Catholic Girlhood, Ideas and The Novel)* that she is not entirely "serious"? She has, in fact, been consistently serious for years; her recent work has had neither the savage humor nor the forbidden flavor of gossip that made *The Group* such a commercial success. She has stopped writing "sexy" books. She is no longer eccentric (the Vassar girl turned bohemian), and seldom dangerous; it is a rare diplomat's wife who likes to collect enemies. Why, for that matter, should a woman in her sixties, with a life's work behind her, want particularly to be risqué? On the other hand, why should such a woman be so eager to remove herself from her sphere of influence? Whatever the motive, McCarthy has backed off, as far as is reasonable, from the world that attracted and repelled her, and gave an edge to her wit.

She came to that world from a considerable distance. As a child, living in Minneapolis, she wanted to be an actress. Later, in boarding school, she conceived the desire to be a writer, "getting up at four in the morning to write a seventeen-page medieval romance before breakfast. . . ." She was "composing a novelette in study hall about the life of a middle-aged prostitute ('Her eyes were as turbid as dishwater')" when the idea of going East, and becoming a Vassar girl, took hold of her. The Vassar girl, as she soon discovered, "will have chosen Vassar in all probability with the idea of transcending her background." McCarthy not only transcended hers, she erased it. The orphan from Seattle was replaced by a sleek, sophisticated young woman who, in time, became the theater critic for the *Partisan Review,* the wife of the formidable author and editor Edmund Wilson, and one of the most visible literary celebrities of her day.

She wrote, in her fiction, about failed marriages and complicated affairs, about women who were trying to elude the commonplace. The details of their lives were remarkably similar to the details of McCarthy's own life, and these women often resembled her. When

Martha Sinnot, in *A Charmed Life*, defied her husband ("she
immediately distributed the guilt by setting down one pail of garbage
and slapping him across his grinning face") it was hard not to think of
Mary and Edmund Wilson. Yet she herself was wary of these
resemblances; her life, to her, was one thing, her fiction another. She
was careful not to glamorize herself—in print, at least—or to deceive
anyone about who she really was.

Memories of a Catholic Girlhood was a systematic attempt to
extricate the real Mary McCarthy from the mass of uncertain details
surrounding her history. She analyzed her orphaned, lonely childhood, rejecting its pathos; she probed her memory to try to
distinguish the realities of her life from its fantasies. She told each
autobiographical story, then corrected it, separating real memories
from insubstantial ones, and fiction from fact. Coming after a
particularly choice memory, such corrections had a tart flavor, a
cleansing effect. That effect remains the strongest virtue of Mary
McCarthy's writing, though the appetite for it is, arguably, her most
obvious personal vice.

She believed, and still does, that (in Martha Sinnot's words), "the
hardest course was the right one; in her experience, this was almost
an invariable law. If her nature shrank from the task, if it hid and
cried piteously for mercy, that was a sign that she was in the presence
of the ethical." Mary McCarthy continually set herself challenges. She
has not always acted morally, as she readily admits; but she considers
it a moral obligation to answer for her actions. If she has lied or
(worse) behaved in a cowardly way, she is the first to accuse herself.

For a woman so scrupulous about her motives, it would be heresy
to retreat, knowingly, from any situation. When she has retreated in
the past, it has nearly always been because circumstances took her
unawares.

In an essay called "My Confession" (confessing is a kind of legal
skill with her) she tells how Trotsky's fate was decided by his decision
one day to go duck hunting. He got wet during the hunt and caught
the flu, which made him miss Lenin's funeral and the subsequent
political struggle that changed the future of Russia, and decided his
death. "One can foresee the consequences of a revolution or a war,"
wrote Trotsky with an existential shrug, "but it is impossible to foresee
the consequences of an autumn shooting trip for wild ducks." Muses

Mary McCarthy, "It may be that the whims of chance are really the importunities of design. But if there is a design, it aims, in real lives, like the reader's or mine or Trotsky's, to look natural and fortuitous; that is how it gets us into its web." Trotsky shrugs, McCarthy investigates. She is shrewder than he is.

She is always trying to foresee consequences; it would not be in her nature to do otherwise. One of the stories she tells in *Memories of a Catholic Girlhood* is about a decision she once made, as a student in a convent school, to lose her faith. The motive, as she says, was attention-getting: if she could claim something so outrageous, the older girls would notice and admire her. "'Say you've lost your faith,' the devil prompted, assuring me that there was no risk if I chose my moment carefully. Starting Monday morning, we were going to have a retreat, to be preached by a stirring Jesuit. If I lost my faith on, say, Sunday, I could regain it during the last three days of retreat, in time for Wednesday confessions."

But for Mary McCarthy, with her Catholic's instinct for renunciation, this retreat became a spiritual crisis: she really did lose her faith. Having lost it, she felt, and still feels, obliged to live with the consequences. "Unregenerate," she calls herself, and that obstinate refusal to take the easy way out is, with her, a point of pride. "If," she writes, "the kind of God exists who would damn me for not working out a deal with him, then that is unfortunate. I would not care to spend eternity in the company of such a person."

McCarthy seems, to her admirers, an extremely forthright woman, exacting and scrupulous. To her critics, she seems devious and vindictive, and a sham. That is probably because her actions do not invariably match the standards she sets for herself and for others. Nevertheless, as Doris Grumbach puts it in her biography, McCarthy is, in spirit, "the reformer who is willing to discard the baby in order to be permanently rid of the bath water."

In general, McCarthy assumes, she will tend in the wrong directions—a Freudian transcription of original sin—but her better part will object, and hopefully in time. "The moral part of her," Martha Sinnot (Sin-Not) realizes, "seemed to square its shoulders dissociating itself from the mass of weakness that remained. . . . The lawgiver was impractical, a real lady, disdaining to soil its hands. . . .

Martha could have laughed aloud, except for the pride and awe she felt in the acquaintance."

Mary McCarthy seems, at this point of her life, to be living fairly comfortably with the lawgiver, the lady. She has become cautious, and she tends to measure her words. She is writing more slowly now—not, as she points out, because of age; because of perfectionism. That she should have gravitated toward Maine, where pride, willpower, and stubborn speech are a form of good breeding seems, upon consideration, natural. If she has retreated from the world she knew, she has probably by now understood her motives, and corrected them. The reasons for leaving are not, necessarily, the reasons for staying away.

She seems, in some ways, a size too large for this daintily proportioned part of the world—the "'stranger to this ground'" as Grumbach has called her, "orphaned, excluded, the Westerner come East, the Catholic among Protestants, the end girl of the rooming group, the American abroad." A Western-born woman, her feet are built for long strides. Here, she measures her steps. She fits into this decorous space the way an ingenious salesman will fit an oversized foot into a shoe, making everything "snug." She moves discreetly here, because here the oldest definitions apply: it is only by tucking in tight, by pinching around the edges, that civilized life takes shape.

Mary McCarthy is a proud woman, with a grim (if ironic) sense of mission. New England offers a context for that stripped-down pride; it is America without varnish, without excuses. And Maine, that proud syllable, is New England unregenerate; propriety with a sheet of snow, legitimacy with a widow's walk, morality with an evergreen tip.

If she has retreated here it is, possibly, another kind of retreat—the military kind. Castine, in Colonial days, was famous for it: the kind of retreat armies make when the old position becomes untenable, to realign themselves on new ground. There is the sense, with Mary McCarthy, of a shoring up of forces—against age, or her own rebellious instincts. Perhaps living with a diplomat has helped: to a certain extent she has learned the art of equivocation. That is an art of survival, at its best.

She is, in some real sense, an American classic. If she was ever propelled by ignoble impulses, she has since made them honorable.

Her ancestors were "wreckers," land pirates on the Nova Scotia coast who lured ships to their destruction. Grumbach calls their descendant, Mary McCarthy, a wrecker too, and rightly, because that is the impulse that produced some of her wickedest work. Those pirate ancestors gave birth to solid citizens, and wrecker Mary McCarthy finally became legitimate. That is in the American tradition, the legacy of scoundrels to their heirs.

She is walking toward the camera now with slow, even steps, her arms swinging military style, between twin rows of plantain lily down her front path—Mary the martinet. She even favors, in her clothing, regimental stripes, echoed by the upholstery on her furniture. Her posture is excellent. She is wearing long white stockings with dark, buckled shoes, like those worn by the founding fathers whose enormous cartoon portrait hangs in her front hall. She is, consciously, her own ancestor. Her own uncompromising judge.

Mary McCarthy 'Set the Standard' for Distinguished Visitors

Dixie Sheridan/1982

From *Vassar Views*, 67 (April 1982) 1,2,4. Reprinted by permission of Dixie Sheridan.

"Mary McCarthy set the standard for what I know will be a long line of Distinguished Visitors. The program exceeded our highest expectations and was an exceptionally exciting week at Vassar."

That was President Virginia B. Smith's assessment of the inauguration, in February, of the President's Distinguished Visitor program, which is designed to honor Vassar alumnae and alumni and to offer students the example of persons of genuine achievement.

Arriving at Vassar directly from her Paris home, Ms. McCarthy plunged into a week of activities, starting with a welcoming party that was already in progress at Pratt House, her residence for the week.

Ms. McCarthy, a Phi Beta Kappa graduate with the class of '33, was a highly visible figure on campus, working far more than a 40-hour week. Ms. McCarthy spent 13 hours working with nine different classes. These classroom visits, along with several combined classes and luncheon and dinner meetings, brought a total of almost 200 students and 21 faculty members in close and personal contact with the Distinguished Visitor.

On Tuesday, her third day on campus, she was greeted by a crowd of 350 students and faculty members who gathered in the Villard Room to listen as Ms. McCarthy fielded questions raised by the audience and by faculty panelists Thomas Mallon, assistant professor of English; David Schalk, professor of history; Brett Singer, visiting lecturer in English; and Peter Stillman, associate professor of political science. Ms. McCarthy began the program with a reading from her book, *The Mask of State: Watergate Portraits*. Although a number of her 20 books deal with political and social issues, Ms. McCarthy said that she was "not political at all" during her years at Vassar. "I was a royalist, actually," she quipped. "Of course, you can't really be a royalist in this country . . . that was my tragedy."

She recalled with particular relish, however, discovering John Dos Passos's *The 42nd Parallel* in Rose Peebles's course, Contemporary Prose Fiction. Inspired, Ms. McCarthy read all of Dos Passos's works in the Vassar library and was "set on fire" by what she found, especially his pamphlet on Sacco and Vanzetti, which she termed "brilliant."

"Elizabeth Bishop ('34) was to the Left of me," she said. "Later in life we reversed roles." Hitler and the Depression politicized the young Mary McCarthy, but she resisted the temptation to use her fiction as her forum. "The novel is not the right place to deal with political emergencies," she said. "I think it's a very inappropriate place to deal with such things."

Ms. McCarthy delivered a major public lecture entitled "Some Narrative Techniques and Their Implications" in the chapel on Wednesday evening before a capacity crowd of 1,300 that included special guests of the college from the Poughkeepsie community and several members of the class of 1933. Using as examples works as diverse as *Don Quixote, The Captain's Daughter, Silas Marner, Lolita,* and her own *Memories of a Catholic Girlhood,* and writers ranging from Faulkner to Joyce to Hardy to Saul Bellow, Ms. McCarthy set up criteria for distinguishing three forms of fiction: the tale, the romance, and the novel.

Just prior to the lecture, President Smith presented Ms. McCarthy with a hand-cast sterling silver medal commissioned especially for the Distinguished Visitor program from Elizabeth Jones '57, the chief sculptor-engraver of the U.S. Mint. The medal, measuring 2¾ inches in diameter and suspended from a rose grosgrain ribbon, is a bold architectonic rendering of Taylor Gate. An open book, a symbol of learning as well as of Ms. McCarthy's art, is shown on the reverse.

A press conference on Thursday gave the world outside Vassar the opportunity to hear from Mary McCarthy. The press conference was followed by a luncheon for the Distinguished Visitor and alumnae journalists, at Alumnae House. Articles and photographs chronicling Ms. McCarthy's week at Vassar appeared in *Time, Newsweek,* the *New York Times,* the *Poughkeepsie Journal,* and several other publications.

On Friday, still energetic and gracious despite her grueling week, Ms. McCarthy joined three Vassar faculty authors, Beth Darlington,

Walter A. Fairservis, Jr., and Donald J. Olsen in an autograph party at the Vassar Cooperative Bookshop. The bookshop sold more than 350 volumes of Ms. McCarthy's works, and she signed nearly 500, adding a personal message in each.

Later that afternoon, Ms. McCarthy's son, Reuel Wilson, a professor of Slavic languages at the University of Western Ontario, flew in from Canada to join his mother for the weekend and for a party in her honor at the president's house on Saturday evening. Vassar music faculty Blanca Uribe, Carol Wilson, and James Armstrong performed works by Purcell, Scarlatti, and Mozart in an after-dinner musicale. The evening, and Ms. McCarthy's week as the President's Distinguished Visitor, ended with a champagne toast and thanks from President Smith.

Ms. McCarthy later wrote of her week on campus, "My New York stay was pale in comparison with Poughkeepsie . . . it was an unbrokenly splendid time."

The eminently quotable Mary McCarthy left the campus a storehouse of new treasures. All who heard her have their favorites.

—"I think what one has written takes precedence over what happened."

—"I couldn't stand my narrative writing class at Vassar. It was so boring. We all wrote the same thing and then had to read what each other wrote. I think we hadn't had enough experience to write a story—our experience was too fragmentary. We did better in English 105 where the assignments were freer. I remember Miss Kitchel saying, 'Girls, hand me your effusions.'"

—"I don't know about taking notes. I almost never took notes in class. It keeps you from remembering. It's like using a camera; it's bad for the visual memory."

—"I don't go out to lunch—that's my one rule."

—"I can't go on to page two until I'm satisfied with page one—like having something solid to walk on. So when I'm finished, I'm finished except for a little tinkering."

—"It's harder to write fiction. I probably feel closer to my fiction. When fiction is finally done, it has more of oneself in it."

—"It is better to go outside than inside when you're young, but don't look at subjects as subjects of writing. It's gone once you look on it as a subject for writing. Instead, try to render it as it was/is. Doing portraits of people is a good exercise, just as if this person were sitting for you. It's very hard."

—"I think I'm getting on another Flaubert binge. Two years ago it was Victor Hugo. Tolstoy I can read over and over, forever. Stendhal, Shakespeare, George Eliot. Jane Austen is much more re-readable than Eliot. Next maybe Conrad or *Moby Dick*.

—"I didn't want to teach. I didn't want to do journalism. I didn't particularly want to write, although I knew I could do it—it's something that came with me. I wanted to be an actress."

Seeing Mary Plain

Thomas Mallon/1982

From *Vassar Quarterly*, 78, No. 3, (Spring 1982), 12-15. All rights reserved to and reprinted by permission of Thomas Mallon.

I had known the face, and in a way we'd known each other, for ten years, but we'd never met. I'd known it from dust jackets and magazines, and as she came through the door of Pratt House at 7 p.m. on Sunday, February 7th, directly from Paris to a welcoming cocktail party, I took pleasure in seeing she was beautiful in the way she was supposed to be: the smile flying towards the gray hair, narrowing the green eyes above the definite nose. After ten years of waiting to see McCarthy plain, it was a relief to find that she wasn't. It would have defied all I knew about her; it would not have made *sense*, and sense (not sensibility) was a value I had learned from her books more than anyone else's. So I took pleasure in discovering that this bit of the world had tested out and measured up. My first sight of Mary McCarthy was, appropriately enough, a triumph of reason.

And her own of me was a bit of the same. As we stood, moments later, in the living room, I approached her. She took in my age, perhaps the traces of an Irish name in my face, whatever seemed plausible inference from the thesis I'd once written about her, the letters I'd sent and she'd answered.

"Miss McCarthy, I'm Tom Mallon."

The smile snapped up like a shade. She put out her hand: "I guessed!"

I overrated innocence—ethically, psychologically, erotically—even before I lost it; that's one of the reasons it was so difficult to shed. But it went, and much of it went in a season: the summer of 1973. I had just been graduated from college, winning prizes for the achievements of a mind I feared was more nimble than deep; bearing a fellowship to Harvard, a place I did not want to be in the fall; worrying about my father, who was in the hospital beginning the seven long years of his dying. I was at the beginning of a very bad year, although I didn't yet know how bad. I took the prize money and

223

went to Paris, where I decided I would solve my perplexities about myself and the future. All ribs and hair, I bicycled about the city, trying to "find" myself in a place where there was no objective reason to look for it.

Except perhaps—for a piece of it—on the rue de Rennes. That was where Mary McCarthy lived, and, since I was going to be in Paris after graduation, she had invited me to visit her. The invitation had come after she read my senior honors thesis: "Excited Scruples: Ideas of Human Responsibility in the Writings of Mary McCarthy." *All* the writings: in the summer of '71 I'd read a new novel called *Birds of America* and then gone on to her fifteen other books. They dealt with what that novel I'd read had been about—namely, politics, manners, ethics, literature, travel, art, human oddity. I had a rather Joycean notion that a senior thesis should encyclopedically touch on as many genres as I'd been exposed to in the past four years. Long before it was time to pick a subject, I became convinced that Mary McCarthy was the only feasible one. I asked Elmer Blistein, my Shakespeare professor at Brown, to be my advisor. As knowledge and English departments are organized, this proposal made little sense, but he agreed, not because he took me seriously, but because he still loved the Renaissance idea of polymathy and knew my chosen author had it.

A year later the thesis had gotten me my honors. Mary McCarthy read it, liked most of it, and sent me her best: "I wish you luck for your future. Do you plan to be a writer? Critic? Novelist? Poet? Teacher?"

Five good questions. I don't remember exactly, but I think I probably hoped she could help me answer some of them.

But when I came calling on June 14, 1973, Mary McCarthy was not at home. She had gone to Washington to cover the Senate Watergate hearings. Her not being there was a disappointment whose intensity I can't convey clearly, because it was partly a function of that awful summer. A few weeks later I was back in New York; she sent a note thanking me for the verbenas I had left with the *gouvernante*.

"I love emergencies," she says. Several instructors are in the Alumnae House pub having dinner on Tuesday evening, and she is explaining how she negotiated the municipal chaos of Paris in May

1968. By now we're friends; Mary has been here for two days and this is our fifth encounter. She has already visited two English classes, a philosophy seminar on her friend Hannah Arendt, had lunch with students in the English department's creative writing courses, and— just before dinner—been part of a gathering in the Villard Room, "open to the entire college community" and billed as a discussion on current politics and literature between Mary and several members of the Vassar faculty. As hundreds of people drank tea, videotape cameras turned, and photographers moved about, she began the event by reading from *The Mask of State,* the Watergate book that took her away from the rue de Rennes nine summers ago:

"If the various Watergate inquiries, trials, civil suits, and grand jury hearings are, as I feel, steps toward purgation, cathartic efforts, on the part of the country as a whole, direct expiation is being suggested, though, only to those pale or pink-faced young men, wearing earnest glasses, who have appeared before the Ervin Committee. It is as if they were expected, through type casting, like little oblates, to expiate all the nation's sins against its own conception of itself."

She then entertained questions about the present American mood, and whatever hopes she had for the future. Most of those hopes had until recently been settled on Poland. They had not been extinguished, but were now more difficult to hold. As for America itself: "I feel very, very discouraged about this country." I knew what she meant, but I wondered if for once she hadn't picked the best word. The energy of her answers somehow contradicted the faintheartedness of "discouragement." Pessimistic, perhaps; but too endlessly interested, too quick and too unappeasable, to be discouraged.

She responded to a question about why she had turned to journalism rather than the novel where Vietnam and Watergate were concerned by saying that the novel is not well suited to political emergencies. I think about this later in the pub when she talks about May '68, and once more when she is at the last stop on Tuesday's rounds: a visit with students in the department's expository writing classes. This is not one of the week's high points. By now it's past eight o'clock in the Old Faculty Parlor in Main, and the participants seem a bit too tired to allow this particular occasion to reach a critical mass. I ask Mary why she will invariably be called a novelist before anything else, even though she has probably written more words of "expository" prose than fiction. She says she understands the tendency to rank fiction as a higher art than nonfiction, and indeed tends to view her own novels as her most important work. I smile, and because I'm tired, nearly laugh: it's not the answer I'd been hoping she'd give a class of non-fiction prose writers. She's unloaded my question.

As we leave the room, and walk along the second floor of Main, she asks me what time students go to bed nowadays. Very late, I tell her I suspect. I also think that she probably needs sleep herself. I wonder if we aren't scheduling our Distinguished Visitor like a minor candidate in the New Hampshire primary. But she has refused to strike anything from her itinerary.

And at 11 p.m. on the following day, after visits to Twentieth Century American Literature and an interdepartmental course in the use of literary manuscripts, and after her lecture in the filled chapel on "Some Narrative Techniques and Their Implications," she is back in the Villard Room at a reception. Students circle her and ask questions. She answers them with seriousness and engagement. She is clearly enjoying, not just enduring, this. There is a rightness to the whole picture. The bordeaux ribbon of the medal given her in the chapel even matches her dress.

On Thursday, Mary and I are sitting over plates of pasta. She eats with more zest and discrimination than I do. We have been here since seven thirty. I am supposed to be conducting an interview, but it is past ten and I haven't asked any questions. I have, in fact, brought no pencil and paper to the table. Mary and I have become friends over the last few days, and the idea of interviewing now seems a way of becoming less, rather than more, acquainted.

So, instead, we talk. Conversation moves in its associative way from the small to the sublime and back. We talk about cities (she can't go to London with the same feeling now that Sonia Orwell has died), Maine, the Irish, my father, changes in the Vassar curriculum (the healthful reintroduction of a foreign language requirement). We pick up the threads of two conversations we've had earlier in the week: one about Diana Trilling's book *Mrs. Harris* and its peculiar phrase "moral style," the other about Keats's Odes, which I'd been teaching to freshmen in the afternoon: " 'Beauty is truth, truth beauty.' " We agree that the two ideas are different, and that "moral style" is a bad phrase, but we part company over one implication of Keats's line. She thinks there is a connection between beauty and goodness. I say I doubt this: what about people? Yes, she says, you would probably find beauty in those you knew were good. I hesitate, and then say that finally I can't agree: one would be seeing what one wanted to see. Later on I'll think again about this and be sad to realize that I believe what I said, and deeply, too.

She's down to smoking two Lucky Strikes a day. (The other night at dinner she said that the press corps at the war crimes trial of Captain Ernest Medina had warmed to her when they discovered she smoked that serious, filterless brand.) I get her a light, and use the opportunity to ask her about something that has been on my mind since Sunday.

"You didn't like it when I offered you my arm the other night," I say, laughing. I had extended it to her while we were navigating an icy path to a car door. I had wondered why she didn't want it: some sort of vanity? No: I have heard her attack the myth of the pleasures of aging. A sense of the gesture's outmoded gallantry? No: the only uneasy (but, finally, hissless) moment at the Tuesday symposium had been her pronouncement: "I'm not a feminist."

She looks at me kindly, as if afraid I may have been hurt by some misinterpretation, and explains that for the last year or so she's had some trouble with her balance that a doctor only now seems on the verge of pinning down. When, to my presentation of an arm, she'd responded, "Well, if it's out, I suppose I'll have to take it," she hadn't been irritated by my offer, just reflexively determined to oppose by herself this condition that's been bothering her. She explains how she and her doctor have just about reasoned their way through to what the trouble is. She enjoys this explanation, as well as the probability that her deductions are going to be proved right. For a moment the physical irritant has become an intellectual pleasure.

I finally give in to asking an interviewer's question—the wholly unimaginative one about what it feels like to be back at Vassar. She tells me she has enjoyed the week, has been charmed by the students. "One girl came up to me at the entrance to the library and said, 'Your eyes really *are* green.' She said I'd referred to their being green in one of my books, but when she'd seen me the day before she thought they might be hazel. But now, she told me, she saw they really were green."

She likes this story, and I like it, too. She tells me that she feels it probably would not have happened elsewhere than Vassar—not, say, at the University of Maine, where she was writer-in-residence last fall. The spontaneous presumption of it seemed to show that the girl was embracing her as "one of the family."

"It's all here—even my automobile accident!" It is Saturday morning in Pratt House, and the sun is coming into the living room. Tortoise shell glasses are over the green eyes now, and Mary is looking into her college records. The dean of studies has sent the folder over from the basement of Main Building. Mary wants to look through it as part of the research for what her publisher calls an "intellectual autobiography." The automobile accident is preserved in an administrator's note to professors asking that Mary McCarthy be excused from classes for several days.

"German!" she says, in amused amazement. She is reading a letter she wrote in 1929 to Helen Sandison, who at that time was chairing the committee on admissions and would become her favorite English teacher. It lists the things she hoped to study at Vassar; as things turned out, it would be decades before she got to German.

The folder yields up the mail of half a century ago: a brief letter from Harold Preston, Mary's grandfather, requesting application forms, seems to bear all his civic rectitude in its pledge to get the papers "properly" on file. A Vassar warden's report, a picture of Mary at Annie a letter of recommendation above a woman's Scottish surname. "That's Miss Gowrie," Mary says, handing me the letter and identifying the passionately disciplined schoolteacher in *Memories of a Catholic Girlhood*.

Mary selects the materials she wants copies of. She is pleased with the trove and content to close the folder. Her eyes, throughout its examination, have been keen with an unsentimental avidity.

Now, though, the tortoise shell glasses have come off, because we are saying good-bye and taking pictures. It is cold on the porch, but we are without coats for the sake of the photographs. The five of us here permutate for the different cameras. Reuel Wilson, Mary's son, is with us, and in a gesture that breaks through some momentary shuffling and indecision, Mary draws him to her right side and me to her left. She puts her arms around us both, we smile, and the picture is taken.

After seven days—and ten years—of knowing her, I wanted to tell her something grateful and inclusive. But sense came to my rescue and I made a simple good-bye. We said we would see each other again. I kept it simple because I realized that there is no quick and accurate way one can thank someone for some of whatever clarity one's mind has, much of whatever feeling one brings to books and politics—and the sustaining revelation that there will never be anything so glamorous as the grammar of a sentence.

The Unsinkable Mary McCarthy
Carole Corbeil/1982

*Her perspective is always feminine: Antigone grown up,
her absoluteness not diminished as she takes on sex. She
has never been easy on herself or her characters, or tried
to make anyone look better.*
—Mary Gordon in a review of Mary McCarthy's latest
and, according to Miss McCarthy, last novel, *Cannibals
and Missionaries.*

Mary McCarthy, who is taking part in the International Authors'
Festival at Toronto's Harbourfront, is now 70 years old. Her face is
the face of a woman who has led, to borrow a title from one of her
novels, *A Charmed Life.* It is remarkably unlined, at once intelligent,
mischievous, and subtly demanding: it is either the face of someone
who has never had to lie, or hide, or suffer for very long, or a face
blessed by remarkable genes. "I like life," she says, toward the end of
the conversation, "I have always liked it." She stops then, to point at
her forehead. "Not up here, of course, I haven't always liked it up
here."

Her fiction (from *The Company She Keeps* to *The Groves of
Academe* to *The Group,* to name a few), and her critical and political
essays (*The Writing On The Wall, On the Contrary:* Articles of Belief,
Vietnam, Hanoi, and the recent lectures collected in *Ideas and the
Novel*) have always been informed by a highly moral point of view.
Satirists are always closet moralists, and Miss McCarthy is no
exception. Morals, however, like anything else, are subject to change,
to the whims of fashion, and Miss McCarthy's particular brand of
morality, has, in recent years, fallen into desuetude.

In describing her Protestant grandfather, who, "was much more
admirable than all of (her) horrid Catholic relations," Miss McCarthy
is describing what she has strived to become: "He was scrupulous,

230

with a very active conscience, but he was also remarkably tolerant and unbigoted." A Christian who does not believe in God, Miss McCarthy has exercised her active conscience on Vietnam as well as on Watergate. In fiction, this lofty aim is often reduced to penning malicious portraits of hypocritical intellectuals who are led astray by wanting to control the world, but Miss McCarthy has always held her standard of integrity with aplomb.

In the thirties, when she entered the literary world of New York as a recent graduate of Vassar, she was often called a blue-stocking. (Today, incidentally, she wears beautiful white lace stockings: one of the advantages of living in Paris, she says. She divides her life, which she shares with her husband James West, between Paris and Maine.) The stylish, lucid, and often vitriolic drama reviews she wrote for the Partisan Review are still remarkably readable, and it is obvious that, right from the beginning, she never allowed such condescending epithets to cramp her style. She was not, she elaborates, ever trying to cut a figure; venomous *bon mots* came very naturally to her.

She has never felt disadvantaged by her gender, and has always been attached to the esthetics of domesticity. "If you're the exception," she says, speaking of that time, "like the exception Jew, things, rather than being more difficult, are actually easier. I don't think there ever is discrimination against exceptional people, you see. It's the average person who has to contend with discrimination. And exceptional people can always escape, even if it is only into their dreams. I suppose average people can also escape into their dreams, if they have any. I'm sure they must, but I can't speak from experience there."

She had always wanted to marry. That she has married four times, she says, laughing but emphatic, is obvious proof that she is the marrying kind. "I like to serve," she says. "Obviously, I don't like serving 100 per cent of the time. Some men like to serve, too. In any case, that's the way I am. There is this terrible virus of the notion of equality which has crept into the race, which has destroyed possibilities of happiness for so many people. You're not supposed to serve now, you're not supposed to look up to anyone. I think it is a marvellous feeling to look up to someone. Right now I feel terribly deprived. So many of the people I looked up to have died."

Edmund Wilson was *not* (the emphasis is hers) one of those

people. Miss McCarthy, who was married to the late pre-eminent American literary critic for seven stormy years, says that if anything, he looked up to her. "He admired my literary gift. He was very good that way. He was an admirable public person, but not an amiable private person. He loved talent and encouraged it."

The story that Wilson at one point shut her into a room and demanded that she write fiction is true. "One day he just sort of harrumphed and said you're limiting yourself into this critical trap, drawing up every play that comes your way. You've got to write fiction. He put me in this little room and I wrote the first story of The Company She Keeps, and in a sense I've never looked back."

Wilson may have been personally detestable, but Miss McCarthy says with some admiration that when their son was born (her only child), he was the first to suggest that they hire a nurse so she could go on writing. "That really freed me," says Miss McCarthy, "rather than hiring a cook, or someone to clean."

She began The Group, which was published in 1963, in 1952, and it was written in fits and starts between other books. "My publisher had the first two chapters locked in a drawer for years. The chapter where she loses her virginity was considered unpublishable." What initially stopped Miss McCarthy from going on with the novel was "this feeling that I was being too cruel to those girls. I kept punishing them, banging them into the ground." Every once in a while, however, she would look at early chapters and think them quite good.

It was not until she met her current husband (he was married, she was married, they were waiting for a divorce) and followed him to Warsaw, that she managed to finish the novel. (She has been married to West for 21 years now, which she considers to be quite a coup. "Things have always cracked for me after seven years. Multiples of seven also do it, like fourteen or twenty-one). Did her critical faculties ever block her fictional facility? "No. Maybe it has, but I didn't feel it. It was marvellous preparation. Criticism teaches you to express yourself clearly, with some pungency, it teaches you to organize your emotions."

Apart from her Western sense of Christianity, which she says has clearly dominated her thinking, Miss McCarthy says she "inherited an abhorrence of the will from reading Shakespeare. I am against vows, against the will as it manifests itself, and vows are a way of turning the future into a project. In Shakespeare, there is this great suspicion of abstraction, of the works of the will. He is always on the side of fools, of nature, and nature is the force which is always giving the will its come-uppance.

"The idea that people of intellect are admirers of abstraction is totally wrong, I think it is probably the opposite. In Shakespeare, in Tolstoy, there is this great tenderness for the concrete, for life, which I find admirable." Outsiders might regard her as a willful person, but Miss McCarthy protests that she is dominated by what she calls "negative will," a kind of negative will power which she has had to fight all her life. Although not compulsive, what she wants is often "bad for her," she says, and she has to trick herself into action, such is the weight of her lack of will.

"Hannah Arendt and I used to talk about the will, about this aspect of the will. She was always at home with thinking but not with willing. She developed this concept of the anti-will, which immediately creeps in when you will something. But I don't think that any writer has ever dealt with this subject of the will in its purely negative aspect."

The only way, she says, she has ever been able to come to terms with it, is by using "a recipe," she "learned from Kierkegaard a long time ago." Miss McCarthy was teaching at Barnard at the time, had a child of 7, and found it tremendously difficult to motivate herself "domestically." She had been reading Kierkegaard's account of how he broke his engagement to a woman so he would be free to marry her. (He never did marry her, but that's not the point.) "So," says Miss McCarthy, "I applied the Kierkegaard principle to doing the dishes. I would sit in the kitchen, and decide not to do them. As soon as I did this, they would do themselves. You have to be sincere, to truly decide not to do something, though, otherwise it doesn't work."

Miss McCarthy is now working on an "intellectual autobiography." She says she's too old to write novels. "I don't notice things any more, what people wear, the way they talk. It's just a fact. I don't think anyone over 60 has ever written a good novel."

Mary, Still Contrary

Carol Brightman/1984

From *The Nation,* 238 (19 May 1984), 611-618. Reprinted by permission of *The Nation.* Copyright © 1984 by *The Nation.*

Brightman: When you left the United States in 1960 was it because you felt you could no longer function as a writer in America?

McCarthy: I don't know if it was hard to function as a writer, but as a person, yes. I think there was a certain flight. I don't know if it was from America or from New York intellectual life. Before Jim [West] and I were married we were living in Warsaw, never sure we would ever get our divorces. I would have these dreams where we're sitting there in Warsaw, and we know a few Poles but we hardly see anybody, and I'm reading Hegel. I'm just sitting there reading Hegel. I really did develop a kind of horror of the sort of tinniness of New York intellectual and literary life.

Brightman: Did something happen around the end of the 1950s that made it difficult to be a part of that life?

McCarthy: What happened, of course, was the whole McCarthy period and the reaction to the McCarthy period, and both were terrible. The McCarthy period itself was worse, but the counter-hysteria was also sometimes very false and self-loving. I was involved with Dwight Macdonald's [*politics*]. That had died. A great many things had died. Then I tried with some other people to start a magazine [*Critic*] that never got off the ground. *Critic* was a reaction against the McCarthy atmosphere and *The Nation, The New Republic* and *The Reporter.* They were just so dead, so weak and timid. A combination of hysteria and cowardice. I did some work for *The Reporter,* and I know how cowardly Max Ascoli was.

Brightman: In her book about you, *The Company She Kept,* Doris Grumbach described *Critic* as politically "middle of the road." What does that mean?

McCarthy: I don't know what that means. It certainly was to the left of *The Nation* and *The New Republic,* but we weren't all of the same views by any means. It had Nicola Chiaromonte, who was to

234

me the most important figure, and Dwight McDonald and Hannah
Arendt and Arthur Schlesinger and Dick Rovere. They were certainly
much more classically liberal, but they were also independent.

The problem for the new magazine, of course, was to get money.
We figured we could do it for $28,000 a year. We had something
quite inexpensive in mind. But as soon as I started trying to raise this
money and seeing all these people, we immediately got involved in
something much more expensive, because nobody would give me
$1,000 unless I wanted to spend $50,000, and so our budget went
up.

It was not going to be only political; there was going to be quite a
strong cultural side—looking into phenomena that hadn't been
looked into, like Levittowns, for example. And *The New Yorker*
wasn't doing that kind of journalism then. Now it's more or less all
been done.

Anyway, I finally succeeded in getting promises for about $60,000,
and by that time I was completely broke. I had spent the whole
winter working on this, so I hadn't earned any money. And I quit. It
was all this business of pledges. The strange thing was that the only
people who were truly helpful were Republicans—whereas the
Democrats, they were awful. I remember when I first met with
Marietta Tree, her opening remark was, "My dear, I'm flat as a
pancake!"

Brightman: Meaning what, that she was—

McCarthy: Broke, yes. I was eating all this rich food and drinking
cognac with these people and they were telling me they didn't have
any money.

Brightman: Did you see working on this magazine as a way of
making a connection between your writing life and your social
concerns?

McCarthy: I've always had quite an attraction to communal
enterprises and things guided by friendship, or I used to have
anyway. And I thought we were going to have an awful lot of fun
doing it. Then the usual thing developed; people became very
hateful. I got word from Alfred Kazin that my quitting had been a
betrayal. He hadn't done one thing; he hadn't given us the price of a
postage stamp. So I went back to writing. I was working on *A
Charmed Life* and doing magazine pieces like "My Confession,"

which was a reaction to [Whittaker] Chambers. When we didn't get anywhere with the magazine—and all that disappointment with the Democrats—I suppose that was very offputting.

It was shortly after that that I got into doing the European books, the art books. That began in 1955. The Venice book [*Venice Observed*] happened by chance; then I did the Florence book [*The Stones of Florence*] on my own initiative. I had an absolutely marvelous time. I was very happy through all that. That was when I discovered what sculpture was all about. I discovered the ideas of art.

Brightman: What was it that you discovered?

McCarthy: That sculpture is civic: these are the pillars that uphold the civic life. Painting has a thin and flimsy quality by comparison. It has this element of witchcraft. Hannah Arendt was very helpful in these discussions. We used to go down to Princeton and listen to the Gauss lectures—she had given one set—and come back on the train, and we would have a lot of conversations on the difference between painting and sculpture. Until then, I had much preferred painting to sculpture.

Brightman: Do you still feel that way about sculpture?

McCarthy: The trouble with modern sculpture is that when it's bad it's so ugly; it's so big and ugly, much more so than painting, whose very flimsiness makes it somewhat harmless. There are a lot of those columnar and pillarlike forms in Brancusi's work at the Guggenheim, and suddenly you see all this and its relation to the idea of a republic. I think I am really a republican—I mean with a small "r." I've never liked those late Medici. I like old Cosimo, the most democratic of the Medici or at least the simplest in his manners.

Brightman: Wouldn't you describe yourself as a democrat with a small "d" for the same reason?

McCarthy: I've tried all my life to be a democrat, but I think I'm really a republican in this sense: I believe in the institutions of a republic, the protection of laws, starting with the protection of the rights of the individual. I have a great suspicion of the demos. Society needs the protection of institutions. Of course, things can reach a point where an outbreak of democracy is terribly exciting and liberating and oxygenating. But it doesn't seem to work out very well at the stage we're living in now.

Brightman: What stage would you say we are living in now? The institutions of this country seem very weak.

McCarthy: We're not living in a republican society at all.

Brightman: Certainly. But it's not a demos either.

McCarthy: It's more a demos of the belly. Even that isn't democratic, or rather it's not egalitarian, in that everybody is fed up to here, but the quality of what he's fed differs greatly. It's terrifying. There is satisfaction delivered in the form of cars, television and the usual packaged foods, convenience foods.

Brightman: That's just a holding action, don't you think?

McCarthy: No, I think it's forever. I've been going to super-markets all my life and I've always wanted to write an article entitled "Let Them Eat Cake." Marie Antoinette had the right idea, from the point of view of those in power, about what to do with the plebs. Anyway, your heart leaps up when you see somebody taking out a bag of oranges.

Brightman: I read your essays in *The Seventeenth Degree* when they were first published in *The New York Review of Books;* I read them again recently and it seems to me they stand up as the only writing about Vietnam that actually shows Americans who the North Vietnamese leaders were as individuals. "To this fastidious man," you wrote of Pham Van Dong, "bombs were a lowgrade intrusion into the political scene, which he conceived, like the ancients, as a vast proscenium." I think you captured his conservatism and audacity perfectly.

McCarthy: I suspect that Pham Van Dong's ascendancy at the time that you and I were there* had a lot to do with the fact that he was really the carrier of Ho Chi Minh's values and that with the death of Ho Chi Minh, Pham Van Dong became something of a figurehead. I haven't seen any of the Vietnamese that I used to know for years. They used to look me up in Paris, but I don't think they come there anymore. The last time I saw Nguyen Minh Vy was at the time of the carpet bombing when I went out to see what one could do, and he was rather ironical. I wanted to go to Hanoi and get bombed—

Brightman: What year was that? 1972?

McCarthy: Yes. I wanted to go to North Vietnam, and I was trying to get the Pope to go. I thought it would be great if the Pope got hit by an American bomb, and I don't mean it against the Pope, really. I was also trying to get the bishop of Harlem to go. I was trying to get various Americans to go but not one would touch it. It was like that magazine, exactly, a real *déjà vu.*

Brightman: People were retreating to their burrows then, weren't they?

McCarthy: And they had the most terrible excuses. Granted, it was a rather chimerical project, but you couldn't get one taker. Anyway I did go to see Vy and he said, "You don't want to go to Hanoi, you want to go to the White House." At any rate, in a few days it was over. And so, where are we?

Brightman: By your own account, Vietnam certainly succeeded in setting a great many American intellectuals into a kind of action we haven't seen since. It seems a long time ago. Getting back to your supermarket, I wonder if we've reached a stage where consumerism has become a substitute for either civic life or political life?

McCarthy: For a while the uprisings in Poland seemed to break that mold. Something could happen there. Poland was always my other touchstone. That's where Jim and I met, and before we got married I kept going back to Warsaw; we would have lived there, except things worked out differently. It wasn't the best period then, but a good deal of the spirit of the 1956 revolution was still there. The people had a marvelous sense of freedom which was electrifying, and they were fearless—unlike the Russians, I must say. The Poles believe that they're very prudent and cautious but they are not.

Brightman: That seems to change when they come to America, doesn't it?

McCarthy: The ethnics. The ethnics certainly do not seem to be a courageous people. It may be only the intellectual class who are—except that those young workers [in Solidarity] whose pictures appeared in the paper, I've never seen such handsome young men. Maybe it has something to do with not having all those consumer goods. You know, we haven't had a worker in this country that looked like that in fifty years. Railway men used to be very good-looking in this country, very handsome. And an occasional telephone lineman.

Brightman: Twenty years ago I did a masters thesis at the University of Chicago about three woman writers who greatly interested me. One of them was you, and it was *Memories of a Catholic Girlhood* and early stories like "The Man in the Brooks Brothers Shirt" that set you apart as a master of observation whose writing nonetheless honors the unruly truths of the heart. Today it seems to me that your essays about Vietnam possess both qualities in equal abundance, while a recent novel like *Cannibals and Missionaries* seems more remote from immediate experience.

McCarthy: Actually what I put in that novel was a real experience of trying to get a delegation to go to Iran.

Brightman: You mean that trip really happened?

McCarthy: Yes. But in actual fact it was to investigate torture. There was this character who came to see me in Paris and stayed on my sofa for about six weeks with his folders, and I was writing all these people like Ramsey Clark and Bishop Paul Moore. All that was true, including the fact that the committee that he talked to me about turned out not to exist—like the disappearing rabbi in the novel. One's life does tend to repeat, yes.

Brightman: Still there is something missing for me in the novel. I was caught up with your writing at times, with the feel you had for the female academic for example, the older one, Aileen, and with the way you just let people *be* by showing how they moved or how they talked. But then when they all got blown away I didn't feel any concern.

McCarthy: Well, you're not meant to.

Brightman: You're not meant to?

McCarthy: Not really.

Brightman: Are the characters meant to be less real than characters in other novels you've written in recent decades?

McCarthy: I would say that Peter Levi is more real in *Birds of America*. That's the one that's closest to the Hanoi experience, both in time and everything else. I interrupted *Birds of America* twice, first to go to Saigon and then to go to Hanoi. I said to myself, How can I be writing about a 19-year-old boy, draft-bait, and this war is going on and I'm not doing anything! So I felt I couldn't go on; it would be too false to be close to the hero, or think I was, and just be writing a novel.

Brightman: When you were in Hanoi you told Pham Van Dong that you were not sure you could write a book, yet with all your furious note-taking it seems to have written itself. You could not hold yourself back.

McCarthy: That was the thing. I got back to Paris and wrote "Hanoi" right off, which is what I did after Saigon too; only it was during the events of 1968 in France, and I had the most terrible time getting the copy out to *The New York Review.* Nothing was functioning in Paris, and I was just shut up in my apartment, without electricity sometimes. But I was working very fast against time to get that out—except the final chapter, which was written more slowly.

Brightman: How do you feel about that writing today?

McCarthy: I haven't reread it since it appeared in *The Seventeenth Degree.*

Brightman: Here's an observation you made in the book, and I'm curious to hear if you have anything to add: "Since the 'brand' of radicalism we preferred had no appeal for the masses (only the C.I.A., as it turned out, was interested), we had no clear alternative but to be 'believing' socialists and practicing members of capitalist society."

McCarthy: That's still true. Perhaps I'm a little bit less believing, and more practicing.

Brightman: I'm curious as to whether you have given any thought to what that contradiction means.

McCarthy: I thought that somehow this experience in Vietnam was going to change my life. I didn't go there with that purpose, but while I was there I thought it would. And it did not.

Brightman: It didn't?

McCarthy: No. It sharpened some perceptions for a while and then they wore off. It flared up again with the Christmas carpet bombing in 1972, then it vanished and I went back to writing a book about the Gothic and I went on an English cathedral tour, taking notes.

Brightman: Have there been other events that brought you to that pitch and that did in fact change your life?

McCarthy: Yes, but those are intellectual things that haven't changed my life in terms of where I live or how much money I have. One was my friendship with Nicola Chiaromonte which I think was probably *the* crucial event in my life. It was not a love affair in any

respect. I met Nicola Chiaromonte around 1943 through Dwight
Macdonald on the Cape.

Brightman: I don't know Chiaromonte by the way.

McCarthy: He was an Italian anarchist, fought in the Spanish
Civil War, was in Malraux's air squadron, and in *L'Espoir* he's the
flyer or mechanic who's always reading Plato and who's very
awkward. Both parts are very true to Nicola's character. Then he
came to America as an antifascist refugee during the fall of France,
and eventually began writing for *Partisan Review, The New Republic*
and Dwight's *Politics*. In the Spanish Civil War he became completely
disillusioned with the idea of war as a means of solving anything
political and became an anarchist/pacifist and worked with left-wing
anarchist groups in France.

Brightman: Was it a core of ideas or a perspective on history that
he passed on to you?

McCarthy: It was a kind of seriousness, a kind of thoughtfulness.
The summer after I left Edmund Wilson, Reuel [her son] and I lived
in Truro, and the Chiaromontes lived not far from us; we used to pass
their cottage on the way to the beach and we had many beach
picnics and talks at night by the fire. I was going off to teach at Bard,
to begin to make my living. I was going to teach the Russian novel.
And I was translating Simone Weil that summer. It was all part of the
same ambiance. We talked about Tolstoy and about Dostoyevsky,
and the *change* from someone like Edmund and his world was
absolutely stunning.

Nicola did not like Dostoyevsky and he had an absolute passion for
Tolstoy. Anyway we would talk and it had never occurred to me
before to think of those two writers as anything but two writers—as
Edmund would have looked at them. One might have said that of
course T. was a much better stylist and D. wrote bad Russian and so
on. But that was a completely empty literary point of view by
comparison. And in some way a self-satisfied point of view: it really
didn't involve thinking about what these writers were saying! Talking
with Nicola Chiaromonte was an absolute awakening, and I never got
over it.

Brightman: Was that really different from the way Edmund
Wilson looked at things in *To the Finland Station?*

McCarthy: Well, yes. I don't want to put him down too much but he had no moral core, Wilson—or any of those people around *Partisan Review.* It never occurred to them that there should be a connection between what they read and wrote and their own lives, how they were living and what they believed in.

Hannah Arendt, she is the other person in my life who, I would say, made a change, but not so dramatic.

Brightman: She lectured at the University of Chicago when I was a graduate student, and I used to sit in on the Eichmann lectures. It was very exciting then, that kind of passionate intellectual involvement with the world. Later I felt she got herself stuck behind a kind of elitism that allowed for very limited behavior on the part of different classes and groups.

McCarthy: I really do not think there was any elitism in her. I think that what you mistake for classes in society in her work are categories. She was corseted in her own categories. She seemed to need them to be able to think.

Brightman: It's in *On Revolution* that that rigidity comes out.

McCarthy: I think that's her weakest book.

Brightman: It's not really about modern revolution. It's more a classical treatise on the idea of revolution.

McCarthy: Yes, of course. There are wonderful things in it, but she thinks that revolution should only make political change, not social change. What is a revolution if it doesn't make any social change? I don't think she ever faced the contemporary fact that you can no longer separate these categories.

Brightman: Have you interested yourself in any feminist issues that have come up in the past twenty years?

McCarthy: It just does not say Hello to me at all.

Brightman: Really? Because it comes wrapped up in too much righteous rhetoric?

McCarthy: That too, but there are a lot of things that come wrapped in rhetoric besides feminism. I certainly don't like the tone and the shrillness and the self-pity. I loathe the emotion of self-pity.

Brightman: It's very dangerous in personal life.

McCarthy: But I'm sort of Uncle Tom from this point of view; I'm quite aware of that.

Brightman: You mean you've made your way in the world of men?

McCarthy: Yes, yes. Or I'm an "exception Jew."

Brightman: You never realized you were inferior? (laughing)

McCarthy: No, I've always liked being a woman. I had a lot of trouble, especially with Edmund Wilson.

Brightman: Did you have competition problems?

McCarthy: No. He was excellent on that score. It was that he was a terrible bully and a tyrant and paranoid—a rather pitiable man in a way, like a minotaur. But in terms of work he was marvelous. He made me write. I would never have written fiction, I think, if it hadn't been for him.

Brightman: You never had trouble working after you had a child? You never got caught up in that ancient history that overtakes you when you're a mother?

McCarthy: I did sometimes, but Edmund always insisted that I have a nurse, and sometimes we had a cook.

Brightman: But you were never limited by the expectations or training or socialization of being a woman?

McCarthy: No. I think it may be because I'm an orphan.

Brightman: Because you had to make your own way as an orphan first rather than—

McCarthy: As a girl.

Brightman: There were also some men in your life early on who supported you.

McCarthy: My grandfather was absolutely marvelous.

Brightman: And even argued with you.

McCarthy: Yes, and wanted me to do what I wanted to do. He liked that and respected it. I've had very good luck in men, and most of the men I've known have been like that.

Brightman: How is it then that in so many of your stories the relations between men and women are so embattled?

McCarthy: Really?

Brightman: It comes out most strongly in the early short stories in *The Company She Keeps*, and in *The Group*. There's such a frustration with the limited rituals of behavior that exist between wives and husbands in particular.

McCarthy: Well, that's just bourgeois marriage!

Brightman: But that's basic to feminist literature, and you've described that piece of life with as much clarity and horror as anybody else, yet in your public life as an essayist or speaker, you have made no pronouncements.

McCarthy: I think feminism is bad for women. I mean, it induces a very bad emotional state.

Brightman: Which is self-pity?

McCarthy: The self-pity, the shrillness and the greed. There's an awful greed and covetousness there too. And what else? I've never met an intellectual woman who was a feminist—except my friend Barbara Deming. And she's a lesbian so it's a little bit different. And she's such a dear feminist, she's not really as militant as she ought to be from her own point of view.

Brightman: What was the trouble you had with Edmund Wilson?

McCarthy: He was very hard to oppose because he was so stubborn and so mean and violent when drinking. When I inherited a little bit of money from the McCarthy family—and I was earning a little bit of money from my writing—he made me put it into his bank account. And, of course, I couldn't have signature power on his bank account. I had to ask him for a nickel to make a telephone call.

Brightman: That's pretty incredible.

McCarthy: The signature power idea gave him the horrors, but it sort of did me too, because if it was a joint account and I was putting my own money in and he had signature power, that didn't look too good to me either. Anyway, I fought. I finally thought it was absolutely mad. Maybe I was going to a psychoanalyst at that point who said that perhaps I could have my own bank account, though usually they tell you to avoid change in your life arrangements. I took a stand and Edmund gave in and I had my own bank account and that was the end of it.

Brightman: Well, a good part of feminism is rooted in that kind of frustration in personal relationships.

McCarthy: I don't believe in equality in personal relationships, whether it's between two men, whatever. It's absolutely meaningless and silly.

Brightman: What about the public issues that have been fought over during the last twenty years, the right to a legal abortion, for example?

McCarthy: I'm for that. But that has nothing to do with feminism.

Brightman: Can you explain why it doesn't?

McCarthy: To me, it's just a question of freedom. If men could have abortions I'd be for that.

Brightman: Who wouldn't?

McCarthy: No, of course I'm for free abortions. I had quite a lot of abortions and I think they are rather damaging psychically, but that doesn't mean that I think people should not be free to have them.

Brightman: Yet you're detached. It surprises me somehow that you are not stirred by the struggles of women to change the laws and institutions that hem them in at a time when both domestic and economic responsibilities are theirs.

McCarthy: I've always liked being a woman. And it seems to me that one of the problems of a lot of feminists is that they don't like being women.

Brightman: What has being a woman meant for you?

McCarthy: I like the so-called domestic arts, cooking and gardening. I like clothes very, very much. I'm not interested in makeup or beauty aids but I am interested in beauty, let's say. I'm so happy that I don't have to dress like a man. What makes women want to get into pants all the time I don't understand! I also like the social gifts that women develop, almost as a species I would say, which are the gifts of observation and analysis. I think that does come from their historic position of having to get their way without direct—

Brightman: Confrontation. We have to know what we're up against.

McCarthy: Yes. And I like both the male voice and the female voice.

Brightman: There's not much of a feeling in what you've written for children, or for the experience of being a mother.

McCarthy: No, I enjoyed that. It's so far away now. I've never been mad about children. But certain specific ones I have liked.

Brightman: Did you see the French documentary that was made a few years ago about Simone de Beauvoir?

McCarthy: Yes, I saw part of it in Paris.

Brightman: She's asked why she never had children, and she says that given the conditions that mothers face in this society—limited child care, little help from fathers—it's impossible to be a writer and have an independent existence and follow one's curiosity and have a child, period. I was moved by that because theoretically she was correct—I know that from hard experience—but nevertheless one does those things.

McCarthy: Of course!

Brightman: You take on life even when it's—"wrong." I agreed with her and yet I was repelled. For a woman who thinks of herself as a leader of a women's movement, hers struck me as a strange kind of statement. I suppose she was just making a pronouncement out of her own experience.

McCarthy: I would think that the reason Simone de Beauvoir didn't have children is that she was really a shriveled up old maid.

Brightman: Really?

McCarthy: Yes.

Brightman: What is it about her that you don't like?

McCarthy: Everything. How *dare* she talk about injustice to women when she has put herself on the map solely by attaching herself to Sartre, *soley. Sartre et moi.* He made her. She's not utterly stupid; she would be a good "B" student somewhere in the intellectual world, maybe not even a "B" student. It's bad enough that she has cribbed from him, but when you add to it this language about the oppression of women, and how as a woman she's deprived—

Brightman: I've not heard that language.

McCarthy: She doesn't say Sartre deprived her of anything; I don't mean that. She speaks of herself as deprived because of her sex, discriminated against and so on. In fact, she *made* it through her sex by attaching herself to this man, and many others of us have made it through our sex; but it's most ungrateful in her case. (laughing)

Brightman: You mean to bite the hand that feeds her?

McCarthy: I've only met her once but I gather she's an absolutely horrible person; she's extremely jealous. Nathalie Sarraute claims that she would not permit Sartre to see her. They were friends, and he wrote an introduction to one of Sarraute's books. According to her,

Simone de Beauvoir permitted him to have those little girls because it didn't threaten her position, but Nathalie was her own age and a highly intelligent woman with an original mind. Anyway, according to Nathalie, she broke them up; and it happened not only with her but with other intellectual women. Sartre by all accounts was a very sweet and kind man, and in some way he pitied this woman.

Brightman: De Beauvoir?

McCarthy: Yes, for her limitations and perhaps for her greediness and ambition—that I don't know.

Brightman: It's hard to imagine that they could have maintained the relationship they did over all those years—

McCarthy: Don't you think some relations are maintained through pity?

Brightman: Yes, perhaps in marital relations where there's a real dependency that gets under way, but Sartre and de Beauvoir maintained a different kind of arrangement with much more tension in it. What did they call it? "An essential love with contingent love affairs."

McCarthy: I think the only way that he could stay with her was to have pity for her.

Brightman: Is that widely believed in France?

McCarthy: No, that is my opinion. She has a great cult in Paris. But she's not well liked, let's say, outside her cult of feminists, and not by all feminists either. I can't stand the way she writes; it's so dull. And I think there's also some element of a blackmailing soul in her. The way she puts out damaging things—about Camus, for example, or about Merleau-Ponty.

Brightman: You don't object to her being a fighter—

McCarthy: No, she's a dirty fighter.

Brightman: I'm interested in knowing what the cutting edge will be in the intellectual autiobiography you have begun to write.

McCarthy: I don't know; I hope that in some way this interview may be helpful. It has to be honest. It cannot start from a pinnacle of complacency. The very idea of writing your intellectual autobiography implies that it is a success. You know, look how I evolved, and now here is where that idea of mine—now in full panoply—was born. There's a danger there.

Brightman: Is there a parable or a moral that you start with?

McCarthy: No, I'm going to try to find that. I want to bring out something American also. I don't even know how American I am— I suspect I'm very American.

Brightman: Do you think an intellectual history will help you do that?

McCarthy: More than?

Brightman: A social history?

McCarthy: No. It will be about people. The first sentence is about the time I first became conscious of the fact that there was such a thing as an intellectual.

Brightman: When was that?

McCarthy: I was about 14. I knew that there were people who wrote books, there were artists; but the idea that there was such a thing as an intellectual had not crossed my horizon until I was about 14. It was a young man. He was quite a bit older than I was, but by chance I knew him and had a kind of girlish crush. He was actually very darling; he was a campus intellectual and edited the magazine.

Brightman: You began to see that as a possible avenue for something to be?

McCarthy: I just became conscious that there were these people and that they were different from other people.

Brightman: It sounds like the style will be very much like *Memories of a Catholic Girlhood.*

McCarthy: Yes, yes.

Brightman: And you will be studying where ideas started—for you—but starting with the social experience. That sounds exciting.

McCarthy: And it will contain a lot of portraits, some of people that nobody has ever heard of and some that are well known.

Brightman: And what interests you is to see if in doing these portraits, bringing these people alive—some of them are probably dead, right?

McCarthy: Most of them are dead.

Brightman: That you will find out more about what they had to say.

McCarthy: Yes, and about how ideas develop in this country. I think there is in my mind an American tincture to this.

Brightman: Something along the lines of *The Education of Henry Adams?*

McCarthy: There's quite a bit of complacency there.

Brightman: I don't mean the content of it but the idea of looking at one's education as a way of understanding one's place in the world.

McCarthy: Yes, yes. And you know, I think that getting to know Hannah Arendt and Nicola Chiaromonte, and becoming very close to them—probably that was Europe! You know, I've never thought of that until this minute. Hannah and Nicola had one striking thing in common: they were both Europeans. They both were Platonists too, incidentally, or Socratics, rather. And when I was talking before about the radical difference I felt with Nicola from what I was used to with Edmund and his circle, what I was listening to on the beach was Europe.

Brightman: You don't think you're coming full circle to becoming a royalist again, do you?

McCarthy: No, no! I realize that I'm extremely conservative.

Brightman: God and the king are dead.

McCarthy: I think I've always been extremely conservative. I feel I'm the only one! I mean, the idea that someone like William Buckley is a conservative is just totally laughable. Nobody who believes in the capitalist system can possibly be a conservative, because it's a contradiction in terms.

Brightman: Why is that?

McCarthy: Because of the growth ethic that is built into the system. Everything has to be in continual growth and presumed evolution. A true conservative wants to preserve something resembling a golden age. Not only would he be against nuclear power—that goes without saying—he would also have to be against crossbreeding.

Brightman: Crossbreeding of what?

McCarthy: Plants.

Brightman: Do you think there is a "golden age" in your memory?

McCarthy: Not in *my* memory. But I think we were in much better rapport with nature, certainly, in the past. Some things have obviously been gained. Maybe the vacuum cleaner is an improvement. But I think air travel is absolutely ruinous. Aside from getting us into wars, it distorts our relationship with nature. And I think our perception of the world and our values stem absolutely from the possibility of some reasonably true perception of nature—which is gradually disappearing, and will soon become impossible.

McCarthy Is Recipient of MacDowell Medal

Samuel G. Freedman/1984

From *The New York Times,* 27 August 1984, Section C, 14.
Reprinted by permission of *New York Times* (August 1984).
Copyright © 1984 The New York Times Company.

PETERBOROUGH, N.H., Aug. 26—Mary McCarthy, literary lioness, received the Edward MacDowell Medal here today for her career as an author. She proceeded to show that, at the age of 72, she still has her growl and her claws.

"As a person and a writer, I seem to have had little effect on improving the world I came into," Miss McCarthy said in her acceptance speech at the MacDowell artists' colony here. "I can see deterioration in every area of life. The belief in progress that animated my youth has vanished."

The only exception, Miss McCarthy went on, is in the invention of labor-saving devices, all of which she appears to abhor. In her rambling, 20-minute acceptance speech, she reviled Cuisinarts, word processors and credit cards. "The more labor, the better," she said. "I like labor-intensive implements and practices, even if I cannot persuade anyone to agree with me."

That would hardly mark the first time Miss McCarthy has staked out the unpopular position. Her opinions have ignited so many artistic and political brushfires over the decades that she once kept a file folder in her Paris apartment labeled "Controversy."

Miss McCarthy assailed J. D. Salinger when he was at his height and defended James Farrell when it was chic to dismiss him. She was a stout anti-Stalinist from the time of the Moscow purge trials, yet she remains far to the left in American politics and visited North Vietnam during the war.

And in the incident that brought her perhaps more fame than any of her books, Miss McCarthy was sued for libel by Lillian Hellman in 1980, after calling her "a bad writer and dishonest writer" on "The Dick Cavett Show." Miss Hellman's $2.25 million suit never reached trial before her recent death, but it polarized American intellectuals, revived the split between American Stalinists and anti-Stalinists of the 1930's and cost Miss McCarthy $26,000 in legal fees.

Still, Miss McCarthy declared in an interview here Saturday night that she regretted none of it. She added that had she known in advance that Miss Hellman also had received the MacDowell Medal, in 1976, she would "probably not" have accepted hers today. (But she also pointed out that the MacDowell Medal—instituted in 1960 in memory of the American composer and given to such luminaries as Aaron Copland, Georgia O'Keeffe and Thornton Wilder—went in 1964 to the critic Edmund Wilson, her former husband, giving the honor credibility with her.)

"I'm absolutely unregenerate," Miss McCarthy said of her comments on the Cavett show. "I suppose that if I had thought about it, I might have. . . ." She paused. "No. If someone had told me, 'Don't say anything about Lillian Hellman because she'll sue you,' it wouldn't have stopped me. It might have spurred me on. I didn't want her to die. I wanted her to lose in court. I wanted her around for that."

On the literary front, however, Miss McCarthy expressed some regrets, both about her own stature with critics and about what she considers a decline in literary standards since her days of setting them on the Partisan Review.

"I felt at that time that we were fighting the literary battles," said Miss McCarthy, "and we expected someone else would pick up the weapons. But no one did. We were trying to insist on artistic standards—trying to deflate what we considered false reputations—and we were pretty good at it. No one ever took our place. If it was J. D. Salinger, no young people would criticize him. It had to be me."

Miss McCarthy herself has been a prolific writer—with more than 20 books of fiction, essays and reportage to her name—and yet, today's recognition notwithstanding, she has not generally been accorded a place in the pantheon of American letters. Her last two novels, *Birds of America* and *Cannibals and Missionaries,* both received tepid responses, and many of her earlier novels, such as *The Group* and *A Charmed Life,* were labeled roman à clefs—or, as one critic once put it, "clever, malicious gossip."

"I think I've gotten a raw deal, especially on the last two novels," Miss McCarthy said. "When I was in Paris, there was a French student who was doing a thesis on the literary criticism of my books. She went through all the clippings I had in my attic and showed me the results. I had thought my press was better than it actually was."

But she continued, "Who's going to esteem you—that's the question. To be disesteemed by people you don't have much respect for is not the worst fate."

In part, Miss McCarthy said, her combative streak derives from her Irish ancestry. She also had to become a fighter and a survivor in childhood, when, after the death of both her parents in 1918, she was placed in the household of cruel guardians. And finally, she speaks of the thespian blood in the family. Her brother Kevin is an actor, and Miss McCarthy said she held ambitions for the stage until her boyfriend savaged her performance as Leontes in a college production of *The Winter's Tale.*

Now, there are a few signs of slowing down, or of summation. Miss McCarthy is recovering from surgery on her scalp—a subject on which she will not elaborate—and wore a cloth hat to cover it today. She had to deliver her address from a chair. And her current project is a self-described "intellectual autobiography" tentatively entitled *How I Grew.*

But if anyone expected a humbled dowager today, Miss McCarthy disappointed. "Why should I care that I have lived my life as a person and as a writer in vain?" she asked rhetorically of an audience of several hundred. "Most of our lives are in vain. At best, we give pleasure to some. I had hoped to turn around the readers of *The Group* by going to Vietnam and writing against our involvement. Maybe in that case, my voice among many was heard. Once a girl thanked me in Harvard Square. That was one high point and I suppose so is this medal. But I wonder if anyone will listen to me make a pitch for Mondale."

Raucous applause rose from the crowd.

Mary McCarthy smiled and said, "Maybe so."

Mary McCarthy, '33, Sends Papers to Vassar

Deirdre Carmody/1985

From *The New York Times,* 1 May 1985, Section B, 1, 2. Reprinted by permission of the *New York Times* (May 1985). Copyright © 1985 by New York Times Company.

POUGHKEEPSIE, N.Y.—Folder after folder. Crammed in cardboard box
atop cardboard box. Stashed row upon row. On shelf after shelf in
the basement of the Vassar College Library.

These are the papers of Mary McCarthy—novelist, essayist, journalist, critic and best-known member of the Vassar class of 1933—that
have just been acquired by the college. They contain more than
6,500 pages of typescripts, manuscripts, legal papers, galleys and
notes.

The collection, which will be available to students and scholars
when it has been catalogued, is a treasure trove for those who take
their literature and their gossip seriously. It includes hundreds of
personal letters from friends and writers like Robert Lowell, Hannah
Arendt, Stephen Spender, Sonia Orwell, Dwight MacDonald and
Elizabeth Hardwick, as well as correspondence and legal papers
detailing Miss McCarthy's stormy marriage, her second, to the critic
Edmund Wilson.

A letter from Miss McCarthy to Miss Arendt, her close friend,
shortly after the death of Miss Arendt's husband, tells about a visit
from Stephen Spender, who intimated that the poet W. H. Auden, an
avowed homosexual, had just proposed marriage to Miss Arendt.

"It is true," Miss McCarthy said the other day in a telephone
interview from her home in Paris. "I think Auden was slightly put up
to it by Stephen Spender. Hannah was absolutely devastated by this.
She felt that he was asking her for shelter and that she could not do
it. She felt that somehow it was an unfriendly act on her part to
refuse."

In the folder marked, "Correspondence With Edmund Wilson,"
who died in 1972, are three tiny pieces of paper. Written in pencil in
her precise handwriting is Miss McCarthy's note to Mr. Wilson telling
him she is leaving him.

"Dear Edmund," she wrote. "This is the note in the pincushion. I'm afraid I don't see what else there is to do. Perhaps the fighting is mostly my fault, but that's not a reason for our staying together.

"I'm sorry," the note says at the end. "This could probably all be managed with less éclat, but the only way I can ever break off anything is to run away." It is signed "Mary."

One folder contains reaction from Vassar alumnae to the 1963 novel *The Group,* a fictionalized account of the lives of some members of the class of 1933.

A member of the class of 1917 writes:

"My head droops in shame, my pride is gone and I deny any association with my Alma Mater. *The Group* is a catalogue of venery, a disgrace to the printed word and a blight on the reputation of a fine institution. It will bring a vicarious thrill to the 'underprivileged' and an impetus to the oversexed."

Miss McCarthy's novels include *The Company She Keeps, The Groves of Academe* and *A Charmed Life.* Last year she received the National Medal for Literature and the Edward MacDowell Medal for her outstanding contribution to literature.

She said that over the years several institutions had approached her about donating her papers. At the time, authors were entitled to sizable tax deductions for donating their works to educational institutions, but she said that idea was repugnant to her.

"Why would someone like to give their papers during their lifetime?" asked Miss McCarthy, who is 72 years old. "There's time enough when they're dead."

But the tax law has been changed, and writers are no longer able to take such deductions. The result has been that colleges and universities usually have to pay to acquire the collections of prominent people. When the president of Vassar, Virginia Smith, first approached Miss McCarthy two years ago about acquiring her papers, Miss McCarthy said she was "really strongly tempted and then I have nice feelings about Vassar."

Both Miss McCarthy and Miss Smith declined to say what Vassar was paying for the papers, but Miss Smith emphasized that the cost was being financed by outside donations, not the college budget.

Miss Smith said that the acquisition was in line with Vassar's tradition of having students deal with original source material whenever possible. She also made the point that with the increased use of word processors, on which mistakes can be deleted by simply pressing a key, there will no longer be first drafts with the crossouts and revisions that are so dear to scholars.

What will not be available in the collection for some years are the correspondence and legal papers about the lawsuit brought by the late Lillian Hellman, the playwright and memoirist, against Miss McCarthy. In an appearance on the Dick Cavett Show in 1980, Miss McCarthy called Miss Hellman "a bad writer, overrated, a dishonest writer." The $25 million suit never reached trial before Miss Hellman's death last year, but it polarized intellectuals.

Asked if she had anything to add about the Hellman lawsuit, Miss McCarthy said she would rather not talk about it. Then she paused and said, "I don't think the gossip about that woman will subside for a long time."

Miss McCarthy, when asked for guidance as to what might be of particular interest in the more than 6,000 papers that make up the collection, suggested a number of folders that a reporter might want to browse through. Among these was the Edmund Wilson folder, which contains letters from their early courtship and during their stormy marriage from 1938 to 1946. In the folder are also legal papers in connection with their separation and the custody of their son, Reuel.

In a deposition taken Feb. 23, 1945, Miss McCarthy who was 17 years younger than Mr. Wilson states:

"Before we were married he gave the appearance of a man of quiet habits with an interest in books, pictures and music. He was well known as a literary critic and I had admired his work even before I met him. During his courtship he held out great promise of a quiet settled life and the rearing of a large family.

"Directly after our marriage I discovered that he was addicted to drink and our life together became a series of violent episodes. After I became pregnant he began beating me with his fists, he would kick me out of bed and again when I was on the floor. A short time before our son was born he knocked me down in the kitchen and kicked me in the stomach. At times he would hold me down on the bed and when I opened my mouth to scream he would hit me on the face and about the body. I was distraught and did not know what to do in my condition.

"Since the birth of our son I have tried to see this marriage through but from its inception to the present time I have been compelled to suffer physical and mental humiliation at the hands of the defendant. This has occurred in the presence of strangers, in the presence of friends, before our servants, the defendant's daughter by a former marriage and even before our son who is now 6 years old. He has publicly accused me of infidelity. He has made this accusation before our son."

An undated deposition from Mr. Wilson states:

"At no time did I ever attack her. I have found it necessary to protect myself against violent assaults by her in the course of which she would kick me, bite me, scratch me and maul me in any way she could. She has even gone so far as to break down a door to my study to get at me and she has on other occasions pushed paper under the door to my study and set fire to it.

"Plaintiff is the victim of hysterical delusions and has seemed for years to have a persecution complex as far as I am concerned. She seems to believe that I have attacked her and struck her on occasions when nothing of the sort has happened."

And in a letter, dated July 13, 1944, Mr. Wilson writes to Miss McCarthy:

"It may be that you and I are psychologically impossible for one another," and adds, "I have never wanted things to be as bad as that because I have really loved you more than any other woman and have felt closer to you than to any other human being."

Our Woman of Letters

Michiko Kakutani/1987

From The *New York Times Magazine,* 29 March 1987, 60, 61, 70, 74, 75. Reprinted by permission of *New York Times* (March 1987). Copyright © 1987 by New York Times Company.

It is easy to picture Mary McCarthy at home in France—that "unsentimental country," as she once wrote, "where icy reason had its temples." The classicism and chilly intellectualism of Paris complement her own rational turn of mind, just as the city's magisterial architecture, its fine restaurants and couture clothing seem to have been designed with her highbrow estheticism in mind.

Last September, six people were killed and another 60 wounded in Paris when a bomb exploded across the street from McCarthy's building on the Rue de Rennes, but while the writer still has nightmares about terrorists, her apartment seems a perfect refuge of civility and order. With its stiffly upholstered furniture, the living room is not exactly comfortable, but it's lovely to look at, all the same. Pale pink tulips and a pot of Japanese azaleas echo the pink in the William Morris wallpaper. And everywhere, small, pretty *objects*—butterflies frozen in glass, a tiny brass umbrella, a persimmon carved from ivory—catch the sunlight.

From her perch on a pink chaise longue, McCarthy serves tea and spice cake, and presides over the afternoon. The gaminlike beauty she possessed in her youth has given way to a more stately mien, but her conversation remains animated by the same mixture of girlish charm and intellectual brio shared by all her heroines.

Over the years, in fact, McCarthy has written tirelessly about her own life, busily mythologizing herself in the process of inventing a gallery of alter egos. As she readily points out, she is Meg in *The Company She Keeps*—the clever Vassar girl, "a princess among the trolls." She is also Martha, the truth-telling "bohemian lady" in *A Charmed Life*. She is Kay, iconocast and scoffer in *The Group.* And she is Rosamund, the ardent and willfully noble esthete in *Birds of America.*

257

A more factual portrait of the author was provided by *Memories of a Catholic Girlhood* in 1957, and with the publication next month of *How I Grew*—the first volume of her autobiography—the self-portrait of the young Mary McCarthy will be complete. At least two more volumes are planned, and when completed the autobiography will minutely document McCarthy's own life and more than five decades of intellectual life in America.

At 74, McCarthy has written 19 books, achieving recognition as a novelist and critic, as well as a journalist and cultural historian. Taken together, her books attest to a classical, all-round literary career in a narrow sense, the books chronicle the follies and preoccupations of McCarthy's own liberal intellectual set, but they also open out onto broader issues: sexual freedom in the 1930's, radicalism in the 40s and 50s. Vietnam and the social upheavals of the 60s. Watergate and terrorism in the 70s. Whatever the subject, the voice has always been consistent. The point of view is always moral (at times, moralistic), the angle of vision, feminine, the tone, logical and cool.

Unlike the work of Philip Rahv or Edmund Wilson, McCarthy's criticism does not demonstrate a consistent set of radical attitudes toward politics or books. Instead, it comprises an anthology of reactions to various phenomena: literary, social and personal. At worst, there is a tendency to go for shrill one-liners at the expense of larger truths (of *The Iceman Cometh,* she wrote, O'Neill "is probably the only man in the world who is still laughing at the iceman joke"). But at their best, McCarthy's essays—and her superb cultural history, *The Stones of Florence*—display a keen intelligence and freshness of perception, coupled with common sense and an old-fashioned belief in social responsibility.

"I see her in the Voltarian enlightenment tradition," says Karl Miller, the editor of *The London Review of Books.* "Her distinctiveness in America relates to her being some sort of European intellectual, but at the same time she's rather thoroughly American—someone who is bright and optimistic and practical."

Although McCarthy has by no means confirmed her gadfly activities to the printed page (she even tried to get a Vietnam protest, based on a refusal to pay taxes, off the ground), her social utopianism has been blunted in recent years. "Through the Vietnam period one had certain hopes," she says. "Not that I personally counted on being so instrumental, but that certain beliefs I cared about and groups I cared about had a chance at least of bringing about a better, more interesting course of history." She now feels, however, that she has not had "the slightest effect on public behavior."

As a young girl growing up in the Pacific Northwest, Mary McCarthy had an image of herself "starring, shining somehow." In the years since, she has constructed one of the most annotated of literary lives. Robert Lowell addressed her as "our Diana, rash to awkwardness," blurting "ice-clear" sentences above the "mundane gossip / and still more mundane virtue" of her colleagues. In "Pictures From an Institution," Randall Jarrell reputedly drew a wicked fictional portrait of her as a ferocious lady novelist who "had not yet arrived even at that elementary forbearance upon which human society is based." And Norman Mailer simply dubbed her "our First Lady of Letters": "our saint, our umpire, our lit arbiter, our broadsword, our Barrymore (Ethel), our Dame (dowager), our mistress (Head), our Joan of Arc."

Memoirs about the New York intellectuals who came of age during the 1930's are flecked with references to McCarthy, and central to all of them is an image of combativeness and radical dissent. William Barrett, a *Partisan Review* editor, saw her as "a Valkyrie maiden, riding her steed into the circle, amid thunder and lightning, and out again, bearing the body of some dead hero across her saddle." And Alfred Kazin portrayed her as the owner of "a wholly destructive critical mind." She had, he wrote, an "unerring ability to spot the hidden weakness or inconsistency in any literary effort and every person. To this weakness she instinctively leaped with cries of pleasure—surprised that her victim, as he lay torn and bleeding, did not applaud her perspicacity."

What was it about McCarthy that inspired such attention? In large part, of course, it was her fiercely adversarial literary and political stands: her vitriolic theater columns in *Partisan Review*; the public skirmishes with Philip Rahv, Diana Trilling and Lillian Hellman; her impassioned pronouncements on Watergate and Vietnam. She defended Hannah Arendt and William Burroughs when it was easy to assail them, and attacked J. D. Salinger, Kenneth Tynan and Arthur Miller when others were celebrating their oeuvres.

To this day, McCarthy appears astonished that everyone does not share her own lofty standards, knowledge or even expertise at spelling. She tends to address almost any subject with directness and precision. She talks in detail about her three recent operations for hydrocephalus (otherwise known as "water on the brain"). She casually names various real-life models for characters in her fiction (the bright young woman journalist in *Cannibals and Missionaries* was based on Renata Adler; the Senator in that same novel, on Eugene McCarthy). And she is equally candid about her confrontation with the late Lillian Hellman—a confrontation that has roots in the split over Stalinism within the intellectual left during the 1930s. Hellman had responded to McCarthy's calling her a "dishonest writer" on a 1980 Dick Cavett show with a $2.25 million lawsuit, and McCarthy now says, "I still feel disgusted by the amount of lying that didn't stop after my remarks on that show." "I wanted it to go to trial," she adds, "so I was disappointed when she died."

The thing about McCarthy's pronouncements is that they are delivered with a distinctive style and flash; and as Elizabeth Hardwick has noted, this "romantic singularity" has helped her to "step free of the mundane, the governessy, the threat of earnestness and dryness." Indeed, when McCarthy first appeared on the literary scene, she must have seemed like some sort of Shavian heroine: this would-be actress who used her theatrical instincts to call attention to herself and who, as William Barrett recalled, intended "to hold her own with men—both intellectually and sexually."

Her short story "The Man in the Brooks Brothers Shirt," which chronicled a casual one-night stand on a train, created an uproar when it appeared in 1941. *The Group*, which included an almost clinical chapter on diaphragms, became a much talked-about best seller in 1963.

Thanks to such outspokenness, Mary McCarthy has been held up as an early exemplar of feminist ideals, but she has little patience with the women's movement, which she sees as a by-product of women's "loss of function in the domestic sphere." "I don't care for the whole self-pity business," she adds. "I'm not such a fool to think that relations between any two persons who live together can be divided up in absolute equality—somebody has to give more."

McCarthy's independent-minded women all share an anomalous dependence on men ("the mind was powerless to save her," thinks one heroine. "Only a man . . . ") and the author freely acknowledges

the large role that men—as mentors, husbands and friends—have
played in her career. It was Philip Rahv, then an editor of *Partisan
Review* and her live-in boyfriend, who helped her get her first literary
job: writing theater reviews for the magazine (the other editors
figured she must know something about drama, since she'd been
married to an actor, Harold Johnsrud). And it was her second
husband, Edmund Wilson, who got her started writing fiction. He put
her in a room, she recalls, and admonished her to stay there until she
had finished a story.

At home, certainly, McCarthy seems less the acid-tongued sibyl
portrayed by her colleagues and more the pleasant, convent-
educated homemaker, cheerfully nattering on in her low, Julia Child
voice. She has always demonstrated in her writings an ability to com-
bine the personal and the didactic, the cerebral and the feminine;
and in conversation, too, she moves fluently from discussions of
Kantian ethics to analyses of Fanny Farmer.

McCarthy's sentences tend to be as symmetrical and as Latinate as
those in her books. But she also speaks with girlish enthusiasm,
exclaiming excitedly over bits of found knowledge and news. The
correct pronunciation of Kierkegaard; the exact date of a meeting, the
alternate name for a chaise longue—all are pieces of information to
be pinned down, then happily filed away, until they may be properly
displayed for the edification of others. Once noted, nothing is
forgotten. To this day, McCarthy remembers everything from the sort
of breakfast buns her young son once liked to eat at a certain coffee
shop to the dirty verses Edmund Wilson composed about other
writers ("the next one on the list is Malcolm Cowley / Who edited
The New Republic so foully . . .").

Friends note that McCarthy has mellowed over the years—largely,
they say, as a result of her 25-year marriage to James West, a former
director of information for the Organization for Economic Cooperation and Development, a Paris-based group that promotes worldwide
economic growth. In Paris and at their summer house in Maine, the
Wests maintain a hectic social schedule; and in McCarthy's capable
hands, picnics, birthdays and holidays tend to become special
occasions. In such respects, notes her brother Kevin McCarthy, the
actor, she has succeeded in "reconstituting" the life they once had
with their parents.

As Mary McCarthy has recalled, their parents possessed a romantic singularity. The former Tess Preston was reputed to have been "the most beautiful woman in Seattle," and her husband, Roy McCarthy, radiated a wild, extravagant charm. Life with them seemed, in retrospect at least, a sweet idyll with May baskets and valentines, picnics in the spring and fancy snowmen in the winter. Then it abruptly ended. Both Roy and Tess McCarthy died during the flu epidemic of 1918. Mary and her three brothers ended up living with relatives in Minneapolis.

It was a harsh and incomprehensible exile, for if the children's previous life had been Edenic, this new one was Dickensian. They were made to stand outside in the snow, for three hours at a time, and they were routinely beaten with a razor strop.

Although McCarthy's grandfather would later take her away to live with him in Seattle, the years in Minneapolis had lasting consequences. They made her aware of the possibility of starting over, of inventing a self, as an orphan, out of the raw materials of will and imagination. And they also made her aware of "the idea of justice"— an idea, she says, that informs nearly everything she has ever written.

"It wasn't only the sort of divine justice that took our parents away from us and set us down among these awful people," she says, "but also the difference between our lives with our parents, which was so spoiled and delicious, and the life in that dreadful house in Minneapolis. And then the fact that I made my escape, while my brothers were left behind. There was certainly a great deal of injustice there— that I was the lucky one."

As her brother Kevin sees it, their experience as children also had the effect of turning them into critics. "I always thought," he says, "that Mary was busy criticizing the great mistakes that were made back then. It's trying to make things nice again, seeking to regain paradise. And in doing so, you have to show how things went awry.

"I would think a kind of detachment happens," he continues. "Something goes so wrong it silences you. But at the same time, there's a tremendous amount of anger. And I think Mary's stifled anger and my stifled anger have a lot to do with who we are and how we've conducted our lives. We had to suppress these things, and it manifested itself by finding fault with things. I think Mary, through her talent, has released a lot of that—using the tools of language."

His sister is less given to looking at their lives in such psychological terms, for she feels that Freudian theory leads to a kind of emotional determinism, in which will and intellect are diminished. When it is pointed out that all her novels involve groups of one sort or another—closed communities of bohemian artists, academics and so on—she acknowledges that some underlying longing for family definition might, just might, have something to do with it. But she would prefer to think of the phenomenon as a manifestation of her "political utopianism." "I don't like these biographical explanations," she says. "I like to think things come out of the mind."

McCarthy had last taught at Bard College in the 1940s, and when the school offered her a teaching chair two years ago, she eagerly accepted. She is now dismayed, however, to find that her students seem "almost totally ignorant of the whole period spanned by my life, to say nothing of what happened before."

Given her hectic writing and lecturing schedule, her recent illness and the strain of juggling several households, one wonders why McCarthy even took on the additional responsibility of teaching. Like many things in her life, it seems largely a matter of will and drive— a sense of duty to her own credo of self-reliance.

"I remember Lizzie [Hardwick] and me saying to each other—this was perhaps 25 years ago—that we never woke up in the morning without a feeling of intense repentance and a resolve to be better. I don't do that anymore—or almost never. But I do have this idea of improvement, if not in one's powers, at least in one's vision, in one's understanding. I couldn't live without feeling I know more than I did yesterday."

Certainly these imperatives to better oneself lend a certain puritanical quality to McCarthy's life. Though she and her husband covet such niceties as an antique Mercedes convertible, though they insist on buying the *best* bottled water, the *best* meat and fish, these luxuries seem less frivolous indulgences than eccentric manifestations of her obsessive insistence on high standards. In other respects, their Paris apartment is modest, even spartan. There are no fancy appliances in the kitchen and no television. When McCarthy is writing, she takes only 10 to 15 minutes for lunch, and spends her free time studying German.

In a sense, there have always been two sides to McCarthy. In both *How I Grew* and *Memories of a Catholic Girlhood,* there is a die-

hard, impetuous romantic, who worships Byron and writes outlandish stories about suicide and prostitution. And there is the self-
conscious, persevering puritan, who wants to win a pink ribbon at
school for good conduct. The first wants to become a famous actress;
the second pictures herself as a Carmelite nun.

Failing to win sufficient attention by being a good student, the
young McCarthy will determine "to do it by badness." She will
pretend to lose her faith (and in so doing, actually misplace it). She
will lose her virginity at 14, renounce her family's bourgeois roots,
and become a "wayward modern girl." In becoming a writer,
however, she will also develop her rational, objective side; and like
Flaubert and so many other reformed romantics, she will attempt to
submit her wilder impulses to her perfectionist drive.

"I've often thought," she says, "that I have very little will in terms
of abstentions, restraining, though that's been very much developed
in me in later years. But when I was young, assertion of the will was a
force almost to throw off self-control.

"Of course, one's tastes also change a bit," she goes on. "One is
no longer tempted by certain things that were temptations in the
past. For example, I was terribly tempted by detective stories when I
was young, and I'd swear off them as though I were swearing off
drink. Now, I don't think I've read one in 25 years and I have no
inclination to read one. Nor do I have an inclination toward light
reading. I enjoy things that are harder more."

Curiously enough, the same impulse informs McCarthy's writing
career, which includes eight novels. On the whole, her essays and
journalism possess an organic assurance—a style, a voice, an
originality—that is missing in her fiction, and McCarthy herself says
she finds "that writing anything from a book review to a book about
Watergate is easier than writing one chapter of fiction."

"That may mean that I have no natural talent for fiction," she says.
"It must mean that, or that it isn't at least as accessible to me as the
other. But I prefer, in the end, writing fiction because you're creating
something that wasn't there before. That's where you're really
contributing something to the world's treasure."

Indeed, McCarthy's fiction has the distinct feel of being a willed
creation. With the exception of her first novel The Company She
Keeps (which melded autobiography and a highly personal voice to

produce a wonderfully immediate series of interconnected stories),
the novels each began with an idea. *Birds of America*, a sentimental
study of an idealistic boy's coming of age was meant to "be a novel
about the idea of equality and its relation to nature." *The Groves of
Academe,* a brittle portrait of a Machiavellian academic, was supposed to raise the question, "Where is the justice for an impossible
person?" And even *The Group*, that gossipy chronicle of eight Vassar
women, was conceived as "a history of the loss of faith in progress."

Their execution tended to be equally didactic: after a chapter or
so, says McCarthy, she would ask herself a series of questions and
then proceed on the basis of the answers. The problem with this
approach, of course, is that the narratives tend to become mannered;
the voice, more and more detached. In his review of *The Group,*
Norman Mailer concluded that McCarthy was really "an engineer
manqué in literature." And Hilton Kramer, reviewing *Birds of
America*, was even harsher: "the truth is—dare one say it?—that
Mary McCarthy cannot write a novel. She lacks the essential fictional
gift. She cannot imagine others."

McCarthy herself acknowledges the limitations inherent in her
mode of comic detachment. "Laughter is the great antidote for self-
pity," she writes in *How I Grew.* "Maybe a specific for the malady,
yet probably it does tend to dry one's feelings out a little, as if
exposing them to a vigorous wind." "There is no dampness in my
emotions," she adds, "and some moisture, I think, is needed, to
produce the deeper, the tragic, notes."

Although McCarthy says she hopes her fiction has moved in a
"direction of greater objectivity" over the years, she points out that
she "can't get away from autobiography." Indeed, read together, the
novels form a sort of ongoing narrative of her life. *The Group* was
based heavily on her own schoolmates at Vassar, and *The Company
She Keeps* serves as a virtual chronicle of the author's own
adventures in New York during the 1930s.

Like the heroine of that book, McCarthy says she was an essentially "nonpolitical person" who fell, quite by accident, into the
middle of one of that period's great ideological debates. She was at a
party in 1936, she recalls, when she was casually asked two
questions: Did she think Trotsky had a right to asylum and did she
think he had a right to a hearing? Without thinking much about it,

she answered yes to both questions. The next day, she says, "I got a letter from something calling itself the Committee for the Defense of Leon Trotsky, and there was my name on the letterhead. I was furious.

"I was just about to call the committee to tell them to take my name off that list when I began to hear that a number of people—including Freda Kirchwey, the editor of *The Nation,* and God knows who else—had dropped off the list. And as soon as I heard that, naturally I turned completely around and felt very glad I hadn't asked them to take my name off because I would have had to be in the company of people like that."

Even though she began reading more and more Marxist literature, she recalls that the "P.R. boys" (Phillip Rahv and the rest of the *Partisan Review* crowd) "were always afraid I'd commit some awful bourgeois error." Similarly, she says, when Edmund Wilson—who was regarded by Partisan Review editors as an eminent elder statesman—asked McCarthy out to dinner, "the boys" worried that she would embarrass them all "by having the wrong literary opinions."

They needn't have worried. Wilson, who was then 42, soon asked the 25-year-old writer to marry him. McCarthy, who was then living with Phillip Rahv, demurred. "I told Wilson I'd live with him," she says, "but I did not want to get married. But I guess I felt guilty. I felt, somehow, since I'd gone to bed with Wilson that I should marry him. It was wrong, of course. I wasn't in love with him, and I was kind of in love with Rahv." She and Rahv, however, were "fighting all the time" ("class and race warfare," as she recalls), and McCarthy found herself increasingly drawn to Wilson's promises of quiet domesticity. "The next thing I knew," she says, "I was sitting next to this stranger on a train to get married."

The marriage lasted seven years. Some years after that, in her novel *A Charmed Life,* McCarthy portrayed a loud, unattractive intellectual named Miles Murphy, who "wanted to be another Goethe and had ended up as a rolling stone"—a character widely believed to be based on Wilson. Wilson ignored the book—unlike Rahv, who reacted to McCarthy's teasing portrait of him in *The Oasis* with a lawsuit (later dropped).

You could not treat your life-history as though it were an inferior novel and dismiss it with a snubbing phrase," says Meg in *The Company She Keeps.* "It had after all been like that. Her peculiar tragedy (if she had one) was that her temperament was unable to assimilate her experience; the raw melodrama of those early years was a kind of daily affront to her skeptical, prosaic intelligence."

It is an outlook common to many of McCarthy's heroines, and one suspects that their creator, too, shares this unwillingness to trust in fate—this desire to make sense of life through rules and definitions, this instinct to control disorder through intelligence and logic.

Her own life, after all, seems to have had more than its share of accidents and chance occurrences. Had her parents lived, she once observed, they would have been "a united Catholic family, rather middle class and wholesome," and she might very well have ended up "married to an Irish lawyer and playing golf and bridge, making occasional retreats and subscribing to a Catholic Book Club."

In *The Company She Keeps,* Meg dreams of having a "brilliant career," of becoming "a great writer, an actress, an ambassador's gifted wife." As her autobiography makes clear, McCarthy not only cherished similar dreams herself, but she also succeeded in using her will and intellect to become that imagined person. After years of feeling like an outsider—the orphan in a strange household, the young woman from the Far West at Vassar, the "bourgeois" theater critic at *Partisan Review*—she now seems, in Meg's (and Chaucer's) words, "my own woman well at ease."

Though she contemplates no further novels, McCarthy says she hopes one day to write a study of Gothic architecture. In the meantime, there are at least two more volumes of the autobiography to complete.

What sort of self-assessment is she making? "Not too favorable," she says slowly. "But then it'd be awful if one formed a favorable assessment of oneself."

Index